THE INSIDE STORIES OF MODERN POLITICAL SCANDALS

How Investigative Reporters Have Changed the Course of American History

WOODY KLEIN

Foreword by Jeff Greenfield

 PRAEGER

AN IMPRINT OF ABC-CLIO, LLC
Santa Barbara, California • Denver, Colorado • Oxford, England

Library of Congress Cataloging-in-Publication Data

Klein, Woody, 1929-
 The inside stories of modern political scandals : how investigative reporters have changed the course of American history / Woody Klein ; foreword by Jeff Greenfield.
   p. cm.
 Includes bibliographical references and index.
 ISBN 978-0-313-36513-3 (hard copy : alk. paper)—ISBN 978-0-313-36514-0 (ebook) 1. Press and politics—United States—History—20th century. 2. Press and politics—United States—History—21st century. 3. Investigative reporting—United States—History—20th century. 4. Investigative reporting—United States—History—21st century. I. Title.
   PN4888.P6K57   2010
   973.92—dc22   2010015757

ISBN: 978-0-313-36513-3
EISBN: 978-0-313-36514-0

14 13 12 11 10   1 2 3 4 5

This book is also available on the World Wide Web as an eBook.
Visit www.abc-clio.com for details.

Praeger
An Imprint of ABC-CLIO, LLC

ABC-CLIO, LLC
130 Cremona Drive, P.O. Box 1911
Santa Barbara, California 93116-1911

This book is printed on acid-free paper ∞

Manufactured in the United States of America

To my friend and mentor, John Hohenberg (1906–2000), professor of journalism at the Graduate School of Journalism, Columbia University, whose caring advice and guidance on investigative reporting inspired me from the outset and for the past 60 years

CONTENTS

Foreword, ix
  Jeff Greenfield
Preface: A Personal Retrospective, xiii
Acknowledgments, xix
Introduction: The Muckrakers' Tradition, xxiii

Chapter 1: Sherman Adams Resigns—Jack Anderson, 1

Chapter 2: The Bay of Pigs Fiasco—Tad Szulc, 21

Chapter 3: Watergate: The Fall of a President—Bob Woodward
  and Carl Bernstein, 39

Chapter 4: Monicagate: Impeachment of a President—Michael Isikoff,
  73

Chapter 5: The Collapse of Enron—Bethany McLean, 91

Chapter 6: Abu Ghraib Revealed—Seymour Hersh, 105

Chapter 7: Domestic Eavesdropping: "The Biggest Secret"—Eric
  Lichtblau and James Risen, 123

Chapter 8: Rendition Exposed—Dana Priest, 145

Chapter 9: Walter Reed Veterans Administration Scandal—Anne Hull
  and Dana Priest, 169

Chapter 10: Guantanamo Detainees' Stories—Tom Lasseter, 197

viii   *Contents*

Epilogue, 219
Selected Bibliography, 221
Index, 231

FOREWORD

JEFF GREENFIELD

As the American newspaper more and more takes on the coloration of an endangered species, an intriguing argument has broken out in preparation for the postmortem: if the newspaper dies, will we be bidding goodbye to a creature that has outlived its time; or will we be losing something that is irreplaceable and critical to a free society?

There is, after all, nothing especially admirable about an information delivery system that requires the felling of countless trees, the transportation of wood, then paper, and then the newspaper itself across crowded streets via trucks that clog the roads and foul the air. And those of us who were poetic about that feel of the newsprint in our hands . . . well, how different are we from our ancestors who might have sighed, "You know, I really need to feel that papyrus under my hands as I unscroll the news"? Even if we are talking not about the form of the newspaper but the institution itself, perhaps it's simply that the time has passed when the bundling of so much disparate information—comics, horoscopes, advice to the lovelorn, high school lunch menus, weather, national and international news, and opinion—was a sensible combination of data. Today, the sports comes via ESPN, the comics come animated, and opinions—unlimited in volume or ideology and covering the entire thoughtfulness–thuggishness spectrum—are free for the asking (whether you have asked for them or not). What then, might we lose if the newspaper dies?

Woody Klein's book provides one powerful answer: for generations, the conglomerate nature of the newspaper, and its profitability, enabled reporters to devote great amounts of time, energy, and publishers' resources to throwing light on dark corners of power, especially political power. Put bluntly, the readers who paid their nickels and dimes for "Dear Abby," "Steve Canyon," or "Omarr the Stargazer" were funding the work of uncovering the abuse of power by officials high and low, in arenas that ranged from kickbacks for paving contracts to the conduct of war—and that is why the most worrisome aspect of the decline of the newspaper is the possibility that, at least for now, there is no clear idea of how and where such journalism will survive.

It is not precisely a blazing new insight to note that the founders of the Republic were certain that an independent check on authority was as essential to America's survival as a standing army or a means to raise revenue. It is practically illegal to convene a journalism conference without noting James Madison's observation that "a popular government without the means to popular information is a prelude to a tragedy or a farce—perhaps both," or recalling Thomas Jefferson's statement that, given a choice between a government without newspapers or newspapers without government, he would unhesitatingly choose the latter. Of course, Jefferson said that before he was president; afterwards, he said, "Nothing is to be believed which now appears in a newspaper; truth itself becomes suspect when placed in that polluted vehicle." And that underscored a critical point: the shapers of the Bill of Rights knew full well that the press could often be irresponsible, inaccurate, indeed completely mendacious. Newspapers in the United States at that time, remember, were more often than not wholly owned subsidiaries of political factions and parties. Yet the Founders still made newspapers the only enterprise specifically granted exemption from substantive government regulation.

Klein's accounts of how the press uncovered some of America's most significant political scandals shows that the Founders knew what they were doing. His survey brings to life Lord Acton's famous observation that "all power tends to corrupt." More intriguingly, this survey reminds us that corruption is a house with many mansions.

Those who have great power may abuse it to get rich, to broaden their sexual horizons, to avoid dealing with intractable dilemmas, to punish their political enemies, or—most chillingly—to pursue what they are certain are noble ends by means forbidden to them by law or simple human decency. In almost every case, the work of exposing such wrongdoing is laborious, time-consuming, and unglamorous (having your story made into a movie and finding yourself played by Robert Redford is generally not the fate of the investigative reporter). Moreover, like the old-time wildcatter looking for oil, these reporters know that sometimes their work produces only dry holes. But it is work without which the possibility of unchecked power would be much closer to reality.

Woody Klein is, manifestly, the right man to take us on this survey. He has, as they say, "worked both sides of the street"—as a press secretary and for many years as a dogged reporter for the *World-Telegram & Sun* in New York City. In my youth, if a story appeared exposing corruption, neglect, or bureaucratic ineptitude in the inner workings of city government, the odds were pretty good that Klein was one of its authors. From decades of experience and observation, he has selected ten tales that do much more than bring some of the biggest news stories of the last half century to life; they also serve as a cautionary tale about what we will lose should the new forms of journalism fail to find a mechanism to keep investigative journalism alive.

PREFACE: A PERSONAL RETROSPECTIVE

Some reporters have done brilliant work in unearthing wrong-doing by acting as detectives or accountants, and sometimes both.

—John Hohenberg, *The Professional Journalist: A Guide to Modern Reporting Practices*

This book is the inevitable product of my career-long passion for investigative journalism. Long before Bob Woodward and Carl Bernstein became household names, I first became enthusiastic about this kind of proactive journalism when I was a student at the Graduate School of Journalism at Columbia University in the 1950s. I began doing this kind of reporting in 1955 when I joined the *New York World-Telegram & Sun*, after spending a year learning the ropes of reporting on the night police beat on the *Washington Post and Times-Herald*. For a decade on the *World-Telegram*, I was assigned to cover the "housing" beat, which soon led me to firsthand on-the-scene visits to people—mostly blacks and Puerto Ricans—living in dank, gloomy tenement houses in the depths of poverty, mostly in the Harlem and Bedford-Stuyvesant neighborhoods of New York, but also on the Upper West Side of Manhattan where once-proud brownstone buildings that flourished in the 1920s had been divided up by greedy landlords into what was known as single-room occupancy (SRO) apartments. These cramped quarters were often occupied by more than one family, with as many as 10 or 12 people sleeping literally side by side on the floor in unbelievably cramped quarters. It was, to paraphrase Lincoln Steffens (1866–1936), the

famous crusading reporter at the turn of the century, the "shame" of
New York City.[1] Steffens was considered by some the first "muckraker" in American history.[2] With Steffens as a model, I tracked
down landlords who failed to fix building violations and wrote
stories about them.

The tenants, many of whom were being gouged by shady landlords
for high rents just to remain in their dilapidated apartments, frequently called my newspaper with complaints of lack of running
water, electricity, or heat and the City of New York's failure to pick
up their garbage or even clean their streets. Further, they complained
that neither the Buildings Department nor the police responded to
calls for help in bringing their living standards up to the minimum
requirements of civilized society in America in the 20th century.

My interest in exposing the "slumlords" of New York turned into
an obsession. I began to read all of the books of other famous muckraking reporters—especially Jacob A. Riis (1849–1914), the Danish-
born journalist who immigrated to New York in the 1870s and made
it his hunting ground for stories and starkly photographic exposés
of the city's slums that were published in the *New York Tribune* and
later the *New York Evening Sun*, where he worked as a photojour-
nalist. Riis—who developed a close working relationship with then
New York City police commissioner Theodore R. (Teddy) Roosevelt—
was dubbed by Roosevelt as "the most useful citizen of New York."[3]
It was obviously not a coincidence that Riis authored a biography of
his friend, whom he idolized. It was titled *Theodore Roosevelt, the Citizen* (1904). Of this book, one chronicler of the history of muckrakers
stated: "It was full of loyalty and conviction that could not have
been bought at any price: the biographer, although older than his
subject, was never able to discuss him in any other terms than those
of reverence."[4]

Riis wrote many books about his findings, among them *Children of
the Poor* (1892), *Out of Mulberry Street* (1898), *The Battle with the Slum*
(1902), and *Children of the Tenement* (1903). His autobiography, *The
Making of an American*, was published in 1901. Riis was perhaps the
greatest reporter to expose slum conditions in New York City. As a
result of Riis's book *How the Other Half Lives: Studies among the Tenements of New York* (1890), Roosevelt ordered the city police lodging
houses that were featured in the book closed down.

Of all the early muckrakers, Riis inspired me the most. I identified
with him in my fervent desire to carry on his crusade in my newspaper, the *New York World-Telegram & Sun*, to rid the city of slums.

I was working for a successor newspaper to the one Riis had worked for, the *New York Evening Sun*, so I felt a special tie to him. In pursuit of this goal, I reached out to find anyone alive who had known Riis. I looked up the name Riis in the Manhattan phone book and, much to my amazement, I discovered that Riis's widow, Mary, his second wife whom he married in 1907—seven years before he died—lived in an apartment on Manhattan's Upper East Side.

In an interview in 1964 in her apartment, Mary Riis told me: "I don't think my husband would have been very happy with New York today. He would have been disappointed to see our city today." Mrs. Riis, then in her 80s, described her late husband's friendship with Theodore Roosevelt: "Teddy and Jake were more than good friends," she said. "They were like brothers. They got along well together." She added: "But when we had other company, I would have to ask Jake, 'Now you must talk to other people, too.'" When Roosevelt became president, Mrs. Riis recalled, "the president was devoted to Jake. As a result, Jake found himself influential in [national] politics because all of his friends knew he was a close friend of the president."[5]

At that time, I really believed slums could be eradicated, not only in the city in which I lived but throughout America. Lyndon Johnson was president and his "War on Poverty" program was pouring billions of dollars into a nationwide effort to clear the slums once and for all. I was a believer. For that reason, I decided to experience firsthand what it was like to live in one of the worst slum buildings in New York City, located at 311 East 100th Street. It had more violations on it than any other building and housed more than a dozen families in filthy, rat-infested, roach-filled rooms, all without electricity and hot water. The stench from clogged toilets and stale air in the summer was almost unbearable.

Posing as an out-of-work actor, unshaven, wearing torn, dirty clothes, I was gradually accepted as an outsider with nowhere else to turn. I carried only a Social Security card with me. One or two tenants suspected I was an undercover agent looking for drug dealers, but after I failed to arrest several young men whom I found in the basement every few days injecting themselves with hard drugs, I won the trust of those who lived in the building.

After three months, I emerged and returned to my desk in the city room at the *World-Telegram & Sun* to write my series under the banner headline: "I LIVED IN A SLUM." The exposé of this old-law (pre-1901)[6] tenement on East 100th Street brought the wrath of

Mayor Robert F. Wagner down on my newspaper, on me personally, and, perhaps more appropriately, on his housing officials.

Before long, my publisher, Roy W. Howard, of Scripps-Howard Newspapers,[7] on a visit to our city room on Barclay Street in Lower Manhattan, stopped by my desk and asked if I was the reporter who wrote the series on the slums. When I acknowledged my work, he looked at me sternly and said, somewhat impatiently: "Well, son, you've gotten us halfway up the tree. How are you going to get us down?" I took that to mean he wanted me to help solve the problem I had focused on. Accordingly, I called City Hall's housing officials and asked them to devise a plan to solve the slum issue. In return, I told them, my paper would support a plan if we deemed it worthwhile.

I interviewed Mayor Wagner to get his viewpoint on what could be done to solve the generations-old problem. After defending his administration's efforts to hunt down landlords whose buildings had multiple housing violations, he knew I was not satisfied. Finally, he smiled, looked at me, and said, condescendingly: "There's nothing you can do about the slums. You know that. They're always going to be that way."[8] At the time, as a young, idealistic reporter, I thought his comment was cynical. But the mayor did hire a prestigious consultant, J. Anthony Panuch,[9] a New York lawyer and leading authority on government reorganization, to make a thorough study of the city's uncoordinated housing agencies and to recommend comprehensive city policy by February 1960. Panuch himself, at the outset of his probe, said he was "shocked" by the extent to which slums "had taken over the city."[10]

When Panuch's report was released for publication,[11] the *World-Telegram & Sun* took note on its editorial page and claimed credit for pushing the mayor into taking corrective action to solve the "slum problem." We also praised the well-organized, detailed plan in reaction to our series. Shortly after that, I was the recipient of a Page One Award from the American Newspaper Guild of New York in 1960 for my series. That was followed by an invitation from NBC broadcaster David Brinkley to write a TV script about that slum building—by then declared the "worst slum" in New York City by the mayor—for *David Brinkley's Journal*, which aired on November 22, 1961, and July 25, 1962.

In retrospect, I now realize that all of this attention to one particular building—which has since been torn down—and to the slums of New York at that time was to little avail. There was an effort to improve the blighted parts of the city—which has since been continued by successive mayors. With the passing of time, however, and after becoming more realistic in the nearly half a century that has elapsed, I would agree today that Mayor Wagner was partially correct, but with one caveat: the government's efforts to reform housing conditions in the ensuing years, driven to a great extent by newspaper exposés, *have* made a difference. I believe we are much better off today than we were at the turn of the last century. But there remains a huge task ahead in the 21st century to realize the dream of a slum-free New York or, for that matter, a nation without slums.

Notes

1. "Shame" was the word vividly describing the slums of cities. It was first used by famed journalist Steffens, who was the first reporter to be called a "muckraker" as a result of a series of reports he wrote about a number of cities. They were published by *McClure's* magazine under the title "The Shame of the Cities" in October 1902.

2. Louis Filler, *Crusaders for American Liberalism* (Yellow Springs, OH: Antioch Press, 1939), 55.

3. Louis Filler, *The Muckrakers* (Palo Alto, CA: Stanford University Press, 1968), 45.

4. Ibid., 46.

5. Woody Klein, interview with Mrs. Jacob Riis, *New York World-Telegram & Sun*, May 5, 1964.

6. So-called new-law tenements, requiring much safer construction, were built after 1901 when the State of New York passed a reform measure.

7. Roy Wilson Howard was one of the most important journalists of the 20th century. He headed the United Press during its greatest period of growth, turning it into a worldwide news agency. As chairman of the board and business director, Howard saw the Scripps-Howard newspaper chain become the largest chain of newspapers in the United States before his death in 1964.

8. Woody Klein, *Let in the Sun* (New York: Macmillan, 1964), 118.

9. Panuch prescribed a brand-new plan in a special report to the mayor titled "Building a Better New York: Final Report to Mayor Robert F. Wagner," March 1, 1960.

10. Klein, *Let in the Sun*, 128.

11. Summarizing the report, Panuch stated: "In our overcrowded city, where low-income minorities fight desperately for living space in its blighted neighborhoods, slum formation has steadily increased. What appeared to be a manageable problem in the 1930s has assumed staggering proportions in the 1960s in congested New York City."

ACKNOWLEDGMENTS

First, I want to acknowledge the deep commitment—both personally and professionally—of my wife, Audrey Klein, who is always there to provide me with never-ending support. As an editor, her insights and suggestions helped me formulate the content of this book. She has been, at once, my hardest critic and my most enthusiastic reader. It is never easy to live with an author, but she has managed to cope with this writer's idiosyncrasies for the past 48 years. For that I thank her with all my heart.

I should like to express my profound gratitude to Jeff Greenfield, an award-winning senior political correspondent for *CBS News*, for contributing the foreword to this book. Greenfield, a former colleague of mine in the news business, is a commentator on the *CBS Evening News with Katie Couric* and *CBS Sunday Morning*. He has also worked as a senior analyst for CNN, serving as its lead analyst for coverage of the primaries, conventions, presidential debates, and election nights. Greenfield also has reported on the media, culture, and trends for the cable channels. He is principally known for his coverage of domestic politics and media. A one-time speechwriter for Robert F. Kennedy, he has served as a floor reporter or anchor booth analyst for every national political convention since 1988. His experience as an analyst and investigative reporter places him among the elite in the news business today. Greenfield has twice been named to *TV Guide*'s All-Star Team as best political commentator and was cited by the *Washington Journalism Review* as "the best in the business" for his media analysis.

Greenfield has contributed articles to the *New York Times Magazine*, *Esquire*, and *National Lampoon* and has authored or coauthored nine books, including *Television: The First 50 Years* and *The Real Campaign*. His first novel, *The People's Choice* (1995), was named one of the *New York Times*'s notable books of the year. Before joining CNN, Greenfield was ABC News's political and media analyst for 14 years and was with CBS before that. Greenfield has earned a number of awards, including the 2002 Quill Award for Professional Achievement and three Emmy Awards. He graduated with honors from Yale Law School with a bachelor of legal letters degree.

I am deeply indebted to my editors who guided me along the way from conceptual proposal to final manuscript. They are Robert Hutchinson, senior editor, Praeger Publishers; Brian Foster, formerly an assistant editor with Greenwood Publishing; Michael Millman, senior editor, ABC-CLIO, who was enormously helpful down the stretch in helping me shape the final manuscript and getting it on press; and, finally, Erin Ryan, submissions editor of ABC-CLIO.

I also am enormously grateful to Westport reference librarian Nancy Kuhn-Clark, who assisted me in compiling in-depth material from all sources. With her "can-do" attitude, she ferreted out invaluable historical sources in the course of her research, enabling me to write about familiar subjects with a fresh viewpoint. For two years, she responded to every one of my inquiries in a timely, thorough, and caring manner. She was ably assisted by Westport reference librarian Carolyn Zygmont, who helped compile the bibliography.

In addition, I could not have written this book without the advice of Mark Feldstein, associate professor of media and public affairs and director of the Journalism Oral History Project at George Washington University. He is a former TV investigative reporter whose work has won more than 50 journalism awards. He is quoted as a media analyst by the *New York Times*, the *Washington Post*, CNN, NPR, NBC News, ABC News, CBS News, C-SPAN, Al-Jazeera, BBC News, *Newsday*, the *Christian Science Monitor*, and other news outlets. Feldstein's latest book is *Poisoning the Press: Richard Nixon, Jack Anderson, and the Rise of Washington's Scandal Culture*.

I am also especially grateful to all of the award-winning editors and investigative reporters who gave generously of their time for interviews that allowed me to compile the "inside stories" behind the memorable exposés they wrote, namely:

- Ben Bradlee, arguably the most influential American newspaper editor in the second half of the 20th century, currently vice president at large of the *Washington Post* and the newspaper's executive editor from 1968 through 1991, under whose leadership the paper won 18 Pulitzer Prizes. He was at the helm during the Watergate scandal, supervising the paper's entire coverage by Bob Woodward and Carl Bernstein, who shared a Pulitzer Prize with the newspaper.

- Dana Priest and Anne Hull of the *Washington Post*, for their exposé of conditions at Walter Reed Veterans Hospital in Washington, D.C. Priest also won recognition for the *Post* with her award-winning stories on "rendition" during the Iraq War.

- Bethany McLean, a contributing editor at *Vanity Fair* and a former editor-at-large and columnist for *Fortune*, for her initial story on the collapse of Enron.

- Seymour "Sy" Hersh, one of the most prolific and dogged investigative reporters in modern history, who broke the story about the Iraqi prisoner abuse in 2004 at Abu Ghraib jail in Baghdad in the *New Yorker* and authored the book *Chain of Command: The Road from 9/11 to Abu Ghraib*, based on his magazine reports.

- Tom Lasseter, investigative reporter with the *Miami Herald* who, along with Mark Seibel, head of the McClatchy Newspapers Washington Bureau's Web site; Roy Gutman, foreign editor for McClatchy Newspapers; and Warren Strobel, a McClatchy Newspapers foreign affairs correspondent, produced a spectacular series of stories quoting detainees who had been held in Guantanamo Bay and released.

- Michael Isikoff, the former *Washington Post* and then *Newsweek* investigative correspondent who broke the Monica Lewinsky scandal.

- Eric Lichtblau and James Risen of the *New York Times*, who broke the story about the U.S. government's unauthorized domestic eavesdropping on American citizens.

All of these individuals shared their personal stories about their painstaking steps in the course of their investigative reporting to help the author gather the "inside stories" behind their published stories.

Further, in the course of selecting the 10 investigative series for this book, I wish to acknowledge the help of Nicholas Lemann, dean of the Columbia University Graduate School of Journalism; Richard

Tofel, general manager of ProPublica; Jim Eggensperger, Ph.D., of the faculty of Mass Communications Department, Iona College; Investigative Reporters and Editors; the Center for Investigative Reporting; and, the Center for Public Integrity. In addition, my thanks go to Betty Pessagno, an independent professional manuscript editor. And, my appreciation also to award-winning artist-author Tracy Sugarman, for his frontispiece drawings.

Finally, to my daughter, Wendy Klein, I am, as always, grateful for her ongoing encouragement and confidence in me. As an anthropologist in academia with a passion for excellence, she has inspired me to try to achieve the highest quality in my work.

INTRODUCTION:
THE MUCKRAKERS'
TRADITION

The man with the muck-rake, the man who could look no way but downward, with the muck-rake in his hand; who was offered a celestial crown for his muck-rake, but who could neither look up nor regard the crown he was offered, but continued to rake to himself the filth on the floor.

—Theodore Roosevelt

The newspaper industry in America is facing its greatest challenge in history. It is reeling from huge revenue losses and staff cutbacks, including bureaus at home and abroad. The red-ink bottom lines of many newspapers and magazines are forcing publishers to close down as the Internet is rapidly displacing the print media with thousands of news stories around the clock on its myriad outlets in cyberspace or, as some call it, the blogosphere.

In addition, a proliferation of other communications and social media—Twitter, text messaging, Facebook, LinkedIn, YouTube, Skype, iPods, iPhones, Kindles, Plaxo, and Google and other search engines, to name just a few—are distracting readers away from newspapers and other traditional print media.

Perhaps Bill Keller, executive editor of the *New York Times*—a prominent spokesman in the forefront of the effort to save print journalism—expressed the somber mood in the journalism profession best when he stated at the outset of a talk to a group of newspaper editors: "It's kind of like being a motivational speaker in a hospice."[1]

Punctuating this thought with a sense of finality, writer Richard Rodriguez, an editor at *New American Media* based in San Francisco, bluntly stated in a magazine article at the close of 2009: "When a newspaper dies in America, it is not simply that a commercial enterprise has failed; a sense of place has failed."[2]

Speaking of failure, Tom Rosenstiel, director of the Pew Research Center's Project for Excellence in Journalism warned: "The crisis facing newspapers is a revenue problem. Advertising, the economic foundation of journalism for the last century, is collapsing." In a paper entitled "The Future of Newspapers: The Impact on the Economy and Democracy," Rosenstiel wrote in September 2009:

> The consequence is that the amount of our civic life that occurs in the sunlight of observation by journalists is shrinking. I believe we do have a stake as citizens in having reporters who are independent . . . and who, simply by their presence, say to those in power on behalf of all the rest of us, you are being watched.[3]

Indeed, the technology revolution in the realm of news has so profoundly transformed the newspaper business that journalism educators and practitioners at all levels are no longer confident that the traditional printed word in newspapers and magazines—as we have come to know it—will continue to serve as the conscience of a nation. As the late Prof. Ithiel de Sola Pool, a political scientist and founding chairman of the Political Science Department of the Massachusetts Institute of Technology, stated: "Networked computers will be the printing presses of the Twenty-first Century."[4] In sum, the future of the technology explosion in the news business is *now*. Already, some high-tech professionals look down on newspapers as a relic of the past. They use the term "snail paper" for the print newspapers published daily with news on the front page that is already 12 hours old. Others in the newspaper business with a well-honed sense of humor see this as a term of endearment, not derision.

The most comprehensive analysis of the status of the news business in America was released in late 2009 in the report "The Reconstruction of American Journalism," written by Leonard Downie Jr., vice president at large and former executive director of the *Washington Post* and Weil Family Professor of Journalism at Arizona State University's Walter Cronkite School of Journalism and Mass Communication; and Michael Schudson, professor of communications at Columbia University's Graduate School of Journalism.

The report validated previous findings about news enterprises, stating at the outset:

> American journalism is at a transformational moment, in which the era of dominant newspapers and influential network news divisions is rapidly giving way to one in which the gathering and distribution of news is more widely dispersed. As almost everyone knows, the economic foundation of the nation's newspapers, long supported by advertising, is collapsing, and newspapers themselves, which have been the country's chief source of independent reporting, are shrinking—literally. Fewer journalists are reporting less news in fewer pages, and the hegemony that near-monopoly metropolitan newspapers enjoyed during the last third of the twentieth century, even as their primary audience eroded, is ending.[5]

Indeed, there is general agreement among most publications—newspapers and magazines alike—that the newsprint business may be in deeper trouble than most people realize. Perhaps author Megan McArdle, in an article in the *Atlantic* magazine, summed up the doomsday scenario best this way:

> I think we're witnessing the end of the newspaper business, full stop, not the end of the newspaper business as we know it. The economics just aren't there. At some point, industries enter a death spiral: too few consumers raises their average costs, meaning they eventually have to pass price increases onto their customers. That drives more customers away.[6]

For generations, newspapers published in-depth investigative journalism stories by reporters—once known as "muckrakers"—that protected the people from abuses on all levels of government and in other fields throughout the nation. The days of the sensational newspaper scandals appear to be numbered—at least by the standards established by investigative journalists since the founding of our Republic. Gone also is the stereotypical reporter of yesteryear. "Newspaper reporters have long had the reputation of being hard-boiled cynics, boisterous, irreverent, and full of themselves and whiskey. They are suspicious of those in power," is the way they were described in a recent book, *The Muckrakers*, edited by Robert Miraldi, a journalism professor.[7]

Much of that tough veneer has disappeared, yet there can be no doubt that young, idealistic journalists do find a way to unearth wrongdoing and bring it to the public's attention. As one constitutional scholar and media lawyer, Scott Gant, describes the situation: "Journalism is in flux. Most newspapers and magazines face dwindling readership and the loss of advertisers (including highly profitable classified advertisements) as they compete with electronic publications and other sources of information and entertainment."[8]

Some amateur online "journalists" think of themselves as reporters making a contribution to the business, but the jury is still out as to how and by whom they should be recognized or certified as "real" journalists. "Citizen journalism," while valuable, is a concept the vast majority of bona fide, professionally trained journalists—reporters who have been taught by veteran journalists in journalism classes or on the job in newsrooms to learn the generations-old craft of researching, reporting, and objectively writing news—do not accept as real journalism. This issue leads to the three defining questions in the journalism community in the 21st century:

- Who is a journalist?
- Who *decides* who is a journalist?
- And, perhaps the most crucial question: What will happen to investigative reporting?

With the cuts in staff and bureaus being closed down by big-city newspapers, there has been a concomitant cut in the number of reporters assigned to investigative reporting. According to Downie and Schudson's report:

> The number of newspaper editorial employees, which had grown from about 40,000 in 1971 to more than 60,000 in 1992, had fallen back to around 40,000 in 2009. In most cities, fewer newspaper journalists were reporting on city halls, schools, social welfare, life in the suburbs, local business, culture, the arts, science, or the environment, and *fewer were assigned to investigative reporting.*[9]

There is a real danger to the public interest if this becomes a permanent trend. Investigative reporters already face a major hurdle in protecting their sources. On the floor of the Senate in November

2009, Sen. Arlen Specter (D-PA), discussing a bill that would provide greater protection to reporters who cannot reveal their sources, urged strengthening the so-called Shield Law. He explained: "We still get most of our information from investigative journalists. If you can't protect sources, there is a lot of public corruption and private malfeasance that will go undetected and unpunished."[10]

For an in-depth perspective on investigative journalism, it is necessary to look back to the days when this genre of public service reporting came into the forefront. The word "muckraker" is generally interpreted as a pejorative term for an investigative reporter who digs up dirt or spends his or her time in the world of seamy activities. It originated in a period of crusading American journalism at the dawn of the 20th century. The muckraking movement began in 1902 and quickly took on the appearance of sensational journalism. The heyday of muckraking ran almost parallel with the presidency of Theodore Roosevelt, "T.R." or "Teddy" as he was known. The period between 1902 and 1912 is seen by historians as the high point of early muckraking, the so-called golden age of muckraking journalism.

The term was coined by Roosevelt himself. He is credited with giving such reporters their opprobrious name in a dinner address that was supposed to be off the record at the Washington Gridiron Club on March 17, 1906. Roosevelt complained about a dangerous new breed of journalist whose inflammatory writings were sweeping across America. Based on a famous phrase in John Bunyan's book *Pilgrim's Progress* (1678), Roosevelt paraphrased Bunyan and characterized this sort of newspaper reporter as follows: "the man with the muck-rake, the man who could look no way but downward with the muck-rake in his hand, who was offered a celestial crown for his muck-rake, but who could neither look up nor regard the crown he was offered, but continued to rake to himself the filth on the floor."[11]

The following month, on April 14, 1906, Roosevelt used the same quote during an address at the laying of the cornerstone of the U.S. House of Representatives wing of the Capitol in Washington, D.C., once again referring to reform journalists as "muckrakers." There had always been (and still is) a natural tension between the White House and the press in a free society.[12] At the time, Roosevelt was angered by a political exposé published by his nemesis, William Randolph Hearst, in *Cosmopolitan*. One of journalism's greatest investigative reporters, Lincoln Steffens, is said to have called on

Roosevelt the next day and told the president, tongue in cheek, "Well, Mr. President, you have put an end to all these journalistic investigations that have made you." Roosevelt replied "that he had no such intention" and that he was not referring to Steffens.[13] Steffens subsequently wrote in his autobiography: "I did not intend to be a muckraker; I did not know that I was one till President Roosevelt picked the name out of Bunyan's *Pilgrim's Progress* and pinned it on us; and even then he said that he did not mean me."[14]

Steffens remained so concerned about the president's interpretation of the term "muckraker" that he wrote to Roosevelt on March 6, 1907, to explain his view of the muckraker's message. He stated, in part:

> I am not seeking proof of crime and dishonesty. . . . What I am after is the cause and the purpose and the methods by which our government, city, state, and federal is made to represent not the common, but the special interests; the reason why it is so hard to do right in the U.S.; the secret of the power which makes it necessary for you, Mr. President, to fight to give us a "square deal." You ask men in office to be honest, I ask them to serve the public.[15]

Steffens wrote a series of articles under the headlines "The Shame of Chicago" and the same with other cities' names—namely, New York, Pittsburgh, Philadelphia, St. Louis, and Minneapolis—in the progressive *McClure's* magazine. Steffens's articles were eventually linked together in a book, published in 1904, as *The Shame of the Cities*. It soon became a best-seller.

Yet another famous newspaper muckraker, Jacob A. Riis, an immigrant from Denmark, fought his own war against the slums of New York. Riis earned a reputation in his day for revealing the human interest stories of slum dwellers, especially children, for whom he fought hard. He was not altogether successful in getting the slums torn down, but his writings produced action by the authorities. He is remembered widely to this day and had a park in Brooklyn named after him.

Despite Roosevelt's intended use of "muckraker" as a negative, historian C. C. Regier wrote a half century later:

> In time the expression lost most of its unsavory connotation and was even accepted by the reformers themselves. Today the fact that the term came to be used indiscriminately may

be regarded as an advantage, for it would be almost impossible to distinguish the good from the bad and the sane from the sensational in such a way as to satisfy everyone. Classification becomes arbitrary, and we do much better if we simply define muckraking as the exposing of evils and corruption for the real or ostensible proposes of promoting righteousness and social justice.[16]

Prof. Harry H. Stein and John M. Harrison, coordinators of a conference on muckraking held at Pennsylvania State University in the spring of 1970, stated:

> Muckraking has evoked strong, even visceral reactions because it has dealt with the kinds of issues in this [20th] century—prison conditions, abuse of political office, and economic exploitation, for instance—that nearly guarantee such evocations. The muckrakers' words and images have aimed at the penetration of popular ignorance and fatalism to make suffering vivid and indignities real to uninvolved citizens. So muckrakers inevitably have had to defend against libel actions, economic pressures, individual and community harassment, and corrosive private doubts as to their own effectiveness.[17]

Indeed, muckraking is defined in the eye of the beholder. To those who are First Amendment supporters and are keen to see the press unearth wrongdoings, muckrakers in the media are viewed as the last, best hope of keeping a democratic society free, open, and honest. To a majority of sophisticated readers in America, muckraking is seen as an appeal to the moral conscience of society. Author David Protess describes investigative reporting—that is, muckraking—as

> a form of storytelling that protects the boundaries of America's civic conscience. . . . Investigative journalists are reformers, not revolutionaries. They seek to improve the American system by pointing out its shortcomings rather than advocating its overthrow. By spotlighting specific abuses of particular policies or programs, the investigative reporter provides policy makers with the opportunity to take corrective actions.[18]

In the beginning, the muckraking reporters went after corporate and government corruption under the banner of seeking social justice. For the most part, the muckrakers were honest, idealistic, and brimming with righteousness, and they viewed their writings as a moral crusade in the public interest.

Throughout America's history, politics and journalism have been a potent mixture. The passions of newspaper reporters have always been stirred by stories of alleged misbehavior by often righteous, pious-talking political and business leaders—especially occupants of the Oval Office. This has been an essential part of the DNA of American politics from the outset, and as a result, it has stained the legacies of a great many—but not all—presidents. In the best traditions of American journalism, author Suzanne Garment sees political scandal as "a fragment of its historical period, like a finding at an ancient archeological dig; the explorer must piece it together with other evidence in order to decipher an era's message."[19]

Writing in the early 1990s on the trend of the scandals of the prior half century, Garment comments:

> Our time is different from the decades preceding it. Political scandal has proliferated, and thus proliferation reflects not so much an increase in corruption at the federal level as it does our growing capacity and taste for political scandal production. The resulting culture of mistrust has made the always difficult job of governing measurably harder. The climate of sensationalism has contributed to public cynicism.[20]

A more general definition of what constitutes a political scandal involving the White House comes from historian Jeffrey D. Schultz, who states that the wording he and his editors agreed upon is as follows: "Any action that was considered dishonest or a violation of propriety at the time of the presidency or that would have been considered as such had it come to light at the time."[21]

The range of political scandals in the history of the White House is, indeed, all-encompassing—many involving the presidents, others their appointees. Although only a selected number appear in this volume, collectively—since the inauguration of George Washington—presidents or high White House officials have endured a wide variety of allegations of misdeeds and tragedies. These include marital infidelity, financial misconduct, profiting from a conflict of interest, illegitimate children, stealing elections, fraud, kickbacks, influence peddling, drunkenness, homosexuality, illegal use of government funds, extravagant spending on the White House décor, failure to collect taxes, assessing government employees' wages as donations to the party in power, increasing congressional salaries, incompetence, land speculation, swindling Indians of their land, soliciting corporate contributions for campaigns in return for favorable treatment, violation of antitrust laws, illegal outside compensation, and just about anything one can imagine—except physical violence or murder. Any way you look at it, the goal of political muckrakers down through the generations has been to find a major flaw, or wrongdoing, on the part of the president of the United States—perceived as the "Big Kahuna."[22]

This book consists of a collection of 10 major modern scandals since the administration of Dwight D. Eisenhower (1953–1961). They were chosen in consultation with leading academics, journalism practitioners, and media experts—including the Graduate School of Journalism, Columbia University; the Investigative Reporters and Editors organization; the Schuster Institute for Investigative Journalism; and several noted journalism scholars and practitioners—for the reporting of "the inside stories" about how the journalists actually went about ferreting out information in the course of their relentless research.

The primary requirement in choosing those scandals is that each involved a great deal of in-depth firsthand reporting by investigative print journalists. The litmus test was the impact on the political, national security, military, economic, and business communities of the United States. For that reason, they do not include scandals that occurred in every administration, nor was there any attempt to be all-inclusive based on a wide representation of newspapers and magazines.

The purpose of this book is to reveal the anatomy of history-making print scandals for the reader, to tell the inside stories of exactly how some of the most outstanding investigative reporters in America went about doing their painstaking research and writing—with an emphasis on the written word.

For that reason, the following scandals were selected:

1. The resignation of Sherman Adams. President Eisenhower's chief of staff, former New Hampshire governor Sherman Adams, resigned for allegedly accepting illegal gifts from a New Hampshire businessman in return for favors. While never proven, accusations and columns by muckraking columnist Jack Anderson were enough to make the GOP

leaders view Adams as a liability for the reelection campaign of 1958 and, therefore, they persuaded him to reluctantly resign.

2. The Bay of Pigs fiasco. Cuban exiles failed in a CIA-backed plan to land at the Bay of Pigs on Cuba in 1961, recapture the island, and bring down the regime of Premier Fidel Castro. This story was exposed by *New York Times* investigative reporter Tad Szulc, who played a unique role in the unfolding events during the first year of President John F. Kennedy's administration.

3. Watergate. Richard M. Nixon, in 1974, became the first sitting president to resign the presidency, as a result of the Watergate scandal. The landmark exposé by that famous journalism pair, Bob Woodward and Carl Bernstein of the *Washington Post*, brought to light the abuse of power by a U.S. president and a cover-up of his actions. Watergate, of course, was the icon that led the press to add "-gate" to the names of major scandals for years to come.

4. Monicagate. Bill Clinton's history-making sexual affair with White House intern Monica Lewinsky, a sensational story first broken by investigative reporter Michael Isikoff of *Newsweek*, resulted in Clinton's impeachment in 1998.

5. Enron. The collapse of Enron was a story broken by *Fortune* reporter Bethany McLean in 2001. The hugely successful company was a symbol of the excesses, greed, and corruption in the corporate and business arenas.

6. Abu Ghraib. Investigative reporter Seymour Hersh, in the *New Yorker* in 2004, revealed blatant violations by the United States of international and U.S. military law through the use of illegal torture at Abu Ghraib prison in Iraq.

7. Domestic eavesdropping. Called "the Biggest Secret," this was the government's full-scale effort to undermine the Fourth Amendment of the Constitution, which protects the rights of privacy. The story was broken in 2005 by Eric Lichtblau and James Risen of the *New York Times*.

8. Rendition. Exposed by Dana Priest of the *Washington Post* in 2007, rendition of prisoners overseas caused a scandal because of its implications on the legal behavior and moral standards of the U.S. military.

9. The Walter Reed Veterans Administration scandal. Dana Priest and Anne Hull of the *Washington Post* in 2007

uncovered the violation of America's sworn commitment to defend and protect its soldiers.

10. Guantanamo. The violation of the rules of international law at the U.S. detention center at Guantanamo Bay was researched in the Far East by reporter Tom Lasseter, who literally risked his life by following the detainees back to their native countries in Asia to interview them for the *Miami Herald* in 2008.

These are the 10 investigative series of stories that comprise the content of this collection of the inside stories of modern political scandals.

NOTES

1. *Time*, August 24, 2009, 14.

2. Richard Rodriguez, "Final Edition," *Harper's Magazine*, November 2009, 20.

3. Tom Rosenstiel, statement before the Joint Economic Committee hearing on "The Future of Newspapers: The Impact on the Economy and Democracy," September 24, 2009.

4. Ithiel de Sola Pool, *New York Times*, September 28, 1997.

5. Leonard Downie Jr. and Michael Schudson, "The Reconstruction of American Journalism," *Columbia Journalism Review*, October 19, 2009, 68.

6. Megan McArdle, *Atlantic*, October 26, 2009. McArdle is a Washington, DC–based blogger and journalist who writes a blog for the *Atlantic*.

7. Robert Miraldi, ed., *The Muckrakers* (Westport, CT: Praeger, 2000), 1.

8. Scott Gant, *We're All Journalists Now: The Transformation of the Press and Reshaping of the Law in the Internet Age* (New York: Free Press, 2007), 6–7.

9. Downie and Schudson, "Reconstruction of American Journalism," 1; emphasis added.

10. *New York Times*, October 31, 2009.

11. Mark Feldstein, "A Muckraking Model: Investigative Reporting Cycles in American History," *Harvard International Journal of Press/Politics*, Vol. 11 (2), 105–20 (2006).

12. Arthur Weinberg and Lila Weinberg, eds., *The Muckrakers: The Era in Journalism That Moved America to Reform* (New York: Simon & Schuster, 1961), 59.

13. Ibid., 57.

14. Lincoln Steffens, *The Autobiography of Lincoln Steffens* (New York: Harcourt, Brace, 1931), 357.

15. David Mark Chalmers, *The Social and Political Ideas of the Muckrakers* (New York: Citadel Press, 1964), 116.

16. C. C. Regier, *The Era of the Muckrakers* (London: University of North Carolina Press, 1957), 2.

17. John M. Harrison and Harry H. Stein, eds., *Muckraking: The Past, Present, and Future* (University Park: Pennsylvania State University Press, 1970), 11–12, 14.

18. David L. Protess et al., *The Journalism of Outrage: Investigative Reporting and Agenda Building in America* (New York: Guilford Press, 1992), 5, 11, 35.

19. Suzanne Garment, *Scandal: The Culture of Mistrust in American Politics* (New York: Doubleday, 1992), 17. Garment, a resident scholar at the American Enterprise Institute for Policy Research in Washington, DC, has been a professor of political science at Harvard and Yale universities.

20. Ibid., 2.

21. Jeffrey D. Schultz, *Presidential Scandals* (Washington, DC: CQ Press, 2000), xv.

22. *Kahuna* is a Hawaiian word, defined in the *Pukui & Elbert Dictionary* as "Priest, sorcerer, magician, wizard, minister, expert in any profession."

CHAPTER 1

SHERMAN ADAMS
RESIGNS

*Reported by Jack Anderson, Syndicated
Columnist, 1958*

A leader, in accomplishing his task, must at times stand aloof
and use men for the best interests of his task, not of the men. He
must put the nation's interests first, even when he harms,
perhaps unfairly, an Adams; in some cases the good doesn't
triumph, just the better.
            —William Bragg Ewald Jr., *Eisenhower the President*

Sometimes it takes years before a newspaperman investigating a
high White House official finally topples that person from his or
her seat of power. Such was the case for muckraking reporter
Jack Anderson, whose syndicated column, "Washington Merry-Go-
Round," appeared in a thousand newspapers nationwide, more than
any other columnist of his era. His column was arguably the most
influential journalistic source in Washington, D.C., and it always
thrived on political rumors.

Anderson learned his investigative craft at the feet of his mentor,
Drew Pearson, originator of the column. Pearson hired Anderson in
1947 as a "legman"—a reporter who gathered information for him.
Anderson, known for his tenacity, aggressive techniques, and influence in the nation's capital, wrote the column after Pearson's death
in 1969, supported by a varied group of writers and researchers over
the years. Anderson once wrote of Pearson: "From the beginning of
my service with Drew, I was schooled in the relentless Pearson style.
We never conceded the field if there was a sliver of a chance that we
could scoop the competition."[1]

Anderson and Pearson, though using the same tactics, were quite different personalities. Fox News lead anchorman Brit Hume, who once served as an apprentice reporter under Anderson, described Anderson as

> "almost purely a newspaperman. He had dug out many of the exposés that kept Pearson's name in the headlines. . . . [Anderson] was perhaps the most resourceful reporter in Washington. "Drew was more of a reformer," Jack would say. "I think I'm more of a reporter." But Jack was relatively unknown, and he seemed, as one friend put it, "sort of a pastel character" compared to Pearson. . . . Neither was a pundit and neither wanted to be. As Jack once wrote of himself, "I do not observe the Washington scene from Olympian heights. I am neither historian nor scholar. I like to think I am an investigative reporter. I poke into the shadows of government, searching with a small light for the facts that officials would prefer to keep in the dark. I have a tendency to stray from orthodox news trails and I blunder into many dead ends. But while others are occupied with the imposing view out front, I catch an occasional glimpse behind the scenes."[2]

Hume recalled his impression of Anderson upon first meeting:

> He looked and sounded like the man I thought him to be— confident, self-assertive, and even boastful. There was a certain severity both in his voice and his expression. He looked much as he did in photographs, except for one thing. His hair, once parted near the middle, was now combed forward and across the front, apparently to conceal a receding hairline. He was just under six feet tall, with an athletic, muscular build, except for his ample waistline and a certain overall fleshiness that might have been the result of his graduation from being Drew Pearson's legman to a full-fledged columnist. He had a pale complexion and his face was marked by a prominent nose and a stern expression. Once a day, Anderson would turn around in his chair, face the wall, and, in his stop-and-go fashion, pound out the column which would be read several days later by an audience that might number up to 45 million. When he talked of the column and its popularity, a little of the boastful, braying tone returned to his voice.[3]

Hume also related one of Anderson's favorite theories:

> He operated on the same theory as many movie stars, namely, that notoriety is as good as fame. It had been an article of faith with Drew Pearson. "Drew always taught me," he would tell us, "that controversy is good for the column. If you write a column like ours, you've got to be controversial. People will read you even if they hate you."[4]

Anderson, by sheer force of his intimidating personality and his dogged perseverance, eventually closed in on his White House target and broke open one of the most memorable scandals in the capital city's history. It was under Anderson's carefully designed strategy that the column uncovered what has become known as the "vicuña coat scandal," referring to one of several gifts wealthy New England industrialist Bernard Goldfine had given to President Dwight D. Eisenhower's powerful chief of staff, former New Hampshire governor (1949–1953) Sherman Adams. Adams, in turn, intervened in behalf of the businessman with government regulatory agencies. Anderson persevered, and Adams was ultimately forced to resign his post. That was seen as a major journalistic feat.

Adams had such an iron grip on the White House, with Eisenhower's support, that he became known in the press as the "de facto president." Of course, it took time—and a variety of investigative reporting techniques—for Anderson to overthrow this little but powerful man from the Granite State.

It all started innocuously enough as gossip items in two consecutive Drew Pearson columns. In the first, on April 21, 1955—as a result of groundbreaking legwork by Jack Anderson—Pearson alleged that Adams, a slightly built, gray-haired man with little patience for small talk, had intervened with the Interstate Commerce Commission (ICC) to assist Republican friends in two railroad cases. Less than a week later, on April 26, 1955, Pearson reported that Adams had allegedly contacted the Securities and Exchange Commission (SEC) to approve a contract awarded without competitive bid to a private entrepreneur to supply power to the Oak Ridge, Tennessee, and Paducah, Kentucky, atomic plants. Both columns were published without serious incident, but they planted the seeds of suspicion about Adams, whose ensuing White House actions both Pearson and Anderson continued to track in search of a major conflict-of-interest story.

This was no easy task. A highly regarded New Hampshire politician before coming to the White House, Adams had served as chairman of the U.S. Conference of Governors (1951–1952) and was appointed White House chief of staff for the new Republican president, Dwight Eisenhower. Adams took his role very seriously. With the exception of cabinet members and certain National Security Council (NSC) advisers, all requests for access to Eisenhower had to go through Adams, who, it was argued at the time, was the "second most powerful man in Washington" during the six years that he served alongside Eisenhower. In some circles, including the press corps, Adams was known as the "invisible president." Because of Eisenhower's highly formalized staff structure, an organizational format he had adapted from his years in the military, it appeared to many that Adams had virtual control over White House staff operations and domestic policy. (A January 1956 article in *Time* magazine reported that nothing was sent into the president without Adams's approval, which advanced this perception.)[5]

Adams's reputation as a New England Yankee purist enabled him to remain in good standing, despite his sometimes gruff manner and appearing at times to usurp even the president's powers. His troubles began in 1957, a year into Eisenhower's second term, when the powerful Speaker of the House, Sam Rayburn, became disillusioned with the regulatory laws of the Congress. A Special Subcommittee on Legislative Oversight was formed to take on the challenge. Although most of its staff came from the House itself, the committee reached outside for a chief counsel and brought in Prof. Bernard Schwartz of New York University's Law School, a scholarly, intense man known for his integrity. Schwartz wanted to plan a noncontroversial study of the regulatory process, a study quickly approved by Rep. Oren Harris (D-AR), chairman of the subcommittee's parent House Interstate and Foreign Commerce Committee, which would look into the unscrupulous lobbies of the regulated industries.

According to Anderson, Harris had "cleverly produced a prestige name in administrative law who had no experience whatsoever in government, and by his own statement, lacked even those wary instincts which gird the prudent citizen in the presence of congressmen and commissioner." Anderson added that Schwartz

> seemed hardly the white hunter that a safari through the regulatory jungle required. Studious-looking, retiring, at thirty-four the author of several tomes on administrative and

constitutional law, Schwartz was an academic's academic, the holder of five degrees, and a doctor of laws, who had never participated in a court case or a congressional hearing.[6]

As Schwartz would later admit: "I had no idea that there were instances of corruption and improprieties in the regulatory agencies." Anderson saw this as an opening for him to ingratiate himself and "get on a confidence-swapping basis" with Schwartz.[7]

Indeed, when Anderson told Schwartz about the information he had gathered on the Sherman Adams–Bernard Goldfine connection, the diligent professor began following up Anderson's leads. In fact, he widened his investigation to include all of the regulatory agencies. Other reporters, like Clark Mollenhoff of the *Des Moines Register*, also solicited valuable information from Schwartz. "We began to hope," said Anderson of Schwartz, "that we had here not a sheep in sheep's clothing. But a live ram."[8]

As part of his investigative modus operandi, Anderson would always look around for more than one source. He found that source in one of Schwartz's able investigators, Baron L. Shacklette, with whom Anderson nurtured a close collaboration. Out of this alliance between the press and congressional staff grew what Anderson referred to as a "runaway investigation."[9] Indeed, the politicians became so upset with Schwartz that he was fired on February 10, 1958, allegedly because he submitted expense vouchers that showed irregularities. That was just a cover story, however. The fact was that Schwartz was getting too close to embarrassing truths. In a statement to the press the day he was dismissed, the normally low-key Schwartz astounded reporters by telling them he had planned to expose the hold of big business upon the supposedly independent boards and commissions. He promised to bring to light the machinations of the White House clique in controlling the decisions of those agencies. Among the prominent names he mentioned was that of Sherman Adams. While he did not finish his inquiry, he accomplished part of his objective by focusing attention on the regulatory agencies that were supposed to be monitored by Congress.[10]

Anderson took careful note of Schwartz's comments and subsequently increased his courtship of Schwartz behind the scenes as an invaluable source. Anderson related that, by May 1, 1958,

> I had buttoned down the key ingredients of the Adams–
> Goldfine scandal. We knew the story had the potential of

inflicting a crushing blow on the Eisenhower White House. But we also knew that if astutely handled by the White House and played down by a cooperative press, it could be a mere two-day wonder. We decided not to go with all we had up front, but to start off by revealing only fragments, in hopes that the White House would ensnare itself on false explanations which we would then explode, building up the story from week to week and providing time for the professional conflict within the big-time press to generate a crest; moreover, our stories would be couched as an attack on the Harris committee (as it was popularly called) for covering up what we were revealing; only an official inquiry could force the admissions-under-oath from Adams and Goldfine that would finally vindicate our story.[11]

Anderson turned that development into an asset. After some complicated negotiations involving several parties, he obtained and read through the Schwartz papers and, much to his satisfaction, found proof that Adams had indeed interceded in Goldfine's behalf at the Federal Trade Commission (FTC). Anderson could hardly contain his enthusiasm:

> Sherman Adams, by dint of his own administrative drive and Eisenhower's distaste for the nuts and bolts of government and politics, was considered by knowledgeable observers to be the most powerful un-elected official in American history. . . . A sparse, crisp, craggy man, Adams wielded his power in an abrasive and self-righteous manner. Adjectives commonly used to describe him ran to "sharp," "cold," "tough," "brusque," "no-nonsense," "get-to-the-point." White House reporters nicknamed him "the Iceberg" and "the Abominable Nobleman."[12]

In keeping with the plan to report "fragments" of the scandal rather than the entire story at the outset, in a column under Anderson's byline on May 13, 1958, he reported that—during a period in which the House subcommittee was investigating the regulatory agencies—a probe into Sherman Adams's dealings with New England businessman Bernard Goldfine had been dropped for lack of evidence. However, after further investigative digging, Anderson came up with some embarrassing facts: "Federal Trade Commission records show," he wrote, "that Adams intervened to help textile tycoon Bernard Goldfine, who got into trouble with Uncle Sam for mislabeling wool products. After Adams poked his sharply chiseled nose into the case, Goldfine was excused from further investigation with an admonition not to violate the law again."[13]

Anderson continued: "In less than nine months he [Goldfine] was caught pulling the same old tricks. This time the FTC attorney in the case, Charles Canavan, recommended criminal proceedings for 'willful and deliberate flouting of the law.'" Once again, Adams stepped in to help his friend, Goldfine, by calling FTC Chairman Edward Howrey and asking him to meet with Goldfine on April 14, 1958. At the close of that meeting, Anderson wrote:

> a frustrated Goldfine reportedly told Howrey, in the presence of other FTC officials, "Please get Sherman Adams on the line for me." He then told Adams confidently: "I am over here at the FTC. I have been treated very well over here. Thanks for arranging the appointment."[14]

That was more than enough to convince the FTC officials nearby of the veracity of the Goldfine–Adams connection.

It was also sufficient, along with other stories that had come out of the congressional hearings, for the *New York Times* to write an editorial headlined "Mr. Adams' Bad Judgment," published on June 12, 1958, stating, in part:

> Governor Adams, who has spent many years in fine public service, must know that his position as chief of staff to the President is one of the most extreme delicacy and requires avoidance of even the appearance of friendliness—not to mention obligation— to any and all varieties of favor-seekers and influence-men.[15]

In response, White House Press Secretary Jim Hagerty stated in a press conference that Adams had "the full confidence of the president and that the matter would be quickly disposed of. And prove to be false."[16]

The Adams-Goldfine scandal heated up considerably on June 17, 1958, when the "Washington Merry-Go-Round" column revealing the details of the relationship between the two men highlighted the telephone call Adams made to the FTC on Goldfine's behalf. "To understand its true importance," the column reported,

> you have to know first that a call from Adams is considered almost the equivalent of a call from the president. You also have to know that Adams' assistant at that time was Charley

Willis, son-in-law of Harvey Firestone of the Firestone Rubber Co., and that Ed Howrey had long been the attorney for Firestone. He [FTC Chairman Howrey] was a purely political appointment. In addition, it was reported that Howrey enjoyed a close relationship with Adams and visited with Adams' at his home frequently during the early years of the administration.[17]

It had become quite clear during the congressional subcommittee hearings that Adams had seemingly abused his powers as a key figure in Eisenhower's administration. At the hearings, it was revealed that Adams had accepted gifts from Goldfine, who was being investigated for FTC violations. Goldfine was cited for contempt of Congress when he refused to answer questions regarding his relationship with Adams.

Anderson discovered that Goldfine, a wealthy industrialist, had given Adams a large number of presents, including an expensive vicuña coat, an oriental rug, suits, overcoats, alcohol, furnishings, and the payment of hotel and resort bills. Anderson said he eventually found evidence that Adams had twice persuaded the FTC to "ease up its pursuit of Goldfine for putting false labels on the products of his textile plants." When some of this came to light during the congressional hearings, even Adlai Stevenson—Eisenhower's Democratic opponent in 1952 and 1956—abandoned his penchant for civility and publicly accused the Eisenhower administration of "hypocrisy" and Sherman Adams in particular of "holier-than-thou self-righteousness" and "pious preaching."[18]

Anderson's column on June 17, 1958, stirred the White House press corps to demand an explanation from President Eisenhower at a press conference the next day. Following are excerpts from the transcript of the president's opening remarks at the news conference:

Good morning. Please sit down. . . . The intense publicity lately surrounding the name of Sherman Adams makes it desirable, even necessary, that I start this conference with an expression of my own views about the matter. First, as a result of this entire incident, all of us in America should have been made aware of one truth—this is that a gift is not necessarily a bribe. One is evil; the other is a tangible expression of friendship. Almost without exception, everybody seeking public office accepts political contributions. These are gifts to further a political career. Yet we do not make a generality that these gifts are intended to color the later official votes, recommendations, and actions of the recipients. In the general case, this whole activity is understood, accepted, and approved. The circumstances surrounding the innocent receipt by a public official of any gift are therefore important, so that the public may clearly distinguish between innocent and guilty action. Among these circumstances are the character and reputation of the individual, the record of his subsequent actions, and evidence of intent or lack of intent to exert undue influence. Anyone who knows Sherman Adams has never had any doubt of his personal integrity and honesty. No one has believed that he could be bought; but there is a feeling or belief that he was not sufficiently alert in making certain that the gifts, of which he was the recipient, could be so misinterpreted as to be considered as attempts to influence his political actions. To that extent he has been, as he stated yesterday, "imprudent." Now, the utmost in prudence must necessarily be observed by everyone attached to the White House because of the possible effect of any slightest inquiry, suggestion, or observation emanating from this office and reaching any other part of the Government. Carelessness must be avoided.

My own conclusions of this entire episode are as follows: I believe that the presentation made by Governor Adams to the congressional committee yesterday truthfully represents the pertinent facts. I personally like Governor Adams. I admire his abilities. I respect him because of his personal and official integrity. I need him. . . . I believe with my whole heart that he is an invaluable public servant doing a difficult job efficiently, honestly, and tirelessly. Now, ladies and gentlemen, so far as I am concerned, this is all that I can, all that I shall say. If there are any questions from any part of this body, they will go to Mr. [Press Secretary Jim] Hagerty and not to me.

Nonetheless, several reporters asked the president questions, to which Eisenhower replied that Adams may have been "imprudent," but added, earnestly: "I respect him because of his personal and official integrity. I need him."

Those last three words—"I need him"—caught the attention of the media and the public—and have long been remembered as a historical phrase uttered by Eisenhower because it was such an honest statement about how the president felt about Adams. Eisenhower, who had been used to delegating throughout his entire military career, had come to depend completely on Adams.

At this point, Anderson smelled blood. He then turned to yet another investigative tool: wiretapping. In his book, he wrote that he and his old "collaborator," Baron Shacklette, set up eavesdropping gear in Goldfine's suite at the Sheraton-Carlton in Washington on June 29, 1958, to record whatever he could pick up on a microphone.

"The rationale," wrote Anderson,

> was that Goldfine was reported to have hired private investigators to dig up discrediting information about members of the Harris committee (not too hard a task, I thought) and that it was necessary to be able to anticipate and counteract his moves. Shacklette arranged for rooms adjoining various Goldfine suites at the Sheraton-Carlton, set up the eavesdropping gear and invited me to join him to monitor the proceedings. I fully encouraged this official snoopery and assisted with the clandestine arrangements. No ethical problem troubled me at the time. If a government agency, whether the FBI or [a staff member of] a congressional committee, decided to bug someone and permitted me to cover the affair, I persuaded myself that it was the reporter's duty to gain access and to report the news. So I helped Shacklette in registering the various rooms and took to checking in regularly with him and his electronic marvels. I would stay for about an hour at a time.[19]

As it turned out, Anderson and Shacklette were caught in the act by the Goldfine forces one night when they detected something suspicious next door.

> Shacklette explained, with as matter-of-fact an air as he could, that since Goldfine forces were investigating members of the Harris committee, he was keeping a counter watch. I tried to maintain a detached mien of an observer, even when confronted with the embarrassment of being registered in that room under the false name of "Elliott Brooks." I did not realize the trouble I was in until I learned in the morning that some of Drew's [Pearson] closest friends were urging him to suspend

me so as to separate himself from the contretemps; instead, he issued to a clamorous press a paraphrase of Ike's statement on Sherman Adams: "Jack Anderson, of course, has been imprudent, but I need him."[20]

Fortunately for both Anderson and Shacklette, nothing came of the incident other than it being reported on the news and many of their colleagues getting a good laugh at them. But it had considerable fallout. Anderson's adventure into the cloak-and-dagger world, as a matter of record, wound up as a front-page story in the *New York Times* shortly thereafter. Shacklette was forced to resign, but he continued to work with Anderson to uncover the full story behind the Goldfine controversy.

On July 2, 1958, at a White House press conference, President Eisenhower was asked: "Mr. President, many Republicans, including some of your congressional leaders, are saying that Governor Adams should resign, or that you should fire him on the ground that his usefulness has been seriously impaired. In light of this, are you reconsidering your decision to keep him on?" Looking a bit annoyed, Eisenhower replied: "The statement I made to you, ladies and gentlemen, I think about two weeks ago, is no more and no less an expression of my convictions at that time. I have nothing more to say at this time. The hearings are still going on, and I will not make any comment or entertain any questions about that matter."

At that point, the well-respected *Times* reporter William H. Lawrence tossed a hot potato at the president: "Mr. President," he began, "my question concerns not the hearings on the Hill, but rather the responsibility of the Executive [Branch] in enforcing laws. And in that respect have you, as President, caused any inquiry to be made of the Internal Revenue Service as to whether it has audited or approved Mr. Goldfine's corporate tax returns as to whether these claim that gifts to Sherman Adams were legitimate business expenditures?" Eisenhower bristled and said, simply: "I have not made any suggestion of that kind to the Internal Revenue because, until this morning, I had never heard of such a possibility."[21]

The question, however, raised further questions about the Adams–Goldfine relationship. A few days later, the scandal had grown to the point that former President Harry S Truman, known for his caustic commentary, got into the fray with a surprise announcement of his own. In a press interview, he appeared to come to Adams's defense, stating that the government "would be in a bad fix" without Sherman Adams because "he's running it, you know!"[22] That added some levity to the whole affair.

Although Eisenhower had backed up the man whom he most trusted in the White House, historians have come to believe that in his own naïve way, Eisenhower did not really acknowledge the severity of Adams's actions. Politically, Eisenhower was on a downhill slide. The Republican Party was seen by most political observers as being badly hurt by the Adams case.

In his own memoir, Adams recalled how he had gradually come to realize that his actions—though well-intended—were inappropriate. His fall from grace, he believed, really began in the spring of 1958 when he gave a highly inflammatory partisan speech in Minneapolis attacking the Democrats. "I had listened for five years to the criticism the Republican leadership that the White House was being too fraternal with the Democrats," Adams said, "and I made up my mind to give them for once a speech which they should not find fault with." Adams even asked Bryce Harlow, Eisenhower's chief speechwriter, to help him. In the speech, Adams blamed the Democrats for allowing the country to fall behind the Soviet Union between World War II and 1953 in the race to build ballistic missiles, and for "the military catastrophe of Pearl Harbor and the scientific catastrophe of losing our atomic secrets and the policies that had lost China to the Reds and led to Communist invasion of Korea and the war." Looking back on it, Adams wrote:

> I knew, of course, that the speech was a radical departure from the president's own policy of avoiding extremely partisan outbursts, and so I talked it over with him [Eisenhower] before I left Washington. He said he understood that such speeches were part of every political campaign. . . . I found myself warmly applauded, for a time at least, by the right-wing Republicans in Congress, the closest I ever came to being acceptable to the Old Guard. But I was never forgiven by the Democrats.[23]

His speech made page 1 news across the country on January 21, 1958, with the *New York Times* carrying the headline, "Adams Rakes Democrats; Pearl Harbor to Missiles."

"That was in January," Adams wrote, "[but] in June the Democrats had me in a position where one of their investigative committees could level exaggerated charges to square accounts with me for attacking their party."[24] Called to testify before the subcommittee investigating his connections with Goldfine on June 17, 1958, Adams began his opening statement by denying that he had done anything improper in referring Goldfine's requests for information on FTC and SEC rulings, adding that Goldfine's requests "were given no more special consideration than any other requests that we received from private individuals."[25] But he quickly added: "If I made mistakes in giving official attention to his requests, the mistakes were those of judgment, not of intent."

Adams admitted that, even though he did not ask anybody to do anything for Goldfine,

> I did not stop to consider that in making a personal call or an inquiry concerning a matter in which he [Goldfine] was involved I might be giving the officials in the federal agency the erroneous impression that I had a personal interest in their ruling or decision on the case. Sometimes I did not take the time to consider that simply the origin of the call gave it such an implication. This was a blind spot of which I was not sufficiently aware but those were busy days for me and I was continually working under intense pressure. I often acted on the spur of the moment when more reflections would have suggested a wiser course to follow. . . . I said that I might have acted with a little more prudence. This observation was not by any means a slip of the tongue. I said it deliberately; I had been imprudent and I was ready to admit it. As soon as I said it, I could see right away that I had given the reporters what they need to make a sensational story. Everything else that I said at the hearing became relatively unimportant to them.[26]

Adams recalled that he left the hearing with the feeling that his service at the White House was about to come to an end, and he wondered how President Eisenhower would respond to questions about his admissions. Before his meeting with the press the next morning, the president called Adams into the Oval Office, where he and Jim Hagerty and the president talked things over. Eisenhower told Adams that he had written a statement about how he felt toward him and read it to him out loud. He called Adams a man of "personal integrity and honesty" and stated that "no one has believed he could be bought." The president said he believed Adams was telling the truth in his testimony. "I personally like Governor

Adams. I admire his abilities I respect him because of his persona and official integrity. I need him."[27]

That same day, June 17, 1958, veteran *New York Times* columnist Arthur Krock analyzed the effects of the mounting Adams scandal on the administration:

> The Adams episode as thus far on the record could not be more regrettable. Lost public confidence in the maintenance of the proclaimed official standards of the "crusaders" of 1952 would be a national liability. The usefulness of Adams in government, though he is a man whom corruption could never touch, stands tonight badly impaired by an apparent incredible lapse from objectivity where he was concerned, by evidence of a strange belief that it is enough for a man in his position to know his heart is pure. And Republican candidates throughout the country must surmount in some degree an issue [cronyism and corruption] which proved fatal to many Democrats in 1952.[28]

On August 6, 1958, at another presidential news conference, a reporter posed this question: "Mr. President, I want to quote to you in a speech you made to the GOP women in Washington on March 18, 1958. You said: 'The greater the role and responsibility of Government, the greater the importance of uncompromising insistence on the highest official standards all the time everywhere.' Now, sir, I wonder, in view of this, if you can justify keeping Sherman Adams and the girls in the White House who took the gifts from Goldfine on your payroll?" The president answered, briefly: "I made my statement about this subject some time ago. I hope you will remember it."

The president's emphatic statement did not slow the *New York Times*'s momentum. The venerable Krock wrote yet another analysis of the scandal on June 21, stressing the gravity of the situation in a story headlined: "Adams Case Creates Crisis of Confidence; Republicans Fear Disaster."

Despite Eisenhower's strong defense, demands for Adams's resignation mounted. "There was an opportunity for them to remove me from the President's staff," Adams recalled, "and they intended to take advantage of it. I kicked myself for having given it to them."[29]

In early September, Adams took some time off to go fishing with his wife in Brunswick, Maine. While Adams was vacationing, Press Secretary Hagerty indicated that Adams had no "present" plans to give up his job as assistant to the president. Shortly after he arrived in Maine, however, Adams was called back to the White House and informed that contributions to the Republican campaign fund for the fall elections were trailing off, owing primarily to him remaining as chief of staff. At the request of the president, both Meade Alcorn, chairman of the Republican National Committee, and Vice President Richard M. Nixon talked to Adams about the situation. He learned indirectly that the president was troubled, but, Adams insisted, the decision was left to him.

"I worried about the embarrassment that I was bringing upon the president. But I tried to stick it out in my job because I knew that Eisenhower did not want me to resign," Adams wrote.[30] On September 10, however, the *New York Times* carried a story reporting that high Republican leaders were convinced that party pressure would force Adams to leave the White House soon.

The Adams scandal was partly responsible for a Democratic victory over the Republicans in elections in Maine, a traditional GOP stronghold. Party pressure mounted with the passing of each day as the November elections approached. Adams did not take long to make his decision to resign. He flew to Newport, Rhode Island, where the president was vacationing at his home, to review his resignation statement with Eisenhower and Hagerty. The president, looking sober and somber, read the statement Adams had brought with him and nodded his approval. Eisenhower then pulled out a letter which he and Hagerty had been composing and read it to Adams. It was highly complimentary and noted that he accepted the resignation "with sadness." He and Hagerty returned to Washington, and Hagerty arranged for Adams to go on the air that evening, September 22, 1958. Adams read his prepared statement, in which he asserted his innocence of any wrongdoing and said he had served "with pride."[31]

As a footnote to history, Dr. Schwartz, the man who started the controversy by leaking information to Anderson, told the *New York Times* shortly after Adams's resignation that there was a need for "a thorough investigation which the House committee has not given yet." He added: "People in the future, no matter how high they are, are going to say: 'Look at Sherman Adams, and he was practically President, and he got caught.'"[32]

Even after Adams's resignation, the subject came up again on October 1, 1958, in a news conference at the White House, when Eisenhower was asked: "Can you clear up the conflicting stories about the resignation of Sherman Adams? One story is that you instructed

Meade Alcorn to get his resignation; the other story is that he gave it voluntarily. Can you clear up your part in the resignation?" Eisenhower replied, emphatically: "I did not instruct anyone to ask for his resignation. He did resign voluntarily. Now, there is no question that other people advised him very strongly at this time, during these last weeks and months, but he was never advised by me to resign." To the very end, the president wanted—above all—to make it clear that at no time did he, personally, ask for Adams's resignation.

To understand the full measure of Sherman Adams the man, one of the best accounts of Adams's White House years is included in a book written by William Bragg Ewald Jr., a speechwriter for Eisenhower. Ewald, who worked alongside Adams in the White House, described Adams as having a reputation "as the meanest, rudest, most laconic man in the world, a wiry New Hampshire lumberjack with a gruff exterior concealing a heart of stone."[33]

"I always admired him and I liked him, but he had enemies," Ewald told me in an interview. "He called the shots, but he'd hang up on people in the middle of a conversation. He would do rude things to people unnecessarily. I never asked him why he went out of his way to offend people. This was his manner. He was brisk, very quick, and loyal to Eisenhower. He wanted to do what the boss wanted, not what he wanted. In some cases, he had had rather deep-seated differences with Eisenhower and various people in the administration, but he was an absolute loyalist. I liked him. He could be rude and he could be curt with older people—people who had some stature in the political world—but he never was a bully with younger people on the staff. Adams was always quite gentle, kind, and friendly to them. He loved music—he learned a lot of it at Dartmouth College. He'd go to concerts and he would sincerely enjoy great music, singing hymns in church.

"Did he do anything wrong? Adams did not realize the damage he was doing. I'm sure that in his heart of hearts he did not believe he had done anything wrong. But people held to the high standards he set for himself and for others. They would say, well, this [involvement with Goldfine] is coming from a guy like Adams who is the high priest of sanitary government. This is unacceptable. And they kept hinting there was something underhanded about it."

Despite Adams's unwavering loyalty to the president, Ewald concluded that Eisenhower had no choice but to let him go. In fact, Eisenhower's poll ratings did not decline from November 1957 to

November 1958, remaining steady at 58 percent, and indicating that the Adams episode did not hurt his popularity.[34] But someone had to be the sacrificial goat. Wrote Ewald:

> A leader, in accomplishing his task, must at times stand aloof and use men for the best interests of his task, not of the men. He must put the nation's interests first, even when he harms, perhaps unfairly, an Adams: in some cases the good doesn't triumph, just the better. These two particular dilemmas of power have been met by all nations in their histories.[35]

Anderson once summed up his own philosophy of the role of an investigative reporter covering the White House:

> We have tried, in our own way, to become a watchdog of Washington, to be numbered among the few investigative reporters who seek to discover what is really happening in the nation's capital. . . . Investigative reporters grate against the political conviviality and easy friendships of official Washington. They avoid the social entanglements that inhibit straightforward reporting about the high and might.[36]

Mark Feldstein, Anderson's biographer and a professor of journalism at George Washington University, is recognized as one of the best-informed writers on Anderson's life. "Anderson," he wrote, "was ahead of his time, anticipating the victims-and-villains entertainment values that have come to dominate 21st-century television news."

> Ironically, despite the black-and-white view he expressed in his column, Anderson's own reporting was itself a far more grayish mix of courageous digging and sensationalistic self-promotion. In many ways, the columnist embodied the contradictions that have characterized investigative reporting throughout American history; from the beginning it has alternated between the high-brow ideals of public service and the lowbrow reality of celebrity gossip. Part circus huckster, part guerrilla fighter, part righteous rogue, Anderson waged a one-man journalistic resistance when it was exceedingly unpopular to do so.[37]

In an interview with me, Feldstein described Anderson as "a bridge for muckrakers of a century ago and the crop that came out of

Watergate. He held politicians to a level of accountability in an era where journalists were very deferential to those in power."[38]

ABOUT JACK ANDERSON

Jack Anderson was renowned for his aggressive reporting techniques and his political savvy. He was born on October 19, 1922, and had a long and successful career as a Washington columnist with enormous influence—all the way up to a president of the United States. He was a journalist who cultivated more discreet sources than anyone could ever count.

A devout Mormon, Anderson started his career as a reporter in Utah on the *Murray Eagle*, then joined the *Salt Lake Tribune* in 1940. He served in the armed forces during World War II in China, where he worked on the Shanghai edition of *Stars and Stripes*. When he returned to the States, he got a job with the famous reporter Drew Pearson, creator of the column, "Washington Merry-Go-Round." After Pearson died in 1969, Anderson took over sole ownership of the column, which, at its height, was published in nearly a thousand newspapers, with a readership of 40 million. He frequently wrote columns based on anonymous sources, whom he protected at all times, thus gaining the trust of high government officials.

Anderson was the recipient of the 1972 Pulitzer Prize in national reporting for his investigation of secret American agreements between the war with Pakistan in 1971. Anderson became controversial when he alleged that FBI chief J. Edgar Hoover was involved with the Mafia and tied to Watergate as well as the assassination of President John F. Kennedy. Anderson was given credit for playing a part in breaking the Iran-Contra scandal under President Ronald Reagan. Anderson was diagnosed with Parkinson's disease in 1986, and in mid-1987 he retired. He died on December 17, 2005, of complications from Parkinson's disease.

NOTES

1. Jack Anderson, *Peace, War, and Politics: An Eyewitness Account*, with Daryl Gibson (New York: Forge, 1999), 82–83.

2. Brit Hume, *Inside Story: Tales of Washington Scandals by the Young Reporter Who Helped Jack Anderson Dig Them Out.* (Garden City, NY: Doubleday, 1974), 9.

3. Ibid., 14.

4. Ibid., 31.

5. Sherman Adams, "The Administration: O.K., S.A.," *Time*, January 9, 1956, 18–22.

6. Jack Anderson, *Confessions of a Muckraker: The Inside Story of Life in Washington during the Truman, Eisenhower, Kennedy and Johnson Years*, with James Boyd (New York: Random House, 1979), 281.

7. Ibid.

8. Ibid., 282.

9. Ibid., 295.

10. *New York Times*, February 12, 1958.

11. Anderson, *Confessions of a Muckraker*, 302.

12. Ibid., 300.

13. Typewritten column by Jack Anderson, May 13, 1958, courtesy of American University Library, Special Collections, Washington, DC.

14. Ibid.

15. *New York Times*, June 12, 1958.

16. Ibid.

17. *New York Times*, June 17, 1958.

18. *New York Times*, June 13, 1958.

19. Anderson, *Confessions of a Muckraker*, 306.

20. Ibid., 307.

21. *New York Times*, July 3, 1958.

22. *New York Times*, July 10, 1958.

23. Sherman Adams, *Firsthand Report: The Story of the Eisenhower Administration* (New York: Harper, 1961), 443.

24. Ibid.

25. Ibid., 444.

26. Ibid., 445.

27. Ibid., 446.

28. *New York Times*, June 17, 1958.

29. Adams, *Firsthand Report*, 447.

30. Ibid.

31. Ibid., 450.

32. *New York Times*, September 23, 1958.

33. Author's interview with William Bragg Ewald Jr., February 20, 2009. Ewald was a former speechwriter for Eisenhower; he served as a member of Eisenhower's tight-knit White House staff and worked closely with Sherman Adams.

34. Data from Gallup polls. The popular World War II commander succeeded in bringing his military might to bear on U.S. domestic reform. He was ranked sixth all-time among all U.S. presidents by the *Times* of London, according to a survey taken in 2009.

35. William Bragg Ewald Jr., *Eisenhower the President: Crucial Days, 1951–1960* (Englewood Cliffs, NJ: Prentice-Hall, 1981), 280.

36. Jack Anderson, *The Anderson Papers*, with George Clifford (New York: Ballantine Books, 1974), 7.

37. Mark Feldstein, "The Last Muckraker," *Washington Post*, July 28, 2004.

38. Author's interview with Mark Feldstein, July 14, 2008.

CHAPTER 2

THE BAY OF PIGS FIASCO

Reported by Tad Szulc, New York Times, *1961*

Castro's victory at the Bay of Pigs defined for the future Cuba's basic relationship with the United States as well as with the Soviet Union.

—Tad Szulc, *Fidel: A Critical Portrait*

On the evening of April 6, 1961, the phone in the White House rang and an editor from the *New York Times* asked to speak to President John F. Kennedy. The editor wanted to let the president know that the next morning the paper would publish a page 1 story by Tad Szulc, their outstanding Latin American reporter, stating that an invasion of Cuba by exiles was close at hand. Szulc was known in his profession and by the Kennedy administration as arguably the best informed and most knowledgeable contemporary journalist on the subjects of Latin America, Cuba, and, in particular, Premier Fidel Castro. Whenever Szulc wrote an exclusive story, politicians—including the president of the United States—had good reason to pay attention.

The *Times* contact read the lead of Szulc's story to the president: "For nearly nine months Cuban exile military forces dedicated to the overthrow of Premier Fidel Castro have been training in the United States as well as Central America." According to one well-informed journalist, Kennedy "blew up, banging the phone down, and throwing around words like 'treason.' Calming down, he telephoned Orville Dryfoos, the *Times*'s publisher, and asked him to kill the story in the national interest."[1]

That was not to be the case.

Dryfoos told the president he would call him back shortly. After finding that some of his editors were threatening to quit if he held the story, Dryfoos called Kennedy back offering a compromise: The paper would run the story under a one-column headline instead of four columns wide, and the story would be moved from the top of the page to the middle, so as not to call as much attention to it. The headline would read: "Anti-Castro Units Trained to Fight at Florida Bases."

By far the most significant concession the *Times* made to Kennedy, however, was that two words—"invasion imminent"—were removed from the text. In addition, the *Times* toned down its story by taking out references to the Central Intelligence Agency sponsoring the invasion—something that Castro had been publicly stating for months. Kennedy did not want to tip off the Cuban leader about the timing or the support of the CIA. (Decades later, the well-known investigative reporter Michael Isikoff, in a book he wrote about the Clinton sex scandal involving a White House intern, wrote: "In retrospect, *Times* executives acknowledged that they had made the wrong decision. Had they run the story [as it was written], the Kennedy administration might have avoided a major foreign policy disaster.")[2]

"I can't believe what I am reading," Kennedy said aloud the next morning when he read the story—even with the deletions the *Times* had made—which had also been carried in a two-paragraph report by the Associated Press, as well as on a CBS news broadcast reporting that there were "unmistakable signs" that "plans for an invasion of Cuba were in the final stages." Said Kennedy: "Castro doesn't need agents over here. All he has to do is read our papers. It's all laid out for him."[3] The president then instructed Arthur M. Schlesinger Jr. "to go to the *Times* with a list of factual errors in Szulc's story." "The unfortunate fact," Schlesinger reported back, "is that we do not have a strong case against the story as inaccurate."[4]

The next day, April 8, on page 2 of the *New York Times* under the headline "Cuban Intrigue Boiling in Miami as Castro Foes Step Up Efforts," Szulc described the worsening situation:

> This is a city of open secrets and rampaging rumors for the legions of exiled Cubans who plot the downfall of Premier Fidel Castro and his regime. Men come and go quietly on their secret missions of sabotage and gun-running into Cuba, while others assemble at staging points here to be flown at night to military camps in Guatemala and Louisiana.

He went on to write that the exiles intended "to gain a beachhead in Cuba to set up a 'Government in Arms' and then request diplomatic recognition by foreign nations."

Ten days later, approximately 1,500 anti-Castro fighters landed on Cuba's southern coast in an area known as Bahía de Cochinos, the Bay of Pigs. The military plan turned into a major disaster—more than a hundred rebels were killed and more than 1,100 others captured and imprisoned.

Szulc's initial story on April 7 turned out to be accurate. Much to the embarrassment of the Kennedy administration, Szulc reported that an army of 5,000 to 6,000 men was planning to liberate Cuba and that many members of this expeditionary force were former companions of Castro in his revolution. He wrote that the recruiting of Cubans had started in the summer of 1960 under the administration of former president Dwight D. Eisenhower, whose military and intelligence aides had drawn up a CIA-backed plan to invade the island and overthrow Castro. Szulc also reported that many of the anti-Castro troops had already been in Cuba for months from hidden bases in the Florida Keys.

Ironically, only days earlier on April 4, the State Department—well aware of rumblings about the growing presence of Soviet advisers in Cuba—had issued a strongly worded 36-page pamphlet written in the White House under the close supervision of the president. Labeling Cuba a "Soviet satellite," the pamphlet called on the Castro government "to sever its links with the international Communist movement" and "to restore the integrity of the Cuban Revolution." The statement also said that the Kennedy administration saw Cuba as "a grave and urgent challenge" that "offers a clear and present danger to the authentic and autonomous revolution of the Americas."[5] In response, the Cuban press charged: "The Government of the millionaire Kennedy may continue plotting defamation campaigns against Cuba, may continue arming mercenaries and preparing war criminals, may continue threatening and insulting, but all it can achieve is that dirty pamphlet."[6] The foreign minister of Cuba charged that the State Department's denunciation of Castro's regime "constitutes formalization of the undeclared war which the United States is making against us."[7]

Meanwhile, Szulc's original story had set off shock waves of activity. In Miami itself, there was considerable anxiety in the Cuban exile community with the *Times* reporting that some 50,000 Cuban refugees were hoping to return to their homeland. The story said that resettlement was the stated goal of the Federal Cuban Refugee Program. Castro himself poured more fuel on the political flames on April 6 by announcing that he would display Cuba's military weapons "to warn his enemies not to attack and to show that all the people of the island support his revolution."[8] On April 9, the leader of the Anti-Castro Revolutionary Council raised apprehensions by stating that "something is going to happen" and that, if there were an invasion, it would be a "fight to the death."[9]

Szulc's exclusive story from Miami was serendipitous. According to one account of how Szulc pieced together his story: "It was typical of Szulc's fortunes that he was only stopping over in Miami between assignments when he picked up the trail of a news story that would come to rivet the world's attention and create seismic and long-lasting consequences for American foreign policy."[10] Indeed, Szulc pounced on the opportunity to weave together stories that had already appeared in his own paper about the restive nature of Cuban–U.S. relations leading up to the invasion. No wonder. He had earned a reputation during his career at the paper for always being alert, cultivating his own sources, and being constantly on the lookout for any tidbits of information that would lead him to a story. He was an exceptional investigative reporter with the knack for drawing out a story like a sponge soaks up water, while other reporters around him could not—or did not have that same sense of urgency and ability to—piece together information to formulate a sound story.

Szulc's suspense-filled stories caught the attention of everyone. As he became more involved in them himself, contacting people who trusted him because of his reputation as an honest and factually correct writer, he reported on April 10 that Castro's forces were mapping out a military plan of their own to thwart the anticipated landings of rebel soldiers as well as to capture rebels who had already landed and hidden in the mountains. Szulc reported that there was indecision in Washington about whether or not to go ahead with the invasion because of legal, military—and perhaps most notably—political concerns. Should the rebels' landings fail, the Kennedy administration would suffer enormous worldwide embarrassment and the new president would experience a significant loss of prestige, Szulc wrote. But the Cuban exiles were more determined than ever and made last-minute preparations in Miami as their plan went forward, Szulc reported on April 11. According to James Reston, a veteran *Times* columnist, the crisis had turned into a "moral" issue. On April 11, 1961, Reston wrote:

> President Kennedy is now deeply involved in a moral and political question that has troubled statesmen and philosophers ever since the days of Pericles. This is how to reconcile the

nation's self-interest with its ideals and treaty commitments. The self-interest of the nation undoubtedly requires the overthrow of the Cuban Government of Fidel Castro, which is providing a political and, increasingly, a military base for communism in the Caribbean. But how far can the United States pursue this objective by secretly arming and training anti-Castro refugees without misleading its own people and violating its treaty commitments under the Charters of the Organization of American States and the United Nations? For a democratic nation whose foreign policy rests on vast catalogues of treaties all over the world and on opposing the use of proxy armies and forces by the Communists in Laos and elsewhere, this is a difficult question.

On April 13, Reston wrote another analysis based on a Kennedy press conference the day before, during which Kennedy said the United States would not intervene in the impending invasion with its own forces and was not going to allow an armada of anti-Castro refugees to launch an invasion of Cuba from Miami Beach or anywhere else in the United States. "This still leaves the main questions," Reston wrote,

> which he could not very well discuss in public: How much will the United States Government help the Cuban refugees? Will it provide them with all the money and arms necessary to launch an invasion, not from American ports and airfields, but from somewhere else? Will it train the refugees in the arts of sabotage and guerilla warfare in Guatemala or elsewhere? And if they get into trouble once they land, will it continue to supply them from there?

That same day, Szulc filed a story in which he reported that the Cuban rebel leaders had rejected Kennedy's opposition to an invasion from the United States and planned to go ahead anyway. The leaders said no steps had been taken to curb their actions, Szulc reported. He followed up with a vividly written story published on April 16 under the headline: "Cuban Rebels HQ; Miami Provides Strange Backdrop for Conspiracy and Plotting." This was the day when the rebels began their initial raids of sabotage in Havana. His story began:

> MIAMI, FLA. April 15—In sparsely furnished apartments, white-framed homes, boarding houses, cheap hotel rooms, in

luxury motels, and in revolutionary headquarters in Miami and its sprawling suburbs, intense men and women are master-minding this week-end a war without mercy against Fidel Castro, their fallen idol.

For thousands of Cubans—and some Americans—Miami has become a metropolis of double life, secret meetings and perilous expeditions. The Cuban love and tradition of conspiracy—and their virtually incurable inability to conspire harmoniously without splitting into a multitude of separate and rival movements—have found in Miami the fertility and the climate of a hothouse, and they are flourishing as never before.

Like a baseball centerfielder who was patrolling the vast ground around him, Szulc was everywhere, day and night, buttonholing anyone who would talk to him. He interviewed a Cuban pilot who had flown his crippled B-26 bomber into Miami and who described the strafing and bombing attacks on Cuban air bases. The pilot, and two other rebel pilots with him, were not identified—Szulc promised to protect their identity—but one flyer told Szulc he had struck three military targets of the Castro regime. The pilot said the air strikes were intended to be part of a plan that would soften up the defense of the Havana government and pave the way for internal uprisings supported by large-scale guerrilla landings from Miami.

The four-column *Times* headline in later editions read: "Castro Foes Bomb 3 Air Bases; 2 of Raiders Flee to Florida; Cuba Is Mobilizing, Blames U.S." Still, Szulc reported, the Kennedy White House made it a point to announce that no U.S. forces had been involved and that the three airmen, who described themselves as defectors from the Castro air force, had been given asylum in this country.

The next day, April 17, 1961, the long-awaited invasion of Cuba began.

Szulc filed a story with the *Times* on April 18, headlined "Anti-Castro Units Land in Cuba; Report Fighting at Beachhead; Rusk Says U.S. Won't Intervene." The story began:

Rebel troops opposed to Premier Fidel Castro landed before dawn yesterday on the swampy southern coast of Cuba in Las Villas Province. The attack, which was supported from the air, was announced by the rebels and confirmed by the Cuban Government. After fourteen hours of silence on the progress of the assault, the Government radio in Havana broadcast early today a terse communiqué by Premier Castro announcing only that "our armed forces are continuing to fight the enemy heroically" and that details of "our successes" would follow. The Cuban government said the attacks had been launched from points in Florida and Guatemala under the direction of the Central Intelligence Agency. At the same time, U.S. Secretary of State Dean Rusk said his country sympathized with those who struck against Castro but emphasized that there was not and would not be any intervention by U.S. forces.

Szulc filed another story on Thursday, April 20, which was published the next morning under the headline "Castro Says Attack Is Crushed; Cuba Rebels Give Up Beachhead, Report New Landings on Island." The story led with: "The Government of Premier Fidel Castro claimed today that it had 'completely defeated' the invasion force that landed Monday." Szulc said the rebels had been overrun and were said to have been on Cuban soil less than 71 hours.

At his press conference at the White House on April 21, Kennedy said little about the Cuban situation, asserting that the facts would come out at a later date. But then one reporter asked: "In view of the fact that we are taking propaganda lambasting around the world, why is it not useful, sir, for us to explore with you the real facts behind this, or our [U.S.] motivations?" Kennedy replied with his now famous quote: "There's an old saying that victory has 100 fathers and defeat is an orphan. And I wouldn't be surprised if information is poured into you in regard to all of the recent activities."

Meanwhile, Szulc's coverage of the war from Miami continued. On April 22, he reported that Castro and his regime were celebrating their ability to repulse the rebels who had landed in Cuba. His piece also stated:

> With their political leadership battered and divided, and with the underground organization in Cuba badly mauled, deep resentment is mounting against the United States, and especially the Central Intelligence Agency, over what is widely regarded here [in Miami] as a monumental mismanagement. As has been an open secret in Florida and Central America for months, the C.I.A. planned, coordinated and directed the defeat on a beachhead in southern Cuba.

The following day, on April 23, Szulc's analysis of the fiasco, "Cuban Problem Remains in Wake of Debacle," was published. He wrote:

> MIAMI, April 22—The seventy-two-hour odyssey this week of a small invasion force of Cuban exiles on the bloody swampland beachhead in Cuba, ninety minutes by air from here, exploded as one of those historic shots heard around the world. The consequences for all concerned are still unforeseeable.
>
> In this stunned city where the rebel army was born from the ranks of thousands of refugees from the regime of Premier Fidel Castro, the facts about the first elements of truth about the week's events were being sorted out from the incredible chaos and confusion surrounding them.
>
> The initial, but very tentative, conclusions emerging from the settling dust of the abortive attacks were that the Castro regime won new even if temporary strength from what was perhaps not so much of its own victory as it was something of a self-inflicted defeat of the rebels and their United States associates.

As Szulc and Karl E. Meyer, the two reporters who knew the story best, wrote in their book published in 1962:

> Operation Pluto—the attack on Fidel Castro's fortress by a band of brave but totally unprepared Cuban exiles—ran its inexorable course toward defeat. When it was over, the incident on the Bay of Pigs earned its place in the annals of modern history as one of the great fiascos in military leadership, intelligence gathering, and psychological preparation and execution.[11]

Any thoughts that the United States may have had about launching its own invasion were quickly put to rest. For one thing, Castro said that if the United States were to attack, he would execute all of the 743 rebel soldiers taken into custody during the war. Szulc's subsequent dispatches reported that the United States had used men from the Fulgencio Batista dictatorship, which had been ousted by Castro on January 1, 1959; that the anti-Castro movement in the United States had abandoned any further plans of military strategy and announced it would depend on the extensive underground network already in Cuba; and that Castro, who had previously framed his revolution in terms of humanistic goals, announced that he would tighten his links with Moscow with May Day approaching under the banner of socialism.

The Bay of Pigs debacle was a tremendous setback for Kennedy. Perhaps *Time* expressed it best in its issue of May 5, 1961, evaluating Kennedy's first 100 days as president: "Last week, as John F. Kennedy closed out the final 100 days of his administration, the U.S. had suffered . . . setbacks rare in the history of the Republic. First came Russia's man-in-space triumph [launching cosmonaut Yuri Gagarin into space]. Then the shockingly bungled invasion of Cuba." A commentary on these early days of the Kennedy administration was published in 2009 in the *New York Times* which reported: "The President was despondent. He suggested to his historian in residence, Arthur M. Schlesinger, Jr., that if [later] he did a book on the administration it could be titled, 'Kennedy: The Only Years.'"[12]

In his 1986 book profiling Castro, Szulc wrote:

> Castro's victory at the Bay of Pigs defined for the future Cuba's basic relationship with the United States as well as with the Soviet Union. He proved both that he had an extremely high military defensive capacity, and that the Kremlin was prepared to act in Cuba's defense. As Nikita Khrushchev said in a note to Kennedy on April 18, 1961: "We shall render the Cuban people and their government all necessary assistance in beating back the armed attack on Cuba." And eighteen months later Khrushchev showed how far he was really prepared to go: unquestionably the Bay of Pigs affair led directly to the Cuban Missile Crisis in 1962.[13]

Szulc referred to that missile crisis of October 1962 as a "historically inevitable consequence of the Bay of Pigs events. The dynamics on both sides of the Straits of Florida had to force a new confrontation—it was like a law of physics—and [the second] time the conflict was enlarged, raised to superpower level."[14]

There was yet another interesting story going on behind this story, namely, the role of the press in reporting the news when national security is endangered. In its essence, behind the scenes there was a tug of war between the media and the White House over the Kennedy administration's policy of secrecy before the invasion. Kennedy took the opportunity to address this dilemma at a luncheon on April 27 in New York before the American Newspaper Publishers Association, where he stated:

> I have no intention of establishing a new Office of War Information to govern the flow of news. I am not suggesting any new forms of censorship or any types of security classifications. I have no easy answer to the dilemma that I have posed, and would not seek to impose it if I had one. But I am asking the members of the newspaper profession and the industry in this country to reexamine their own responsibilities, to consider the degree and nature of the present danger, and to heed the duty of self-restraint, which that danger imposes upon us all.
>
> Every newspaper now asks itself, with respect to every story: "Is it news?" All I suggest is that you add the question: "Is it in the interest of the national security?" . . .
>
> And should the press of America consider and recommend the voluntary assumption of specific new steps or machinery, I can assure you that we will cooperate whole-heartedly with those recommendations.
>
> Perhaps there will be no recommendations. Perhaps there is no answer to the dilemma faced by a free and open society in a cold and secret war. In times of peace, any discussion of this subject, and any action that results, are both painful and without precedent. But this is a time of peace and peril, which knows no precedent in history.

On April 30, 1961, after the Cuban rebels had been thoroughly beaten, Szulc's article in the *Times* reported that the State Department advised all remaining U.S. citizens in Cuba to return to the homeland; Secretary of State Dean Rusk assured a Senate panel that American had no plans "to proceed in any way in armed intervention in Cuba."

Castro's own perspective on the entire affair, which he presented in *Fidel Castro, My Life: A Spoken Autobiography*, many years later, was simply this: "Kennedy, with reservations, scruples and some hesitation, put Eisenhower's and Nixon's plan into effect—he believed the plan developed by the CIA and the Pentagon would have the support of the [Cuban] people, that the people would rush into the streets to welcome the invaders and that the militias wouldn't fight, that they'd rise against the country's government. They may have believed their own lies and propaganda, and they most certainly underestimated the Cuban people and our Cuban revolutionaries . . . A hard defeat for the [American] empire. And a great humiliation."[15]

By June 16, Szulc displayed in his written dispatch in the *Times* his unusual insight, his focus on details, and his ability to interpret and put into perspective what he saw and heard. He wrote that Castro, feeling new strength, was wooing the foreign press:

> In the casual conversations with newsmen that started at a highly informal news conference Wednesday afternoon, continued most of the night at a hotel bull session, and went on all day Thursday during a tour of the invasion beaches that he insisted on guiding himself, he said that it was up to the United States to take the first step towards relaxing the hostile relationship between the two countries. But his attitude and occasional remarks—including studiously respectful references to President Kennedy at a time when the region's propaganda still poured incredible invective on him—were successful in planting in the minds of the newsmen the seed of the suspicion that, feeling very strong, Premier Castro may not like to find basis of agreement with Washington. And, through his artful, around-the-clock performance, Castro evidently sought to create that impression, despite his care not to commit himself just yet.

By mid-1961, Szulc had not stepped foot in Cuba for a year. His dispatches for Miami were based on reliable sources, but not his usual firsthand reporting—something that had been virtually impossible in the run-up to the invasion and during the brief war. So he left for Havana and quickly wrote a stunning firsthand report, entitled "The Two Cubas of Fidel Castro," published in the Sunday, June 25, 1961, *New York Times Magazine*. His first-person article, reporting on the fifth time he had visited Cuba between 1959 and 1961, stated:

> HAVANA, June 25—The penumbral and chilling world of Cuba is the world of fear and hate, and all of the all-powerful secret police—which has now given up its adolescent presence of being merely the Army's Intelligence Department and has matured into the Soviet-style State Security Service operated by its own Ministry. It is the world of the octopus-like Committees for the Defense of the Revolution. These are spreading throughout the island as a legion of informers for whom it is a high moral

virtue to denounce and arrest suspected counter-revolutionaries, be they one's parents, friends, sweethearts or co-workers. In this weird juxtaposition of worlds, you must take your choice in deciding which of them you think really exists.

Out of the ashes of the failed counterrevolution came the rise of President Kennedy's affirmative 10-year Alliance for Progress with the Latin American nations. Only Cuba and the Dominican Republic were excluded from a meeting held in August 1961. A month later, Szulc capitalized on his close, long-standing personal relationship with Castro based—it was known by Szulc's contemporary reporters at the time—on mutual respect (he had interviewed Castro at length two years before). It had also been said that the two men developed a liking for one another—Szulc because of Castro's fascinating, unpredictable flamboyant style; Castro because Szulc's reporting reflected a profound in-depth understanding of Cuban society and of Castro's intellectual revolutionary ideas, and because he never displayed any signs of judging the egotistical Cuban dictator while in his presence. Szulc wrote that this time he found Castro seemingly more confident and relaxed than in the summer of 1959. Szulc wrote that he thought Castro was enjoying his moment of triumph, acting the victorious warlord and the vindicated statesman after the failure of the rebel invasion of his island. He described Castro as harder, tougher, more uncompromising politically and humanly, wedded to newly discovered Marxist beliefs.

After spending many long hours with Castro—a man whose mind Szulc was able to penetrate and comprehend—Szulc wrote:

> One is always tempted to confuse the public personality of a political figure with his behavior in private, and despite my earlier experience in debating with him across a table, I was again discovering the cunning intellectual and immensely convincing conversationalist in this man. . . . The most striking conclusion to emerge from this latest contact with the Cuban Premier [is] his extraordinary boldness and faith in himself. [He acts] as if [he is] not quite believing that he, the obscure Latin-American revolutionary who only five years ago hid in cheap Mexican rooming houses, has rocketed into a world figure. . . . Dr. Castro's egocentricity has reached monumental proportions but, at the same time, there is the inescapable feeling that he observes himself with a detached wonderment. . . .[16]

Throughout the summer of 1961, Szulc continued to file incisive dispatches about the U.S. government's effort to build up the rest of Latin America and show patience with Cuba, pressure from those same countries on the United States for friendly coexistence with Cuba, the brand-new Castro policy of conciliatory reasonableness, an effort by the United States to find jobs for the thousands of skilled Cuban refugees who by then were concentrated in Florida, and, in the fall, a report that Cuba appeared to be heading for new phase of deepening political and economic problems stemming from a lack of jobs that was causing widespread discontent on the island. After readers had been both educated and informed about Cuba more than they ever had been in the past, Szulc wrote another major article for his newspaper's magazine, published on December 31, 1961. He explained, in part:

> A month ago, as if to provide the formal ideological setting for what Castro called "the first Socialist Christmas," the Cuban Government was preparing to celebrate the third anniversary of the revolution that has turned her into the Western Hemisphere's only full-fledged Communist state. . . . Emotional as ever, pounding the table, his voice rising to a crescendo, he proclaimed: "I am a Marxist-Leninist and I shall be a Marxist-Leninist until the last day of my life." Looking back, one tends to see the events of these years merging and blending into a kaleidoscopic set of images. . . . But behind this blur is the thread of a quiet, sometimes invisible, but relentless effort to mold revelatory Cuba into the Communist states that it is today.

By this time, Szulc had come to know Cuba and Castro so well that the *Times* kept him on that beat. It can now be argued in hindsight that that was a wise move because his stories reflected what would build up to a potential worldwide nightmare—the Cuban Missile Crisis of October 1962.

As it turned out, Szulc's pinpoint coverage of events and political strains between the United States and Cuba began with the Bay of Pigs and—without having any idea of what was to come—ended with Szulc's coverage of the missile crisis, yet another feather in his journalistic cap. Thus, without knowing what world-shaking event lay ahead in just a few months, Szulc reported that the United States was already girding for some revenge-seeking action by Cuba for

America's violation of international standards, as Cuba saw it, in helping the rebels invade the island in 1961.

On November 3, 1961, the president's brother, Attorney General Robert F. Kennedy, in an Oval Office meeting with military leaders to discuss Vietnam, raised the question of Cuba. Robert Kennedy was the chairman of the "Special Group (Augmented)," a White House ad hoc team determined to find a solution to the unresolved issue of Cuba. Wrote author Richard Reeves: "Robert Kennedy thought the CIA and everyone else in the bureaucracies were ignoring the President on Cuba." He quoted Kennedy as saying: "There can be no long-term living with Castro as a neighbor. His continued presence within the hemisphere community as a dangerously effective exponent of Communism and anti-Americanism constitutes a real menace capable of eventually overthrowing the elected governments in any one or more of weak Latin American republics."[17]

Szulc, an objective outsider to all of the fury in Cuba, himself became involved with the inner workings of the Kennedy administration. Reeves, a one-time *New York Times* reporter, wrote in his book about Kennedy, "On November 8, Robert Kennedy met with Tad Szulc, the *New York Times* correspondent who had unearthed the timing and details of the Bay of Pigs invasion, and asked him to come over to the White House the next day."

Reeves relates the following dialogue between Kennedy and Szulc:

> "Why didn't you tell me the truth about the Bay of Pigs? That it was going to be a disaster?" asked the President [talking to Szulc].
>
> "Even if I could have gotten in here, which I couldn't, you would have had me arrested," said the reporter.
>
> "You're probably right," said Kennedy. He laughed.
>
> The President asked Szulc about his conversations with Castro over the years, what kind of man he was. He asked whether there was a possibility of dialogue with the Cuban leader. Szulc did not have that much to add to what he had written (unlike politicians, reporters don't hold back the real story if they know it) and he could not figure out why he was there. Perhaps they were considering him for a job. He thought Kennedy seemed a much tougher man than the young congressman he had known years ago. "Hardened" was the word that came to mind.

"What would you think if I ordered Castro to be assassinated?" the President asked.

"I don't think that's a good idea," Szulc said. He was uncomfortable. The idea of assassination was stupid, he thought. "That would not necessarily change things in Cuba. Personally, I don't think the United States should be a party to political assassinations."

"I agree with you completely," the President said. He said he was just testing Szulc, that he, too, thought it was morally wrong. So did his brother, Kennedy added. He talked for quite a while about how wrong it would be.

"I'm glad you feel the same way," the President said finally to Szulc. "That's the kind of thing I'm never going to do. We can't get into that kind of thing, or we would all be targets." Back in his own office, Szulc prepared notes of the conversation, writing: "JFK said he raised the question because he was under terrific pressure from advisers ('think he said intelligence people, but not positive') to okay a Castro murder, said he was resisting pressures."[18]

Fourteen years later, in an article in the *New York Times Magazine*, Szulc added perspective to this incident, saying:

> There was available evidence that both the Kennedy brothers had acted to block [CIA-proposed] Castro assassination plots. President Kennedy discussed the pressures on him to authorize Castro's murder when he received this reporter in the Oval Office in November 1961 for an off-the-record meeting. Speaking in the presence of Richard N. Goodwin, a special assistant to the President, Kennedy went out of his way to emphasize that it would be morally wrong for the United States to become involved in political assassinations. This was two years before he was murdered in Dallas.[19]

ABOUT TAD SZULC

Szulc was no ordinary newspaper reporter. A superb investigative journalist whose assignments carried him around the world in pursuit of exclusive stories, he was ironically perceived as a major threat to the U.S. government by uncovering plots, some involving the CIA. Thus, it came as no surprise to anyone who knew him well in the world of journalism that a CIA dossier, obtained by his newspaper in 1997, absolved him of any illegal activities. It read, in part: "It is important to note that Szulc's activities can be explained by the combination of his personality, ambition, and the demands on an investigative reporter for the *New York Times*. . . . He is an aggressive, sensitive, and persistent journalist with the family connections (Ambassador John C. Wiley) and ability to develop the kinds of contacts appropriate to a successful correspondent for a paper like the *Times*." (Wiley was an American diplomat who was married to Szulc's aunt and had sponsored Szulc's emigration from Brazil to the United States in 1947.)

Intelligence officials conceded they did not have a legal case against Szulc, after the *New York Times* carefully examined declassified CIA papers in 1997. "Yet the culture of the agency appeared to be such that innuendo about his [Szulc's] dealings with Communist leaders and American officials ricocheted around CIA offices throughout his years at the *Times*, and well into his later career as an author and commentator on foreign policy," according to the *Times* obituary. It also stated:

> In postings to Rio de Janeiro, Spain, Portugal, and Eastern Europe, Szulc covered revolutions and Cold War intrigue for the *Times* and wrote a shelf of books, including biographies of Pope John Paul II and Fidel Castro. His curiosity was reflected in his restless fascination with international politics. As a *Times* correspondent from 1953 to 1972, he had a world in which to pursue those interests and a charmed way of being in the right part of it just as the plot thickened. Reporting from Venezuela on the overthrow of the dictator Marco Pérez Jiménez in 1959, he outwitted censors in two of his six languages and became the first journalist to get out news of the coup."[20]

The *Times* obituary also stated: "Possessing nerve, the obligatory trench coat and a supply of cigarettes, Szulc traveled around pulling off one feat after another. Bursting with energy, he would sometimes follow up a stream of important newspaper articles with a more personal account for *Times Talk*, the paper's in-house newsletter—some tale of complication and derring-do meant for the eyes of fellow workers."[21]

Notes

1. Richard Reeves, *President Kennedy: Profile of Power* (New York: Simon & Schuster, 1993), 83–84.

2. Michael Isikoff, *Uncovering Clinton: A Reporter's Story* (New York: Crown, 1999), 335.

3. Reeves, *President Kennedy*, 84.

4. Schlesinger memorandum to JFK, 4/7/61, PO Box 65, JFK Library.

5. *New York Times*, April 4, 1961.

6. *New York Times*, April 5, 1961.

7. *New York Times*, April 6, 1961.

8. *New York Times*, April 7, 1961.

9. *New York Times*, April 9, 1961.

10. Daniel Lewis, Tad Szulc obituary, *New York Times*, May 22, 2001. The *Times* obituary was published the day after Szulc died at the age of 74.

11. Tad Szulc and Karl E. Meyer, *The Cuban Invasion: The Chronicle of a Disaster* (Westport, CT: Praeger, 1962), 7.

12. *New York Times*, Week in Review, April 26, 2009.

13. Tad Szulc, *Fidel: A Critical Portrait* (London: Hutchinson, 1986), 449.

14. Ibid., 456.

15. *Fidel Castro, My Life: A Spoken Autobiography*, with Ignacio Ramonet, translated by Andrew Hurley (New York: Scribner, 2006), 259.

16. *New York Times*, July 16, 1961.

17. Reeves, *President Kennedy*, 264.

18. Ibid., 264–65.

19. Tad Szulc, "The Politics of Assassination," *New York Times Magazine*, June 23, 1975, 60.

20. The biography is based in part on an obituary (see note 10 above) written about Szulc that appeared in the May 22, 2001, issue of the *New York Times*.

21. Tad Szulc Collection of Interview Manuscripts, University of Miami Library, 1984–1986.

CHAPTER 3

WATERGATE: THE FALL OF A PRESIDENT

Reported by Bob Woodward and Carl Bernstein, Washington Post, *1974*

"Oh, my God, this President is going to be impeached."
    "My God, you're right!"

> —Private exchange between Carl
> Bernstein and Bob Woodward, in the
> *Washington Post* newsroom in September 1972,
> only four months after the Watergate break-in.

The most far-reaching investigative political White House scandal of the 20th century began with a seemingly innocuous burglary on the sixth floor of a plush apartment and office complex called the Watergate in the fashionable Northwest section of Washington, D.C.[1] A story on the front page of the *Washington Post* on Sunday morning, June 18, 1972, was headlined "5 Held in Plot to Bug Democrats' Office Here," with the byline of the paper's veteran police reporter, Alfred E. Lewis. It began:

> Five men, one of whom said he is a former employee of the Central Intelligence Agency, were arrested at 2:30 A.M. yesterday in what authorities described as an elaborate plot to bug the offices of the Democratic National Committee here. Three of the men were native-born Cubans and another was said to have trained Cuban exiles for guerrilla activity after the 1961 Bay of Pigs invasion. They were surprised at gunpoint by three plain-clothes officers of the metropolitan police department in a sixth floor office at the plush Watergate, 2600 Virginia Ave.,

N.W., where the Democratic National Committee occupies the entire floor. There was no immediate explanation as to why the five suspects would want to bug the Democratic National Committee offices or whether or not they were working for any other individuals or organizations.

The story went on to report that all five suspects,[2] four of whom were reported to be from the Miami area, were arrested.

The average *Post* reader may have raised an eyebrow or two at the references to the CIA and the Democratic National Committee headquarters but probably left it at that. Nobody could possibly tell what it was all about. However, as noted at the very end of the *Post*'s story in small print, eight staff writers contributed to the story; among them were the names of Bob Woodward and Carl Bernstein, a rare combination of investigative reporters. Neither Woodward nor Bernstein had a clue to the fact that they were on the cusp of what would become arguably the biggest and the most devastating detective story of the 20th century, resulting—for the first time in American history—in the resignation of a sitting U.S. president. Their history-making investigation traced their first suspicions through the tortuous trail of false leads, lies, secrecy, and high-level pressure until, finally, its dramatic climax.

It was more than chance that led Woodward and Bernstein to jump on the story. Bernstein, who had joined the *Washington Star* in 1960 at the tender age of 16 and then the *Post* in 1966 and was covering politics in Virginia at the time, had a knack for digging out stories by—as they say in the business—"working the phones." He happened to be in the city room the Saturday of the arrests going over some notes for another story he planned to write. But the commotion in the city room caught his attention. Bernstein, then 28, a college dropout with a streak of aggressiveness, immediately volunteered to make phone calls.

Woodward's arrival as a staff reporter on the paper had taken an entirely different route. Woodward, 29, a sophisticated Ivy Leaguer, had been accepted into a law school, but he eschewed the opportunity because he subscribed to the *Washington Post*, a newspaper which, he said, "seemed to fit the times, to fit with a general sense of where the world was, much more than law school," and decided he might prefer reporting as a career. He proceeded straight to Executive Editor Ben Bradlee's office at the *Post*. Utterly without experience, he was given a two-week tryout at the *Post* in August 1970.

Woodward did not make the grade, due to his lack of experience, but he discovered nonetheless that he and the newspaper business were meant to be. As he put it: "I left more enthralled than ever. Though I had failed the tryout completely—it was a spectacular crash—I realized I had found something I loved. The sense of immediacy in a newsroom and the newspaper was overwhelming to me." So he went to work on a weekly paper, the *Montgomery County Sentinel*, where he soon became the paper's best reporter because of his perseverance. A year later, he reapplied to the *Post* and was hired, he recalled, on Friday, September 3, 1971, after passing muster with Bradlee, the preeminent newspaperman of his day, known for his outward toughness as an irreverent, charismatic taskmaster and as a brilliant strategist in planning news coverage.[3]

Thus Woodward, who had been working at the *Post* for only nine months, got involved with Watergate when he received a call from the city editor at 9 A.M. on the first day of the break-in and was told to come into the office. He was not especially enthusiastic about investigating a police story—a routine he had been following since he started. Woodward spotted Bernstein hurriedly making telephone calls, one after the other. "'Oh God, not Bernstein,' Woodward thought, recalling several office tales about Bernstein's ability to push his way into a good story and get his byline on it."[4]

This unlikely combo, who had never worked together on a story up to this time, suddenly found themselves teaming up on a story that neither they nor their editors knew would take off. It appeared highly unlikely that the crime had anything to do with the Republicans—after all, the Democratic convention was only a month away and President Richard M. Nixon had a huge 29-point lead in the polls. Still, Bernstein pounced on the story and, as a result of his barrage of phone calls to people at the Watergate office-apartment-hotel complex as well as to Florida, he learned enough about the men from Miami to write a background piece on them. Meanwhile, Woodward rushed to the courtroom to dig up whatever he could at the arraignment. When one of the men told the judge he had worked for the Central Intelligence Agency, Woodward sat up and took notice. This could very well be more than a routine police story, he thought to himself.

It was a lot more, as Managing Editor Howard Simons quickly sensed coming into City Editor Barry Sussman's office to get the details. Simons told Sussman: "That's a hell of a story," and he directed that it run on page 1 the next morning. Sussman asked both

Bernstein and Woodward to return to work Sunday morning and continue digging. They were the only two reporters in the city room that day to follow up on the break-in. By the time they got in, the Associated Press had put out a story that one of the suspects, James McCord, was the security coordinator for the Committee to Reelect the President (referred to by opponents as CREEP). As related in their book: "The two reporters stood in the middle of the newsroom and looked at each other. 'What the hell do you think it means?' Woodward asked. Bernstein said he didn't know."[5]

In an interview with Bernstein, I asked him how soon he knew he was onto a major story. He quickly responded: "That day [Saturday, June 17]. As soon as we knew these guys had those CIA associations, we knew we were on to something. I knew it was a good story with the Democratic National Committee headquarters involved. I thought it might be some kind of political espionage. The question was: What did it mean? My first thoughts were that somehow, for some crazy reason, this must have had something to do with the CIA. And then the next day Woodward and I came in and Sussman told the two of us to follow up an Associated Press story saying McCord was a security coordinator for the CRP. We were a little chagrined that we did not get that story ourselves. Then we started doing checks on McCord and divided the names of office buildings and home addresses and started calling people anywhere we could find them."[6]

On June 20, 1972, reportedly based on a tip from an anonymous source (nicknamed "Deep Throat"), Woodward wrote that one of the burglars had an address book containing the name of E. Howard Hunt, a consultant to the White House, as well as checks signed by Hunt, and that Hunt was linked to Charles W. Colson, special counsel to the president.

A few days later, White House Press Secretary Ron Ziegler, when asked about the break-in, dismissed the incident this way: "Certain elements may try to make this beyond what it is," and he labeled the incident "a third-rate burglary attempt."[7] Those were words that would indeed come back to haunt him and the entire Nixon administration.

Meanwhile, adding to the growing drama, John Mitchell, the former U.S. attorney general and the president's campaign manager, released a statement from Los Angeles saying that none of the suspects were "operating on either our [the Nixon administration's] behalf or with our consent." This quote was included in the first of what would turn out to be hundreds of familiar, double-bylined Woodward and Bernstein stories—this one published Monday morning, June 19, 1972, under the headline "GOP Security Aide among 5 Arrested in Bugging Affair."

I asked Bernstein how he and Woodward determined whose name would go first in the double byline over their stories as time went on. Bernstein replied: "We kind of evolved a rule that whoever had done the principal work on a given story on a given day would have his name go first on the byline. But I bet you if you added them up, half would be Woodward and Bernstein and half would be Bernstein and Woodward. More often than not, I might write the story and Bob would edit the story. Or it could go back and forth between us. Sometimes Bradlee would sit down, type some words and say, 'This is your lead.'"[8]

How important was protecting sources for the Watergate story? "Absolutely essential," Bernstein said in a TV interview. "We did not name a single significant source in the first 150 stories that we did in the first year of Watergate. In fact, we never did. The only people who were identified by name more often than not were telling lies, because they were spokesmen for the Nixon White House. In terms of real sources of information, they were all confidential, every one. It would have been totally impossible to have done the Watergate reporting and identified our sources. When we wrote *All the President's Men*, we went back to all of our sources, and we asked them, could we identify them? Some of them said yes. But Mark Felt—the individual we called 'Deep Throat'—said no. We kept that secret for 33 years because we believe in the confidentiality of sources. I know of very little important reporting of the last 30 to 40 years that has been done without use of confidential sources, particularly in the national security area. What we know about the last five, six, seven presidencies, we know through the use of confidential sources."[9]

To be certain of all the facts, Bradlee initiated a rule that the two reporters had to have two sources for all of the pertinent facts they used in their stories, one as the original source and the second to confirm, though neither had to be publicly named. We knew all the names. Why two sources? "Well," Bradlee explained, "editors do that anyway. If some guy walks into the city room and says he just saw a 12-foot man walking down 15th Street, you want another source. One time, I found that each [Woodward and Bernstein] was the other's source. I told them: 'Don't play that game with me!'" The publisher of the *Washington Post*, Katharine Graham, "spent a lot of time in the city room," Bradlee said. "When we were doing this, it had everybody's interest. She was around a lot. She knew what was happening every step of the way, but we didn't have to ask her permission. We just said, 'This is what we're going to print.' She always contributed."[10]

Our "story behind the story" returns to Saturday, June 17, 1972, when both Woodward and Bernstein undertook one of the most exhaustive day-and-night pursuits of information—much of it, as it turned out, extraneous—ever recorded in modern journalism. Neither of them wanted to take a day off, so passionate were they about putting together the myriad pieces of a more and more complicated jigsaw puzzle. They immediately recognized they were at the beginning of something big, but the possible impeachment of President Nixon was not even a remote thought. The reporters just followed their leads, one by one, step by step.

Even though Bernstein had been scheduled to take Monday and Tuesday off after the initial Saturday break-in, he came into the office with renewed enthusiasm. By this time, he had received a call from someone who identified himself by name but whom he—even to this day—would not reveal to the author of this book because of promised permanent anonymity. The man turned out to be a good source, Bernstein recalls. "I asked this guy, 'Is there was any possibility that the President's campaign committee—or less likely, the White House—could do something as stupid as the Watergate raid?' I waited to be told no. Then, this guy said, 'I know this President well enough that if he needed somebody to do a job like this, and it would not be a shoddy job.'" Bernstein, at this point in our interview, told me as an aside: "What's interesting to me is how much of the perception of what we did has been formed by the movie rather than the book in the intervening years so that even my own memory is somewhat colored by the movie version, which leaves a lot out, obviously, including this stuff I am telling you right now." Returning to his discussion with his source, Bernstein added, "This guy told me it was 'not inconceivable that the President would want to have every piece of political intelligence and gossip available.' I remember writing that paragraph in the book."[11]

Their journey for the truth was a bumpy one. For example, at the very outset, Bernstein recalls, in an attempt to impress his editors so he would be taken off the Virginia beat and permanently assigned to the Watergate story, he wrote a five-page memo outlining what he called the "Chotiner theory"—an idea that Murray Chotiner, an old friend of Nixon's and a specialist in low-road campaign tactics such as manipulating ballots might be a key to unraveling the mystery. However, no evidence was ever developed to indicate that Chotiner was involved. Chotiner died in early 1974. That was but one example of the vast number of leads that did not pan out.

As both Woodward and Bernstein have said so many times over the years, they could not have uncovered the full Watergate story had they not spent a lot of time tracking down leads that never amounted to much. The key, they said, was to be able to separate the meaningful pieces of data from the rest. "That's what good reporters do," said Bernstein. "They listen. And they learn as they go along. Eventually, the big picture becomes clear."[12]

It is instructive to recall the reporters' accounts of those early hours and days when the *Post* first had a real sense of the Watergate scandal, almost accidentally. Bradlee put it this way in his autobiography:

> The best journalists in the world could be forgiven for not realizing that this [burglary at the Watergate] was the opening act of the scandalous political melodrama—unparalleled in American history—which would end up with the resignation of a disgraced President and the jailing of more than forty people, including the Attorney General of the United States, the White House chief of staff, the White House counsel, and the President's chief domestic adviser.[13]

"The *Washington Post*," Bradlee continued, "got off to a running head start on the story early on the morning of June 17, 1972, thanks to Joe Califano, once special assistant to President Johnson, then counsel to both the Democratic Party and the Washington Post."[14]

As Bradlee told it, Califano called Howard Simons, the *Post*'s managing editor, to inform him about the break-in by five men a few hours earlier and said that they were scheduled to be arraigned. Following the chain of command, Simons called Harry M. Rosenfeld, the metropolitan editor, who in turn called Barry Sussman, the city editor. The first two reporters called were Al Lewis and Bob Woodward, whom Bradlee described as "a former Navy lieutenant and one of the new kids on the staff, who had impressed everyone with his skills at finding stories wherever we sent him."[15] As for Bernstein, Bradlee wrote: "The long-haired, guitar-playing Peck's

Bad Boy of the Metro staff, spent most of Saturday sniffing around the story's perimeter as all good reporters do, and was told to 'work the phones.'"[16]

With so much on the line, what did Bradlee say to Woodward and Bernstein at the outset? I asked Bradlee this question nearly four decades later.[17] He replied: "I told them, 'You better be god-damned sure you are right.' We ran more than 400 stories altogether, you know. We bet the whole ranch on those guys." Nonetheless, he admitted, "I watched them very closely. Very, very closely. They're the best." Bradlee said he read the overwhelming majority of their stories, and toward the end he said he wrote some of the leads. "We would fight over stories so much you couldn't even recognize them; you had to have someone [Bradlee himself as executive editor] come in and say, 'This is how we will do it.'"

Asked if he ever had second thoughts during the entire investigation, he replied, succinctly: "None whatsoever." He said the Nixon White House did not try to pressure him personally, but White House officials did try to influence the reporters. "They also tried to reach Katharine Graham. We were boycotted totally. The only two Republicans we spoke to were [Secretary of State] Henry Kissinger and [Secretary of Commerce] Henry Peterson."

The highly respected Bradlee described the *Post*'s initial reaction to the Watergate break-in: "We were flailing, searching everywhere for any information that might shed any light, unaware that we were up against a massive cover-up being orchestrated by the White House. We were picking up the story, knowing it was there but unable to describe what 'it' was, finding what looked like pieces of a puzzle but unable to see where—or even if—these pieces fit."

On the other hand, it soon became clear that the White House had become so concerned with the mounting attention the *Post* was giving the Watergate story that it moved into high gear to try and discredit the newspaper's stories. By the end of that first week, on Friday, June 22, at a press conference, Nixon made his first public comment on the affair. "Mr. Ziegler, and also Mr. [Attorney General John] Mitchell, speaking for the campaign committee, has responded to questions on this in great detail," he said. "They have stated my position and have also stated the facts correctly. This kind of activity as Mr. Ziegler has indicated has no place whatever in our electoral process or in our government process. And, as Mr. Ziegler has stated, the White House has no involvement whatsoever in this particular incident."[18]

While both reporters continued to track down all of the leads they could based on the arrests of the five burglars, something was obviously happening at the White House that they could not foresee. Only nine days after Nixon's statement, Mitchell resigned as manager of the president's reelection campaign, saying that he was doing so at the request of his wife. In the *Post* city room the following day, Rosenfeld, the metro editor, had a quizzical look on his face when he told Woodward: "A man like John Mitchell doesn't give up all that power for his wife."[19]

With the passing of time—and an opportunity to examine all of the documents that were previously withheld during the course of the scandal—Woodward put the entire investigation into perspective in a book he wrote in 2005:

> The outline of the Watergate cover-up was so clear in retrospect. White House counsel John W. Dean III, who later confessed to leading the illegal obstruction of justice on behalf of President Richard Nixon, stated "all requests for investigation by FBI at White House must be cleared through him [Dean]," according to a summary dated six days after the June 17, 1972, break-in.[20]

The *Post* reporters have also since examined—after going through FBI files in 1992 on the 20th anniversary of the Watergate break-in— another White House memorandum dated October 10, 1972, that addressed what Bernstein said was the "key to everything we wrote—that's after we understood this 'political espionage and sabotage operation.' It was a whole other order and finally made sense. The Watergate break-in was not about an isolated incident but part of a vast campaign. I remember writing this, very carefully picking the word 'sabotage' because I stayed up all night writing the draft of this story. We had held the story once until Bob had gone to see Deep Throat to get a little more information. Deep Throat helped confirm it. And the scope of it how big it was—this political espionage or spying or whatever—and I remember very carefully choosing the word 'sabotage' because it was so resonant."[21]

Woodward summed up the importance of the document in his book:

> The [October 10, 1972] two-page White House memo stated that the FBI had learned that Donald H. Segretti, who headed

the efforts to harass Democratic candidates, had been hired by Dwight L. Chapin, the President's appointments secretary, paid by Herbert W. Kalmbach, the President's personal lawyer. Because there was no direct connection to the Watergate bugging, the memo said, the FBI had not pursued the matter. I smiled. Here were two of the reasons the Watergate cover-up had worked at first: Dean's effectiveness in squelching further inquiry; and the seeming lack of imagination on the part of the FBI.[22]

Examining the full background of how Woodward and Bernstein went about their history-making probe requires that the reader know much more about the prior relationship between Woodward and the informant known only as "Deep Throat" in the book *All the President's Men.* This mystery man's true identity was not made public until 33 years later when a high FBI official by the name of W. Mark Felt revealed to *Vanity Fair* in May 2005 that he was Deep Throat.[23]

I asked Bernstein what Felt's motive was in serving as the key Watergate source. Bernstein responded: "To this day, I don't know all of Mark Felt's motives. There's no way to know the motives of another person totally, even a person that you know very well. You could not be in his head. I don't think it's as simple as he did not get [FBI Director J. Edgar] Hoover's job. I think he felt the FBI had been corrupted by Watergate. It's much more complicated than that. It's a human story."[24] In fact, after he came forward, Felt made no secret of the fact that he believed he had had an excellent chance of succeeding Hoover, and the last thing he expected was that the president would bring in somebody from the outside the FBI, namely, L. Patrick Gray.

Woodward and Bernstein, who cited Felt as an anonymous source throughout their months of reporting, had promised Felt they would not reveal his identity until he died or consented to have it made public. The unknown Deep Throat was portrayed in the movie version of *All the President's Men* as a mysterious man (Hal Holbrook) in the shadows behind a garage pillar who gently steered Woodward (played by the cool, calm Robert Redford) along the right path. (Bernstein was played by Dustin Hoffman, long-haired, ragged, and emotional.) Soon after Felt's identity was made public, Woodward rapidly wrote a book, *The Secret Man: The Story of Watergate's Deep Throat*, detailing his prior dealings with Felt, a rather reserved public official whom Woodward had met earlier and carefully cultivated as his main source.

Woodward had first met Felt in the summer of 1969 when the future *Washington Post* reporter was a lieutenant in the U.S. Navy assigned to the Pentagon as a watch officer monitoring worldwide teletype communications for Chief of Naval Operations Thomas H. Moorer, who would later become chairman of the Joint Chiefs of Staff. In his book, Woodward describes his work as "routine and boring" until one night when he was given a package to walk to the West Wing of the White House near the Situation Room. He was 26 and naïve. While waiting to drop the package off, Woodward described a civilian who entered the waiting room with him. He was

> a tall man with perfectly combed gray hair. . . . His suit was dark, his shirt was white, and his necktie subdued. . . . He was distinguished looking [with] a studied air of confidence, even what may be called a command presence, the posture and calm of someone used to giving orders and having them obeyed instantly and without question. He had an air of patience and comfort about him.[25]

Hardly an extrovert himself, Woodward waited a few minutes and then introduced himself. In response, the man offered only his name—Mark Felt. Woodward talked nervously about himself, trying to make a connection of some kind. In a brief exchange, he established that both he and Felt had worked in Congress for men from their home states and both had attended George Washington University. But that was about all. "Felt and I were like two passengers sitting next to each other on a long airline flight with nowhere to go and nothing really to do but resign ourselves to the dead time. He showed no interest in striking up a long conversation," Woodward recounted.[26]

Nonetheless, Woodward—whose calm low-key, slow-talking, matter-of-fact manner has always been one of his strong suits as a reporter, tending to win over those with whom he talked—got enough nerve to ask for and get Felt's direct-line telephone number to his FBI office.

He later sought counsel from his new FBI acquaintance for advice about going to law school. "Somewhat sympathetic to the lost-soul quality of my questions," Woodward wrote, Felt told him, in Woodward's words, to "go with the action." Woodward added: "I was thankful for his advice. Even now decades later [in 2005] I consider his advice a kind of 'Rosebud,' the elusive X-factor in someone's life that explains everything. The Rosebud here was the realization that I was free to choose."[27]

It was not long before he was carrying out Felt's advice to "go with the action." Barely 24 months later, he teamed up with Bernstein. In the meantime, Woodward had resumed contact with Felt on a confidential basis to gain information, on the condition that he promised to leave the FBI and the Justice Department out of it. Felt also insisted on total confidentiality—and not to tell anyone that they knew each other or had talked regularly. Soon, Woodward's relationship with Felt—while still secret—would change dramatically in substance as a result of the death of J. Edgar Hoover on May 2, 1972—only a month and a half before the break-in at Watergate. Embittered that he was not selected by Nixon to replace Hoover as FBI director—instead, L. Patrick Gray, a Nixon loyalist for decades, got the job—Felt nonetheless agreed to Gray's request that Felt run the day-to-day operations of the FBI.

Only six weeks after Hoover's death—on June 17, 1972—Felt was sitting in for Gray, who was out of town. Informed of the five men and the break-in at the Watergate, based on the few facts he was given, Felt knew immediately, "This thing has all kinds of political ramifications and the press is going to have a field day."[28] It seemed ironic that these two very different men—Woodward and Felt, a generation and a world apart in their background experiences and views—would be brought together by circumstances beyond their control to collaborate in what eventually turned out to be the biggest presidential scandal in American history. Woodward's serendipitous meeting with Felt at the Pentagon in 1969 would leave an indelible mark on the history of American journalism.

Woodward wasted no time in contacting Felt soon after the burglary. Felt, Woodward said, could offer no details and "seemed nervous." Nevertheless, based on a cursory review of names and theories, he was assured by Felt that he was moving in the right direction. Still, as Woodward later wrote:

> It would be more than two years before it was learned, from the [Nixon] smoking-gun tapes which forced Nixon's resignation that, on June 23, 1972, the President ordered the CIA to attempt to get the FBI to halt and limit the Watergate inquiry on vague but insistent national security grounds.[29]

Nixon's tape recordings of his own conversations in the Oval Office ultimately did him in. But it was not the first time that a president had used tape recordings in the White House. Franklin D. Roosevelt taped some hours of press conferences on a big prototype, and Harry S Truman and Dwight D. Eisenhower also experimented with it. John F. Kennedy used tape recorders the least, with no confidential information recorded, while Lyndon B. Johnson used the system to record a great many of his personal and business telephone conversations.[30]

Playing two simultaneous but contradictory roles, Felt's position must have been mind-boggling. FBI Director Gray complained to his staff about leaks and someone having a case of "flapjaw." Yet, Woodward wrote in his book:

> The leaks continued, however, and the *Washington Post*'s Woodward and Bernstein team was soon giving their readers details of the investigation, sometimes within hours after the Bureau learned of them. The White House was furious, and [John] Ehrlichman called Gray on the carpet and told him, in no uncertain terms, that the leaks must stop.[31]

Woodward continued:

> What I did not know at the time, but learned much later, was that John Dean [counsel to the President] called Felt and complained about leaks, demanding new steps to silence leakers. Felt refused. He was playing a dangerous game, and it would only get more dangerous.[32]

As for his constant pursuit of Felt while the agent was in the midst of a firestorm in the White House, Woodward writes: "Perhaps Felt tolerated my aggressiveness and pushy approach because he had been the same way when he was a junior FBI supervisor in Seattle." As time passed, according to Woodward, the more consternation Felt expressed, the more Woodward felt that "Watergate was one hell of a story."[33]

He occasionally called Felt at home and, during one visit there during the summer of 1972, Woodward related, Felt told him that the only way they could talk from there on out would be face to face in a place where they could not be seen. They devised a sort of cloak-and-dagger system whereby Woodward placed a red flag in a flowerpot in the front of his balcony and moved it to the rear of the balcony if he wanted to meet urgently. The meeting place, at 2 A.M., would be the bottom level of an underground garage over the Key Bridge in Rosslyn, Virginia. Woodward would arrive by taxi a few blocks from the garage and walk the remainder of the way.[34]

Felt came up with another way to connect: marking Woodward's *New York Times* on page 20 with a circle and the hands of a clock in the lower part of the page.

> The details of what were obviously spy tradecraft, Felt's experience or common sense were appealing. He was taking this as seriously, or more seriously, than I was. In technical journalistic terms, the information he might supply was on "deep background." This meant the information could be used if it were thought reliable or could be confirmed, but no source would be cited—not an FBI, Justice Department or administration source. That way a specific comment or piece of information could not be tracked back to him. How he might have made a daily observation of my balcony [in an apartment house in Northwest Washington] is still a mystery to me.[35]

In the course of his meetings with Felt, Woodward told Felt that Nixon officials were clamming up and that many potential sources were becoming afraid of the two reporters. Felt, he said, told him not to worry about pushing him—that the FBI liked the press and had to rely on people's voluntary cooperation. "Felt's message to me," Woodward wrote, "was unusual, emphatically encouraging me to get in his face."[36]

Discussing this relationship, I posed this question to Bernstein: "Could he and Woodward have uncovered the Watergate scandal without Felt's help?"

Pausing for a moment, Bernstein said: "Yeah, I think the role of Deep Throat is widely misunderstood," said Bernstein. "What Felt did that was clearly invaluable for the first part of our investigation—he confirmed information we had gotten elsewhere. He gave us something invaluable: the certainty that we were right and, given the stakes of this story, it meant that we did not have nearly as much self-doubt as we might have had. We knew where he sat and we knew that if he said, 'You're on the right track, you did your homework, you got it right,' we knew we were solid. I think that because of the drama in the way in which Bob met with Deep Throat in a garage as portrayed in the movie—which by necessity compressed events—that Deep Throat's role became mythic, along with the name, in a way that perhaps it might not have been, and perhaps it was exaggerated. At the same time, I don't want to minimize it in any way because it was so much a part of the thread of our methodology. Bob only had 20 meetings with him."[37]

Nonetheless, it is abundantly clear that had Woodward not met Felt by happenstance in 1969, the *Washington Post* would probably not have been able to put such a glaring spotlight on the Nixon White House and the public hearings that ensued, and Nixon might never have been driven from office. One thing is certain: Felt was critically important.

On September 15, 1972, G. Gordon Liddy, finance counsel to the CRP, and the Watergate burglars were indicted by a grand jury, but neither Woodward nor Bernstein had enough hard information to prove their theory that the Nixon reelection committee had a secret cash fund that had financed the Watergate operation. Woodward was still trying to abide by Felt's admonition not to contact him directly by phone at his office or at home. But, Woodward writes, he broke the rule and asked Felt about a story the reporters had in draft form that "high White House officials" were involved in supplying the money for the burglary. "Too soft," Woodward quotes Felt as telling him ("to my astonishment"). "You can go much stronger," Felt told him.[38]

Both reporters secretly believed in their hearts that their search for the truth could possibly wind up impeaching Nixon. Bernstein recalled a whispered exchange between himself and Woodward in a remote corner of the newsroom in September 1972, just four months after the break-in, when Bernstein said, "Oh, my God, this President is going to be impeached!" and Woodward replied, "My God, you're right!"

The reporters gathered more information by working the phones and came up with what they believed was enough to finally print the story that cash payments had been made to two Nixon operatives. Woodward broke the no-telephone rule again and Felt confirmed the information. "When he heard my voice," Woodward continued, "there was a long pause. This would have to be our last telephone conversation, he said angrily."[39]

But this last call had done the trick. It confirmed that money did, indeed, flow from the White House cash fund—a fact embellished by the scriptwriters of the movie with Deep Throat's admonition to "follow the money," a phrase that does not appear in the book by Woodward and Bernstein because, as Woodward tells it, as best as he could recall, Felt never said those exact words. Soon afterward, on September 29, 1972, the reporters—who by then had been nicknamed "Woodstein" by Bradlee—broke yet another story, headlined "Mitchell Controlled Secret GOP Fund," in which they wrote that the fund fluctuated between $250,000 and $700,000.

Then came one of the most ironic—and personally difficult— moments of their entire investigation: the *Post*'s Justice Department reporter, Sandy Ungar, suggested that they interview W. Mark Felt, the associate FBI director. As Woodward expressed it, "I was in a tizzy." He could not avoid following up on his colleague's suggestion, because it was logical. Yet, at the same time, he had no idea whatsoever of what would happen in such circumstances. Fortunately for Woodward, Felt had an assistant with him and, as Woodward wrote, "A most uncomfortable charade proceeded."

Woodward recalled that he asked Felt some questions about the *Post*'s fact-findings, and Felt refused to answer any questions. Woodward recalled:

> Even in the most useless interview, with the most tight-lipped person, a reporter can generally get something, even if it's a negative. Never has so little been said. I can't even find if I took notes. Felt and I never discussed the meeting, but he mentioned it in his 1979 book as evidence that he had never helped me.[40]

The moment had passed without incident.

By this time, the political atmosphere in Washington was steaming with rumors and innuendos. Further, one of the *Post*'s reporters, scouring the country to determine the "state of mind" of the American electorate, reported that he had found a "distrust and lack of faith in politicians and the government itself." As the *Post*'s editorial page stated, "In a word, the voters are turned off." The editorial went on to charge that

> people in positions of power are engaging in a massive cover-up of essential information about the conduct of public business— whether it has to do with the government's operations or the conduct of a Presidential campaign—which, if better known, might well turn a lot of voters off.[41]

The *Post's* Watergate series was given a tremendous boost of credibility as a historic national story by the dean of television, Walter Cronkite of CBS News. In July 2009, Ben Bradlee wrote a tribute to Cronkite in *Newsweek*, stating, in part:

> In October 1972, Cronkite devoted two segments, back to back, to the Watergate story. The first [on October 27] was 14 minutes, the second [on October 31] eight. I think that second night was curtailed by CBS chairman William S. Paley because Paley was scared of it. The fact that Cronkite did Watergate at all (let alone at that length) gave the story a kind of blessing, which is exactly what we needed—and exactly what the *Washington Post* lacked. It was a political year, and everyone was saying, "Well, it's just politics, and here's the *Post* trying to screw Nixon." We were the second-biggest newspaper in the country trying to scramble for a good story—whereas Cronkite was the reigning dean of television journalists. When he did the Watergate story, everyone said, "My God, Cronkite's with them."[42]

The two CBS newscasts won Cronkite an Emmy for his coverage, an award that he was said to have valued most out of all his others.

As another reporter noted:

> With his steady and straightforward delivery, and millions of viewers tuned in at home, "the most trusted man in America" [Cronkite] gave legitimacy to, what was then a developing story, that ultimately resulted in the indictment and conviction of several of President Richard Nixon's closest advisors, and in the resignation of the President himself.[43]

As Bradlee wrote:

> You could feel the change overnight. . . . A little more than a week after the Cronkite broadcast, Nixon decisively won his reelection campaign. But those of us following the story felt it. Washington people, people who followed national stories—a lot of them who had not decided that we were right changed their minds because of Walter.[44]

In a separate homage to Cronkite in September 2009, Woodward agreed: "There have been a lot of gutsy things done in journalism and television journalism, and I don't know if anything beats that."[45]

Daniel Schorr, a senior news analyst at National Public Radio, worked with Walter Cronkite for 20 years. Commenting on Cronkite's impact on Watergate, Schorr wrote: "*Washington Post* Publisher Katharine Graham acknowledged that, for all of her paper's great work, it was Cronkite's CBS that had made Watergate a national story."[46]

By mid-October, Woodward and Bernstein had come so close to the truth that Nixon and his aides let loose with a triple-headed broadside from the Nixon administration, the CRP, and the Republican National Committee. The attack was aimed at the media in general and at the *Washington Post*'s Woodward and Bernstein in particular. The GOP charged, in effect, that the press was manufacturing a story and that its goal was the impeachment of the president. In response, the *Post* published an editorial on October 18, 1972, strongly backing the two reporters, citing the fact that the only reason they were assigned to the story in the first place was because of the Watergate break-in on June 17, 1972, and the fact that a few of the burglars had ties with the Republican Party. The *Post* declared that any good newspaper would want to find out what they were doing there, who sent them, and who paid them.

Even though the *Post* had stirred up a hornet's nest in Washington and its stories were being circulated throughout the country, Nixon handily won reelection on November 7, 1972, with the largest plurality in American history—61 percent of the vote. Why was there such a landslide in light of what the *Post* had been publishing? There were four reasons: First, the Nixon White House had clouded the public's view of the entire Watergate scandal by consistently connecting the *Post*'s campaign with the campaign of George McGovern, the Democratic nominee. Second, while Woodward and Bernstein had damaged the prestige of the White House, they had not yet found any "smoking gun" unambiguously linking Watergate to Nixon. Third, the McGovern campaign had been unsuccessful in changing the public's perception of the candidate as a "far left" liberal who was so far out of the mainstream that he would not be a good president. And fourth, during the final stretch of the campaign, neither Woodward nor Bernstein could make much headway, running up against a resistance they had not encountered since the June 17 break-in. With the reelection of the president, even the two ace reporters themselves wondered if, indeed, their Watergate probe could be at a dead end.

The day after the election, the *Post*'s editors asked the two reporters to find something—anything—that would take the spotlight off of the *Post* and put it back on the scandal. City Editor Sussman was particularly concerned about the perception that the *Post* had been actively promoting McGovern and thus had failed in its attempts to depict Nixon as the dishonest president that he was.

Like so many investigative stories, there are peaks and valleys, and now they had hit a valley. Accordingly, Sussman wrote a one-page memo, much to Woodward and Bernstein's chagrin, stating:

> Woodward and Bernstein are going back to virtually every old source and some new ones who have shown an interest in talking now that the election is over. Some of our best stories to date were pretty much unexpected and did not come from any particular lines of inquiry, and quite possibly the same will be true now.[47]

The next development in their chase turned out to be a grand juror—a Republican woman who reportedly disliked Nixon—who was willing to talk to them. That was a touchy situation; under the law, reporters are not supposed to talk to grand jurors. But Bradlee figured that since the juror had initiated the contact, the reporters should go ahead, with this admonition: "No beating anyone over the head, no pressure, none of that cajoling," he told them in no uncertain terms. "I'm serious about that. Particularly you, Bernstein, be subtle for once in your life."[48]

Bernstein recalls that critical incident: "I talked to a grand juror. I didn't think seeing a grand juror was illegal," he told me. "The onus is really on the grand juror. Would I do that again? I'm not sure. I doubt it. Clearly a grand juror is subject to a contempt citation and possibly worse. If there are instructions from the judge that jurors cannot talk about the case—and there usually are—it's pretty standard the jurors are not going to talk. You don't see it happen very often. Anyway, on this occasion Edward Bennett Williams was counsel to the *Washington Post* and Bradlee's great friend. The lawyer urged extreme caution. Bradlee was a bit nervous. And then he asked us to call him as soon as we had left the woman's house."[49] She was not home, so the reporters returned the next day, but they learned little—another example of taking a big chance on a lead that did not pan out.

Woodward looked at the grand juror situation this way: "We got legal clearance to go to grand jurors. It's not illegal. It's not a desirable thing to do, but at the same time the abdication of justice was so high we felt we had to go talk to people, but not coerce them, but just to say, we're here. If there is something we should know, will you talk to us? We never got very far with that."[50]

Nonetheless, Woodward was determined to get a list of the rest of the grand jurors and track them down. So he went to the court files and actually memorized the names and addresses because the clerk would not allow any information to be copied. The ethical and legal questions of whether or not to pursue the jurors were debated by the editors, who finally reluctantly agreed to let them go ahead on the condition they did not prod or push any of the prospective interviewees.

They went ahead separately and visited the jurors at their homes. Once again, no success. They all clammed up. In fact, the strategy backfired. One of the jurors complained to the judge, John Sirica, of the U.S. District Court for the District of Columbia. Fortunately for the two reporters, Williams lived up to his reputation as one of the best attorneys in the nation. After talking with Sirica, Williams told Woodward and Bernstein: "John Sirica is some kind of pissed at you, fellas. We had to do a lot of convincing to keep your asses out of jail."[51]

As it turned out, both reporters were subsequently called into the courtroom by Judge Sirica on December 19, 1972—as a result of another case against the *Los Angeles Times*—but neither was singled out by the judge, who simply admonished the newsmen gathered there as a group about the legal ramifications of talking to a grand juror. Worried and anxious as they had been at the opening of the session, they were much relieved when they learned they would remain free and not be humiliated by hearing their names mentioned in court publicly. It was a close call.[52] Nonetheless, Bernstein was subpoenaed during Watergate for his sources. However, he worked with his management to find a way out.[53]

In the midst of all this journalistic and political chaos, Woodward and Bernstein signed a contract with Simon & Schuster with an advance of $55,000, a sizable figure, even though neither had written a book before. They would subsequently take six weeks off and go to Florida to write their book, *All the President's Men*, at Woodward's mother's house, while still remaining in touch with the *Post*. They felt they were running out of leads for the Watergate investigation but agreed to remain in touch. The fact that they actually took this interlude is all the more remarkable in light of what was yet to come back in Washington. The book would be published in April 1974, just months before Nixon was toppled from office. An interesting caveat is that, even before they had finished the book, actor Robert Redford approached them about possibly making a movie and gave them suggestions—some of which actually helped them shape the narrative. As Woodward explained it, "Redford's ideas no doubt contributed to the idea of telling the story as a personal one about journalism."[54]

In 1973, the year started off on a good note when the *Post*'s publisher, Katharine Graham—who had up to that time waited patiently through the rapid-fire burst of Watergate stories as well as the White House's attack on her newspaper—asked them to have lunch with her for the first time shortly after the trial of the five Watergate burglars began. The soft-spoken woman whose etiquette and class impressed everyone who worked for her politely asked the reporters: "Is it all going to come out? I mean, are we ever going to know about all of this?" "Never? Don't tell me never," she said with a smile.[55] She proceeded to ask for a briefing on their progress and, half-jokingly, asked them to identify Deep Throat. Woodward recalls freezing up, but nonetheless said he would tell if she really wanted to know, hoping she did not. She said she would rather not be burdened with it.[56]

That was the closest the two reporters came to informing anybody—other than Bradlee—about Deep Throat's identity until Felt himself, at age 91, identified himself on May 31, 2005, on *Vanity Fair*'s Web site in a piece by John D. O'Connor, an attorney acting on Felt's behalf. The article eventually appeared in print in the July issue of the magazine, and Woodward, Bernstein, and the *Post*'s editors confirmed the story.

At the height of the scandal, the *Post*'s competition—especially the *New York Times*—tried hard to keep up with Woodward and Bernstein. The *Times* even hired the well-known investigative reporter Seymour Hersh. As Hersh recalled the matter in a television interview in 2007: "I remember during Watergate when I was playing catch-up to Woodward and Bernstein, who had done such spectacular work. I was asked in the spring of 1972 to do something, I remember thinking, 'Are you crazy?' These guys are writing front-page stories about people whose names I'd never heard of. I didn't cover the White House. I covered the Vietnam War." Nonetheless, in January 1973, Hersh scooped Woodward and Bernstein by documenting how White House hush money had gone to the Watergate burglars.[57]

On June 22, 1973, Mark Felt retired from the Department of Justice, in part because he had seen himself as J. Edgar Hoover's successor and also because he was feeling the pressure of being Deep Throat among people who were ready to arrest that informant. This was only three days before John Dean testified at the Senate hearings on Watergate to charge that Nixon had, indeed, been involved in the illegal cover-up.

The Senate hearings, of course, brought out the existence of Nixon's secret tape recordings of his own conversations with multiple aides about covering up Watergate. By November, Woodward had gathered enough information to know that they were close to breaking the White House. Even though Felt had retired, Woodward asked for another meeting with him on November 21, at which time Felt told him that the tapes had erasures on them. By this time, things appeared to be almost out of control. "We were swimming, really living, in fast-moving rapids," Woodward wrote. . . . "It was only after Nixon resigned [on August 9, 1974] that I began to swim upstream seriously."[58]

It would be an oversimplification to conclude that Woodward and Bernstein alone brought down Richard Nixon. Their articles were the spark that lit the fire in the House and Senate to hold hearings that eventually led to the revelations by Dean, who said he had discussed the cover-up with Nixon at least 35 times; the resignations of virtually all of Nixon's trusted aides around him; the appointment of a special prosecutor; the White House's release—after holding out for months—of the edited transcripts of the Nixon tapes on April 30, 1974; the House passing articles of impeachment on June 30; the release of the actual tapes on July 24; House articles of impeachment from July 27 to July 30; and, finally, in early August 1974, the release of a previously unknown tape from June 23, 1972, recorded a few days after the break-in, documenting Nixon and [Assistant to the President] H. R. Haldeman formulating a plan to stonewall any investigation. This tape was, in fact, known as the "smoking gun" that finally forced Nixon's hand, soon after leading Republican senators informed the president that the Senate had the votes to convict him. More than a quarter of a century later, Woodward disclosed that those tapes reverberated in his mind to the extent that he would actually play them during holidays to remind himself of just how "chilling and horrifying" Watergate actually was.[59]

In my interview with Ben Bradlee, I asked him what he thought the journalistic lessons of Watergate were. He succinctly summarized them this way: "You can't believe everything you hear, including what comes from the highest-ranking and most respected people in the country. They do not tell the truth, and if you keep at 'em you can prove it."

Does he consider Watergate the model for investigative reporting? "I'm sure it is," he told me, "but some of the old-timers like Lincoln Steffens and others did the same kind of reporting. But, you know, I think Watergate was a good one. It's been 40-some years. And we're still talking about it." Asked if he thought investigative reporting was still alive and well, he replied: "Damn right. I'm sure there is a Watergate story kicking around in some local town where some banker is robbing the country blind."

What does he think of the current transition of journalism to the Internet? "I am not an expert on that. You know, obviously, we are going that way. It's probably inevitable. But I think your grandchildren and mine are going to be reading newspapers."

Asked what he was most proud of in the entire Watergate adventure, Bradlee replied: "Coming out on the right side. We had a lot of editors involved. There were a lot of people working on the Watergate stories."

I asked Bradlee: "When Woodward or Bernstein got stiff-armed by high-ranking officials, what did you do?" He answered: "I would sometimes talk with those government officials and we would work out something they could say. There wasn't anything magical. Just because I called them up, they didn't want to help me. If they didn't want to talk, they didn't want to talk. But we could talk it over and we could come up with inventive ways to go around it."

As for the movie, Bradlee said he liked it and that he had met Jason Robards, the actor who played him, and had a picture of Robards and him together. "I thought the movie was great. I thought the director, Alan Pakula, was fabulous. Redford and Hoffman did a good job. Hoffman could imitate Bernstein so well nobody could tell the difference."[60]

In 2008, I asked Bob Woodward what lessons he learned from Watergate from a journalistic viewpoint. "The value of incremental coverage," he replied, "and by that I mean you do big stories—not every day, not every week—but you keep chipping away at it. If you look at the Watergate coverage, Carl and I would do a story and it would be on page B17 of the Metro section. You look for details that tell you something. For example, I remember specifically, it was the kind of expensive $3,000 receiver that had been used by McCord and his team eavesdropping on conversations at the Democratic National Committee. The story itself didn't really tell you anything except that, at that time, that was a vast amount of money. So it wasn't an operation taken on the cheap. And that leads you to the conclusion that spending a couple of hundred thousand dollars is not going to be spent without somebody really high up knowing about it and realizing what it's going for. That was one of the little bricks in the story that helped put it together."

Asked what it takes to be a really good investigative reporter, Woodward responded: "I don't necessarily distinguish regular reporting from investigative reporting. There are fundamentals, and one is to find human sources you can talk to, and as many human stories as possible. There are very few stories that don't have some kind of documentary support like calendars or notes, including unofficial and official records. Go to the scene of the site you are writing about if you can. The power of personal observation is obviously high."

How far can a reporter push people? "You don't want to be rude, but I think you can push people as far as they will let you push them," said Woodward. "If somebody says no on Tuesday, that does not mean they are going to say no next Wednesday. So you keep going back and back and try to convince people that you are sincere in trying to understand the full dimensions of what you are writing about."

I asked Woodward to share what he personally thought the "inside story" of Watergate was. He was quite candid: "It's well known and repeated many times, I guess. We were young, unmarried, we had the support and curiosity of the editors—at the base of all this was Bradlee's instinct for a good story. . . . [With] an editor who believes in you, you can do a lot. It was Bradlee's instinct and open-mindedness. The other thing is, collaboration is very important with creative editors like Bradlee and Howard Simons. Simons kept pushing us. He would say, 'Where are we on the Watergate story? What are we doing?'"

Indeed, Woodward, Bernstein, Bradlee, and the entire *Washington Post* staff did not really know what they had accomplished until the scandal drove a president from the White House and, in doing so, set the standard for investigative journalism that—in the eyes of most journalists—remains unmatched since. Their files and papers from the investigation have since been archived at the University of Texas.

It is instructive to remember that their stories were written using typewriters and dozens of phone books, rather than any of the modern technologies that most newspapers now take for granted. As one pundit put it: "Nobody else cares enough to do the digging to unearth what Watergate reporters Bob Woodward and Carl Bernstein call 'the best obtainable version of the truth.'"[61] And, as one of their colleagues on the *Post*, Michael Dobbs, wrote in his summary of the Mark Felt–Deep Throat revelation in the *Washington Post*: "Watergate was the biggest political story in modern American history."[62]

In the aftermath of Watergate, journalists reached perhaps the highest status in American society. Scores of young students enrolled in journalism schools around the country in the ensuing decades aspiring to have a career like investigative reporters Woodward and Bernstein.

As for his own views on what is often called the "glamour" of investigative reporting, in an appearance at New York University before a group of journalism students, Bernstein stressed the importance of remaining down to earth when undertaking an investigatory assignment. "It's sure a fine endeavor to go into this profession or go into a story thinking you're going to change social norms," he said. "But this doesn't serve you very well, this sort of messianic ideal. There has to be a sense of humility about it. It's about giving an accurate picture of what's going on, of factual reporting."[63]

It was somewhat ironic that, after 33 years, Bob Woodward and Carl Bernstein were not the first to identify Deep Throat. As *Post* media writer Howard Kurtz wrote under the headline "The Post's Lost Scoop":

> How, after 33 years of secrecy, did *The Washington Post* get scooped on its own story about the tantalizing mystery of Deep Throat?
>
> The answer is that Bob Woodward, Carl Bernstein and Ben Bradlee felt they were in a box—the promise of confidentiality made to W. Mark Felt during the Nixon administration—and were not convinced that the 91-year-old former FBI agent was lucid enough to release them from that pledge.
>
> Family members "have said he just doesn't have any memory now," Woodward said yesterday, referring to e-mails he received from Felt's relatives. The dilemma, said Woodward, was whether "someone in his condition and age" was "competent" to make the decision to go public.

"I had been in touch with Mark Felt," said Woodward, the best-selling author who is an assistant managing editor at *The Post*. "How was his health? Had he changed his mind about being identified? This was an ongoing reporting enterprise." Felt suffered a mild stroke in 2001.

Woodward said the *Vanity Fair* story detailing Felt's role came as a total surprise to him when it was released. "I didn't know he was gearing up to go public," he said.[64]

In retrospect, many observers now see Felt as arguably the most important—albeit anonymous—whistle-blower in modern American political history, although Felt himself on several occasions denied publicly that he was Deep Throat.[65] Looking back with historical perspective these many decades later, Woodward and Bernstein deserve full credit for their perseverance in igniting the spark that became a full-blown journalistic and political inferno. It was their dogged research and reporting and their extraordinary perseverance that pushed Congress—acting in bipartisan fashion along with the courts—to bring Nixon to his knees on the edge of impeachment. The Congress of the United States took the lead from the *Post* and made history by concluding that the Nixon administration had made a blatant, illegal attempt to cover up Watergate. In the end, it was that enormous abuse of power and corruption of U.S. government agencies—exposed by Woodward and Bernstein—that brought Nixon down.

The scandal was so huge that ever since Watergate, whenever a major wrongdoing—political or otherwise—erupts, it is promptly given the suffix "-gate." Examples include Monicagate (Bill Clinton; see chapter 4), Travelgate (1993 firings of White House travel employees in Clinton administration), Enrongate (collapse of the company; see chapter 5), Katrinagate (George W. Bush), Rathergate (Dan Rather's CBS report on forged Bush documents), Plamegate (leaking the identity of CIA agent Valeria Plame), and even Spygate (New England Patriots football coach videotaping New York Jets signals), plus many more. In effect, "-gate" has become an accepted part of the lexicon of journalists' reportage when referring to perceived misbehavior, conflict-of-interest, or criminal activities of almost any kind.

For the sake of the historical record, it should also be noted that, belatedly, on May 25, 2008, the *New York Times* published a story entitled "2 Ex-Timesmen Say They Had a Tip on Watergate First."

It cited as its source Robert M. Smith, a former *Times* reporter, who said that two months after the initial burglary he had lunch with Patrick Gray, the acting director of the FBI, "who disclosed explosive aspects of the case, including the culpability of the former Attorney General John Mitchell, and hinted at White House involvement." He said he passed this information along to Robert H. Phelps, a *Times* editor, but the story petered out when Phelps left on a monthlong trip to Alaska. Smith said he disclosed the anecdote in 2009 because Phelps, then 89, had recently published his memoir, *God and the Editor: My Search for Meaning at the New York Times*. Phelps was quoted in the 2009 *Times* story as saying he had "no idea" of what happened to the original tip he received.[66]

Interestingly, this account was disputed in an article in the *Manchester* (New Hampshire) *Guardian* in 2009, in a letter to the editor from Ed Gray, of Lyme, New Hampshire, the son of Patrick Gray. He said his father's appointment calendar showed no reference to a lunch with Smith in August 1972, and he denied that his father passed along any information to Smith or anyone else. "Had my father intended to leak anything about Watergate or any other subject of interest to the FBI, he would have made sure the story got published," he wrote.[67]

Perhaps the impact of Watergate on the national psyche can best be summed up by an observation Ben Bradlee made in a column in his own paper in 1992:

> My overwhelming memory of those 26 months—from the day the five burglars were caught with their rubber gloves on, with the crisp hundred-dollar bills in their pockets and White House phone numbers in their address books, to the President's embarrassingly public final torture—is simply this. No news story has ever grabbed and held Washington by the throat the way Watergate did. No news story in my experience ever dominated conversation, newspapers, radio and television broadcasts the way Watergate did. There were times when you could walk whole city blocks and ride taxis all around town and never miss a word of hearings or press conferences.[68]

One noted historian summarized Watergate's place in history in 2008: "Perhaps Watergate's most lasting effect has been a loss of innocence for the American public as they came to view their government with distrust."[69] As for the many foibles of Richard Nixon, with the passage of time, Woodward put Nixon's fatal flaw in perspective, at a public forum in 2009, when he stated: "Hate was the poison that destroyed Nixon. It was the piston that drove his administration. There has been some rough stuff, serious mistakes and all sorts of problems, but none of the other [Presidents] were haters like Nixon."[70]

Finally, one blogger in 2009 put Watergate in perspective from an international viewpoint as follows:

> It is a story that—if history had not turned out the way it did—would read like detective fiction. Instead, it is the portrait of a President under investigation, with Bernstein and Woodward expertly painting the details. . . . *All The President's Men* captures the feeling of waywardness, despair and isolation that flourished in 1970s America. It heralded in a new era, where the carefree bubble of the 1960s was shattered by mistrust, recession and war.[71]

In the end, Woodward and Bernstein proved beyond any doubt that the public has a right to know. Woodward explained it this way in November 2009: "Politicians want the public's support for what they are doing, but they won't let the public in on the nitty-gritty of what that debate is. It is absolutely essential that we have those details. There is a little bit of the First Amendment in the soul of everyone."[72]

ABOUT BOB WOODWARD AND CARL BERNSTEIN

Bob Woodward and Carl Bernstein are considered in the journalism profession—and by the public in general—as two of the "giants" of modern-day investigative reporting. Woodward graduated from Yale University, after which he joined the U.S. Navy. Upon his discharge, he joined the *Washington Post* in 1970. His first significant byline came with the Watergate break-in story, on which he was assigned to work with the more experienced reporter Carl Bernstein. They were, in fact, seen as the "odd couple" in the city room: Woodward, a sophisticated, smooth-talking, well-mannered Ivy Leaguer, and Bernstein, a rough-spoken, shaggy-haired, old-fashioned, nononsense reporter with a nose for news who had started in the business from the bottom up. Prior to teaming up, the two men had hardly exchanged two words.

Based on their unique experiences during the course of their history-making inquiry, the two reporters took copious notes of their reportorial adventures and, together, wrote the memorable best-seller *All the President's Men.* It was subsequently made into a hit movie that romanticized investigative reporting (with Robert Redford playing Woodward and Dustin Hoffman in the role of Bernstein) to the point where they inspired countless young would-be reporters into journalism.

Bob Woodward went on to write a number of other books, including *The Brethren: Inside the Supreme Court; The Man Who Would Be President: Dan Quayle; Wired: The Short Life and Fast Times of John Belushi; Veil: The Secret Ways of the CIA; The Commanders*, about the 1991 Persian Gulf War; *The Agenda: Inside the Clinton White House; The Choice*, on the 1996 presidential campaign; and *Maestro*, on long-time Federal Reserve chairman Alan Greenspan. In recent years, Woodward has authored four books on President George W. Bush's mismanagement of the Middle East wars: *Bush at War, Plan of Attack, State of Denial*, and *The War Within*. After the unknown identity of Watergate informant Deep Throat was revealed in 2005—when W. Mark Felt, a former top official of the FBI, came forward to confess his role—Woodward wrote a detailed book about Felt, called *The Secret Man*. He also continued to fill the role of assistant managing editor at the *Washington Post*.

Carl Bernstein, the "other half" of the combo that famously broke the Watergate story, attended the University of Maryland, College Park. He and Woodward, as well as the *Washington Post*, shared a Pulitzer Prize for their historic uncovering of the Watergate plot. Bernstein won a second Pulitzer in 1977 for a *Rolling Stone* magazine article, in which he brought to light the fact that the CIA had secretly employed hundreds of U.S. journalists who wrote stories for the agency. Bernstein went on to become the Washington bureau chief for ABC News. He coauthored *The Final Days* with Woodward, which described Nixon's last few months in the White House. Bernstein also coauthored *His Holiness: John Paul II and the History of Our Time* with Marco Politi and wrote a biography of Hillary Rodham Clinton, *A Woman in Charge: The Life of Hillary Rodham Clinton*. Bernstein remains a major player on the national political scene with articles and commentaries on television and has ventured into film making.

Notes

1. This chapter does not attempt to include all of the characters involved in this complex story, just those who were a key part of the reporters' investigative reporting process. The Watergate story has been told and retold so many times that it is sufficient, for purposes of this overview of the "inside story" behind Woodward and Bernstein's exposé, to focus on the methods and techniques both men used in pursuit of what both reporters have since, on many occasions, called "the best obtainable version of the truth."

2. The story identified the five as: "(1) Edward Martin, alias James W. McCord, Jr., of New York City and the Washington metropolitan area . . . (2) Frank A. Sturgis of 2515 NW 122d St., Miami . . . (3) Eugenio R. Martinez of 4044 North Meridian Ave., Miami . . . (4) Virgilio R. Gonzales of 930 NW 23d Ave., Miami . . . (5) Bernard L. Barker of 5229 NW 4th St., Miami." All were charged with felonious burglary and with possession of implements of crime.

3. Bob Woodward, *The Secret Man: The Story of Watergate's Deep Throat* (New York: Simon & Schuster, 2005), 31.

4. Carl Bernstein and Bob Woodward, *All the President's Men* (New York: Simon & Schuster, 1974), 14.

5. Ibid., 20.

6. Author's interview with Carl Bernstein, April 1, 2009.

7. Bernstein and Woodward, *All the President's Men*, 26.

8. Author's interview with Bernstein.

9. Interview with Carl Bernstein, *Frontline*, PBS, July 10, 2006.

10. Author's interview with Ben Bradlee, July 17, 2008.

11. Author's interview with Bernstein.

12. Ibid.

13. Ben Bradlee, *A Good Life: Newspapering and Other Adventures* (New York: Simon & Schuster, 1995), 324.

14. Ibid., 324–25.

15. Ibid., 325.

16. Ibid., 326.

17. Author's interview with Bradlee.

18. Richard M. Nixon, *The Memoirs of Richard Nixon* (New York: Grosset & Dunlap, 1978), 1001.

19. Bernstein and Woodward, *All the President's Men*, 30.

20. Woodward, *Secret Man*, 2.

21. Author's interview with Bernstein, April 1, 2009. The cover name "Deep Throat" was coined by *Post* managing editor Howard Simons as a reference to the famous pornographic movie of the time, which became a mainstream cause célèbre. Simons decided on that name because when Bernstein was in danger of being served with a subpoena, Ben Bradlee told him to leave the city room and go see a movie. That was the film he happened to see. The phrase was also a play on the journalism term "deep background," meaning information provided

by a secret source that, by mutual agreement of both the reporter and the source, would not be attributed directly nor tied to the source's name in any way.

22. Woodward, *Secret Man*, 3.

23. John D. O'Connor, "I'm the Guy They Called Deep Throat," *Vanity Fair*, July 2005.

24. Author's interview with Bernstein.

25. Woodward, *Secret Man*, 17.

26. Ibid., 19.

27. Ibid., 24.

28. Ibid., 52.

29. Ibid., 58.

30. Edward M. Kennedy, *True Compass* (New York: Twelve, Hachette Book Group, 2009), 335.

31. Quoted in Woodward, *Secret Man*, 59.

32. Ibid.

33. Ibid., 63–64.

34. Ibid., 61.

35. Ibid., 65–66.

36. Ibid., 68.

37. Author's interview with Bernstein, April 1, 2009.

38. Woodward, *Secret Man*, 69–70.

39. Ibid., 70.

40. Ibid., 73.

41. *Washington Post*, editorial, October 1, 1972.

42. Ben Bradlee, "Walter Cronkite, 1916–2009," *Newsweek*, July 27, 2009.

43. Ryan Smith, "Cronkite on the Crime of the Century: 'The Watergate Caper,'" Associated Press, July 20, 2009, available at http://www.cbsnews.com/8301-504083_162-5175345-504083.html.

44. Bradlee, "Walter Cronkite."

45. Bob Woodward, speaking via satellite during one of several events September 30, 2009, celebrating Walter Cronkite (who died July 17) at Arizona State University's Walter Cronkite School of Journalism and Mass Communication, Phoenix.

46. Daniel Schorr, *Capital Times*, July 23, 2009.

47. Bernstein and Woodward, *All the President's Men*, 200.

48. Ibid., 207.

49. Author's interview with Bernstein, April 1, 2009.

50. Author's interview with Bob Woodward, October 9, 2008.

51. Bernstein and Woodward, *All the President's Men*, 211.

52. Ibid., 222–24.

53. In a television interview on PBS's *Frontline* on July 10, 2006, Bernstein explained: "There was a civil suit brought by the Nixon re-election committee against the Democratic National Committee for the purpose of trying to find

out how they were getting their information to us, among other things. . . . [When we] knew that the subpoena had reached the building, I went to [executive editor] Ben Bradlee, and I said, 'Look, I just got a call from the guard downstairs that there's a subpoena with a piece of paper with my name on it.' And he said, 'Look, go see a movie while we figure out what to do.' So I went to see a movie; in fact, the movie I saw was *Deep Throat*. I came back to the office, and by then the strategy had been gone over with the lawyers. Our notes, my notes, were transferred to the custody of Katharine Graham, the publisher of the *Washington Post*. Therefore, if anybody was going to go to jail, she was going to go also. As Bradlee said: 'Wouldn't that be something? Every photographer in town would be down at the courthouse to look at our girl going off to the slam.' And Mrs. Graham was ready to go to jail because she understood the principle. I accepted the subpoena, because by then, the custody of my notes had been transferred to Katharine Graham. [Eventually] they backed off. . . . They didn't want to take on Katharine Graham. They took on Katharine Graham by trying to take the licenses of the *Washington Post* television stations away, which was the real money-making ability of the Washington Post Company at the time. It paid a lot of the bills."

54. Woodward, *Secret Man*, 113.

55. Bernstein and Woodward, *All the President's Men*, 236.

56. Ibid., 236.

57. Interview with Seymour Hersh, *Frontline*, PBS, January 8, 2007.

58. Woodward, *Secret Man*, 104.

59. According to a story by Aubry Bracco on news@seacoastline.com, from Exeter, New Hampshire, on October 30, 2009: "Bob Woodward told a crowd at Phillips Exeter Academy on Thursday [October 29, 2009] he and the *Washington Post* staff still pull out the infamous President Richard Nixon tapes each year at the holidays. 'We call them "the gift that keeps on giving'," joked Woodward, the famed journalist who, along with fellow *Post* reporter Carl Bernstein uncovered the Watergate scandal, leading to Nixon's resignation in 1974."

60. Author's interview with Bradlee. Alan J. Pakula, known for his films on conspiracies, used journalists Bob Woodward and Carl Bernstein's book about their Watergate probe as the basis of one of the top-rated films of bicentennial year 1976.

61. Mike Tharp, "The Sun-Star Is Too Small to Fail," *Merced Sun-Star*, April 11, 2009, available at http://www.com/2009/04/11/785832/mike-tharp-the-sun-star -is-too.html.

62. *Washington Post*, June 2, 2005.

63. "Foundations of Journalism" forum, New York University, October 27, 2009.

64. *Washington Post*, June 2, 2005. Kurtz's account continued: "To Bradlee, who was the paper's executive editor during Watergate, there was no decision to be made. 'If you give your word you're not going to do it, you can't do it,' said Bradlee, now a Washington Post Company vice president. 'We were the

only people who were clinically and morally bound not to break this story, so how could we break it?' 'What's more,' Bradlee said of Felt, 'the guy has not got all his marbles. The question was whether he could have given us permission.' . . . 'Look, I have one goal in all this, to try and do it right,' Woodward said." Woodward and Bernstein confirmed Felt's identity as Deep Throat after they had spoken with the lawyer who had written the *Vanity Fair* article.

65. W. Mark Felt, *The FBI Pyramid: From the Inside* (New York: G. Putnam's Sons, 1979), 226, 248. Felt flatly stated: "I never leaked information to Woodward or Bernstein or to anyone else." Felt also wrote that he was aware that he was a principal White House suspect in their zeal to identify Deep Throat, but that complaints to Attorney General Richard Kleindienst, forwarded to Gray and to the president, were dismissed when Gray told Kleindienst that he [Felt] was "completely loyal" and the matter went no further. Felt also disclosed in his book that he once talked to Bob Woodward in Felt's office with his assistant, Inspector Wason G. Campbell, present. He said Woodward had asked him to confirm information Woodward and Bernstein had collected. "I declined to cooperate with him in this manner and that was that," was how Felt put it.

66. *New York Times*, May 25, 2009.

67. *Manchester* (NH) *Guardian*, May 28, 2009. Ed Gray referred readers to his Web site, http://www.lpatrickgrayiii.com, for details.

68. *Washington Post*, June 14, 1992.

69. Mark Grossman, *Political Corruption in America: An Encyclopedia of Scandals, Power, and Greed Vol.2* (Millerton, NY: Grey House, 1998), 481.

70. Quoted in Matthew McGowan, "Thoughts on the Presidency: Journalistic Icons Woodward and Bernstein Bring Their Expertise to UTPB," John Ben Sheppard Public Leadership Institute Distinguished Lecture Series at the University of Texas of the Permian Basin, October 15, 2009.

71. Tom Cowie, review of *All the President's Men*, http://www.upstart.net .au/all-the-presidents-men-review/.

72. Jason Levin, *Indiana Gazette*, November 5, 2009, quoting Woodward on the campus of Indiana University of Pennsylvania's second annual First Commonwealth Endowed Lecture, titled, "From Nixon to Bush: What Can President Obama Learn from the Presidents Past?"

CHAPTER 4

MONICAGATE:
IMPEACHMENT
OF A PRESIDENT

Reported by Michael Isikoff, Newsweek, *1998*

His friends would say he pursued this story like a heat-seeking missile. His persistence resulted in the revelation of the biggest political scandal since Watergate.

—Charlie Rose

The White House exposé popularly known as "Monicagate" was painstakingly researched for more than a year by one of the country's top investigative reporters, *Newsweek*'s Michael Isikoff. It touched off a national political scandal—the biggest since Watergate—and culminated in the impeachment of a U.S. president, the second president in history to face impeachment proceedings, and the first since Reconstruction.[1]

The story broke in an unprecedented, unorthodox way, however. On Saturday night, January 17, 1998, a then-obscure Internet columnist by the name of Matt Drudge sent out a story to his 85,000 *Drudge Report* subscribers online, operating in a brand-new media in the wilds of cyberspace, not a morning newspaper. It marked the official arrival of the digital age in the news business.

Drudge's story was actually about how and why Isikoff's history-making journalistic effort had been temporarily held up by his employer, *Newsweek* magazine. Drudge's story on the Internet began on a note of sensation:

Web Posted: 01/17/98 21:32:02 PST – NEWSWEEK KILLS STORY ON WHITE HOUSE INTERN X X X X X BLOCKBUSTER

REPORT: 23-YEAR OLD, FORMER WHITE HOUSE INTERN, SEX RELATIONSHIP WITH PRESIDENT. At the last minute, at 6 P.M. on Saturday evening, NEWSWEEK magazine killed a story that was destined to shake official Washington to its foundation: A White House intern carried on a sexual affair with the President of the United States! The DRUDGE REPORT has learned that reporter Michael Isikoff developed the story of his career, only to have it "spiked" by top NEWS WEEK suits hours before publication. A young woman, 23, sexually involved with the love of her life, the President of the United States, since she was a 21-year-old intern at the White House.

Twenty-four hours later, Drudge sent out the identity of the young intern. He wrote:

Web Posted: 01/18/98 22:33:48 PST – FORMER WHITE HOUSE INTERN CALLED; NEW BACKGROUND DETAILS EMERGE **World Exclusive** **Must Credit the DRUDGE REPORT** The DRUDGE REPORT has learned that former White House intern, Monica Lewinsky, 23, has been subpoenaed to give a deposition in the Paula Jones case.

Drudge's assertion that *Newsweek* had "spiked" Isikoff's story about an official investigation into President Bill Clinton's relationship with a former White House intern was not entirely accurate. In point of fact, *Newsweek*'s editors had simply decided to hold off publication until several loose threads in the story could be nailed down. Special Prosecutor Kenneth Starr's office pressed hard to delay publication while, unknown to *Newsweek*, prosecutors tried to get Lewinsky to agree to a sting operation against the president or his advisers. In the end, *Newsweek* agreed to hold off reporting the story after extracting a promise from Starr's office that it would receive a complete account for the following week's magazine.

However, there was never any doubt that the story belonged to Isikoff, who had been tirelessly chasing it virtually on his own. Here is one account of what happened:

On January 14, 1998, according to *Newsweek*'s account, Isikoff learned that the special prosecutor was investigating obstruction of justice and perjury in the Paula Jones case, and that

Monica Lewinsky was a target of the investigation. Isikoff continued to report the story for the next three days. On Saturday, January 17, at 12:30 A.M., *Newsweek* editors heard a tape of conversations between Lewinsky and her friend Linda Tripp. As *Newsweek* could not independently verify the authenticity of the recording and some of the statements on the tape raised questions about Lewinsky's credibility, the editors decided to hold the story. *Newsweek* quickly posted an explanation of why it held the story on the Web.[2]

Newsweek's editors later said they did not know how the information found its way into Drudge's hands, but they suspected Lucianne Goldberg, book agent for Tripp and a frequent source for Drudge's investigation. Isikoff had informed her early Saturday night of the magazine's decision to hold off. While reporters for mainstream news organizations found the sexual aspects of the story somewhat risky, there was little disagreement that this was a legitimate news story. This much they knew: the Office of the Independent Counsel was investigating whether Clinton had obstructed justice by encouraging Lewinsky to lie under oath about their relationship. The fact that it was a civil deposition in a sexual harassment case funded by political enemies of the Clintons made it no less newsworthy.

No sooner had the news of Clinton's alleged sexual affair with Lewinsky come out than the national press swarmed all over the story. The next morning, Sunday, January 18, Drudge's story was the main topic discussed by conservative commentator William Kristol on ABC's *This Week with Sam Donaldson and Cokie Roberts*. Sam Donaldson, ABC's White House correspondent, suggested on the program that Clinton might soon resign and added gravely: "If he's not telling the truth, I think his presidency is numbered in days."[3]

By January 19, the Washington bureaus of the major news organizations all knew about the report. Drudge's e-mail dispatch had been seen by a number of influential news editors across the country who subscribed to the *Drudge Report*. They all went into high gear tracking down the story. They knew that when the news combines a married president with sex and a single woman, that is a volatile mix that is bound to raise eyebrows and draw readers or viewers, especially since it involved Bill Clinton, a known womanizer.

A decade later, in 2009, with the advantage of hindsight, Isikoff put the entire episode in context in an interview with this author:

"The Drudge phenomenon," he told me, "was a big deal at the time all this happened. But by now, the Web, bloggers, 24/7 cable has so changed the nature of news that it's almost passé. Of course, all this has dramatically changed the process . . . and put much more of a premium on speed and 'getting stuff out' than previously. But I believe there is still a need, and indeed a hunger in many quarters, for well-researched, well-documented investigative reporting."[4] As for Drudge himself, three years after the fact, a *Miami News* reporter wrote a story about him, with the following assessment:

> Democrats hate him. Journalists scorn him. Most Americans ignore him. Which is fine with Matt Drudge. He's taking it to the bank. "When I look back on it, to imagine that the President would be saying my name over and over again in grand jury testimony, having that bounced around on satellites all over the world—it's pretty surreal," he recalls. "And it took just two fingers, a modem, and guts." He then adds with a snarl: "And not giving a shit!"[5]

On the other hand, since Drudge bathed in his own self-reflected glory at the time, most Internet news analysts today agree that he has lost much of his initial glamour as the wonder boy of online journalism. "One sign that Drudge's influence is on the wane is that he goes to such great lengths to deny it," wrote Evan Porter, in *Columbia Journalism Review* in 2009. Since the Monicagate story, writes Porter, Drudge's power has been diminished by the rapid changes in technology.

> The field of online news has welcomed several explosive upstarts, such as Politico and The Huffington Post. . . . Such sites built on the promise of Drudge, mixing hard news and chatter into a stew that generates enormous traffic and ability to shape the conversation. . . . Drudge is now a middle-of-the-pack niche product. . . . In the age of Twitter, Facebook, and YouTube, community building is the name of the game. But not at the Drudge Report, which remains Drudge's private kingdom.[6]

I asked Isikoff how he felt when Matt Drudge put out the story on the Internet before *Newsweek*'s story got out. Isikoff replied in one word: "Lousy." He went on: "Look, I knew that this was treacherous territory and editors always want to know this stuff, but it is publishing it that gives them pause. They want to know it, but they don't know that they ever want to share it [unsubstantiated news] with the public. I always knew that was a risk."[7]

Although Drudge had technically beaten Isikoff on his own story, as *Washington Post* media writer Howard Kurtz explained subsequently: "In the computer-driven culture of the '90s, *Newsweek* simply resurrected its piece on the Bill Clinton sex scandal by posting it online and putting its people on television." At the very outset, as soon as the *Drudge Report* broke his story, in a 14-hour period, Isikoff appeared on the *NBC Nightly News*, *The News with Brian Williams*, *Today*, and *Imus in the Morning*.[8]

Newsweek's first story online would be followed by more than a hundred stories on the topic that *Newsweek* published in 1998, the majority of which Isikoff had a hand in identifying. Others were written by Isikoff—many with *Newsweek*'s then assistant managing editor Evan Thomas—and the rest under the bylines of more than 20 other *Newsweek* staff writers.[9] It was a blitzkrieg of journalism in a superb effort to cover every possible angle of the story. The magazine even invited some outside "name" journalists and political figures to contribute columns, in particular, four by George Stephanopoulos, former Clinton aide turned TV broadcaster; one by historian Alan Brinkley; two by conservative commentator and journalist George F. Will; one by editor and conservative columnist William Kristol; and "The Kid Question: A Privacy Expert Familiar with Fame on What to Tell the Children (What Children Should Know about Scandals or How to Talk to Children about Public Officials Who Have Affairs)" by Caroline Kennedy. The articles in *Newsweek* published during the year were comprehensive and wide-ranging. They included hard news stories, opinion pieces, educational stories, interpretive and speculative pieces, and stories related to the subject of impeachment and sexual harassment.[10]

Late Tuesday night, January 20, 1998, the story hit the mainstream media. In its early edition, the *Washington Post* announced in a four-column headline across the front page: "Clinton Accused of Urging Aide to Lie; Starr Probes Whether President Told Woman to Deny Alleged Affair to Jones's Lawyers." The story was attributed to "sources close to the investigation." Minutes after midnight, ABC News broadcast a story recapping the *Post* story on its radio network. And the *Los Angeles Times* broke the story in its Wednesday edition with a front-page story headlined, "Starr Examines Clinton Link to Female Intern."

The press quickly went after Clinton the next day, January 21, in an interview with National Public Radio's *All Things Considered*. The colloquy with Clinton read, in part:

> Q: *Many Americans woke up to the news today that the Whitewater independent counsel is investigating an allegation that you, or you and Vernon Jordan, encouraged a young woman to lie to lawyers in the Paula Jones civil suit. Is there any truth to that allegation?*
> A: No, sir, there's not. It's just not true.
>
> Q: *Is there any truth to the allegation of an affair between you and the young woman?*
> A: No, that's not true, either. And I have told people that I would cooperate in the investigation and I expect to cooperate with it. I don't know any more about it than I've told you, and any more about it really than you do, but I will cooperate. The charges are not true, and I haven't asked anybody to lie.

The questioning continued that evening on the TV program *The News with Jim Lehrer*:

> Q: *The news of this day is that Kenneth Starr, independent counsel, is investigating allegations that you suborned perjury by encouraging a 24-year-old woman, a former White House intern, to lie under oath in a civil deposition about her having had an affair with you. Mr. President, is that true?*
> A: That is not true. That is not true. I did not ask anyone to tell anything other than the truth. There is no improper relationship. And I intend to cooperate with this inquiry. But that is not true.
>
> Q: *"No improper relationship"—define what you mean by that.*
> A: Well, I think you know what it means. It means that there is not a sexual relationship, an improper sexual relationship, or any other kind of improper relationship.

Many other media outlets piled on. In an attempt to recover, top *Newsweek* editors decided to put the story online on Wednesday, January 21. The coverage far surpassed that of the O. J. Simpson trial or the shocking death of Princess Diana. According to one source,

Suddenly Americans learned on the nightly news details that would have required a parental-warning label had they appeared in a prime-time show. Night after night television audiences heard about oral sex, adultery, and [Lewinsky's] semen-stained dress. Newspapers and television consistently used phrases such as "sources said" or "reportedly" to bring every lurid detail, allegation, and innuendo to the public's attention. . . . For many critics of the media, coverage of the White House scandal indicated the extent to which tabloid and mainstream journalism had become closely aligned.[11]

Finally, faced by a bevy of correspondents at his next scheduled White House press conference on January 26, 1998, Clinton, clearly frustrated and ashen-faced after getting repeated questions about his alleged affair, gestured his right forefinger at reporters and declared, slowly but emphatically: "I want to say one thing to the American people. I want you to listen to me. I'm going to say this again. I did not have sexual relations with *that woman*, Miss Lewinsky. I never told anybody to lie, not a single time—never. These allegations are false. And I need to go back to work for the American people" (emphasis added). The phrase "that woman" has since taken on a life of its own as one of the memorable quotes from the entire debacle.

According to an article in the *American Journalism Review*:

Only once before—when the magazine obtained an exclusive interview with a Chinese dissident—had it [*Newsweek*] published something in cyberspace first. Yet the saga of the President and the intern would move with blinding velocity. Others had the outline; *Newsweek* had the details. "We concluded, look, it's a huge story and we have something exclusive to add, and it's not going to hold," Managing Editor Mark Whitaker recalls. . . . "Let's do it." Isikoff and Thomas began furiously cobbling together a narrative, taking advantage of months of reporting. "I had drafted a piece the previous week," Isikoff says. "But that's all it was, a draft. But the essentials were there." The essentials came from Isikoff's tireless pursuit of allegations of sexual misconduct by Clinton. Isikoff had long believed there was more to the Paula Jones story and that it shouldn't be dropped.[12]

Newsweek let him keep going.

> "I just knew that very few people in this town who are not part of the organized right-wing obsessives were going to pursue this," Isikoff said. "Reporters were not going to touch this story. They're all queasy about it." The story was 4,000 words, far more than would have appeared in the magazine, Whitaker said. "The ironic thing is by Wednesday, because things had advanced and because the story was breaking," says Whitaker, "we were able to be much more authoritative on Wednesday than we would have been on Saturday."[13]

On January 26, 1998, the *Newsweek* story opened as follows:

> They tried to keep her as far away from the White House as possible, but it wasn't far enough. Last Saturday morning Paula Jones, with her new wardrobe, her new hairdo and—most important—her new legal team, walked into the office of Robert Bennett, the President's lawyer, just off Pennsylvania Avenue two blocks from the White House. There, she sat a few feet away from Bill Clinton as her lawyers asked the President what really happened in that room of the Excelsior Hotel in Little Rock on May 8, 1991. Under a gag order from Judge Susan Webber Wright—who was in the room for the deposition—neither Jones nor Clinton nor their minions would talk about the six-hour session, but it was certainly not friendly.

Despite the damage that had been done by the media, it is instructive to recall that the public was not persuaded. A *Washington Post* poll taken 10 days after the story broke found that 56 percent of those surveyed believed the news media were treating Clinton unfairly, and 74 percent said the media were giving the story "too much attention." A Freedom Forum poll found that the top two adjectives used by Americans to describe the coverage of the story were "excessive" and "embarrassing."

Nonetheless, Clinton was faced by the press again with hostile questions on February 6, 1998, at another White House news conference. Helen Thomas, the United Press International's irrepressible reporter, kicked off the questions by asking: "Mr. President, despite the ongoing investigation, you've felt no constraint in saying what your relationship with Monica Lewinsky is not, was not. So it seems by logic that you ought to be able to say here and now what was your relationship. Her lawyer says—called it 'colleague.' Is that an apt description?"

Clinton responded: "Well, let me first of all say, once again, I never asked anybody to do anything but tell the truth. I know about the stories today. I was pleased that [his secretary] Ms. [Betty] Currie's lawyers stated unambiguously this morning—unambiguously—that she's not aware of any unethical conduct. But this investigation is going on, and you know what the rules for it are. And I just think as long as it is going on, I should not comment on specific questions, because there's one, then there's another, then there's another. It's better to let the investigation go on and have me do my job and focus on my public responsibilities, and let this thing play out its course. That's what I think I should do, and that's what I intend to do now."

Long before Drudge had his 15 minutes of fame, Isikoff had been digging into Clinton's past sexual encounters, beginning when he was governor of Arkansas. Isikoff, who investigated the Jones case from the outset, had covered a little-publicized press conference in Washington, D.C., on February 11, 1994, in the Omni Shoreham's Diplomat Room. Jones, a former Arkansas state employee, had been persuaded by a group of right-wing Clinton haters to tell the media that she had been the victim of sexual harassment by former governor Clinton. The *Washington Post*, for which Isikoff then worked, had been tipped off about the event and had sent two newsmen to cover it. The other reporter, from the Style section, lampooned the press conference, referring to Jones as another "bimbo" in Clinton's long list of what the media labeled "bimbo eruptions."

But, as Isikoff later wrote in his book, *Uncovering Clinton: A Reporter's Story*, "I had a somewhat different perspective." Then assigned to cover the Justice Department, Isikoff—known for his old-fashioned shoe-leather reporting—said he was supposed to be writing about important national issues. But, he quickly added, he "had carved out a far more entertaining subject: investigating allegations of improprieties involving Bill and Hillary Clinton. I had no particular axe to grind. As a college student, in the early 1970s, I had been inspired by Bob Woodward and Carl Bernstein as they uncovered the crimes of Richard Nixon."[14]

Interestingly, Isikoff had been hired by Woodward in 1981 and had looked up to the master investigative reporter as someone he would like to emulate. He succeeded. Isikoff's *Newsweek* exclusive—technically, *he* had broken the story—led Woodward to comment: "He's like the junkyard dog." Woodward added that Isikoff did some "tenacious" and "gritty" reporting.[15] It is, at once, ironic and fitting that in 1999, following Clinton's Monicagate scandal, the *New York Times*'s Frank Rich wrote the following about these two great investigative journalists: "Isikoff is who Woodward used to be. He produced many of the biggest Monicagate revelations, and he challenges authority."[16]

Isikoff, indeed, single-handedly undertook one of the most complex, on-again off-again journalistic adventures. Only a very talented investigative reporter with Isikoff's persistence, doggedness—one could call it obsession—to keep digging no matter where the clues took him, would have been able to stir up enough attention to Clinton's sexual peccadilloes, past and present, that a special prosecutor would be appointed by the attorney general of the United States to follow the same trail—but with subpoena power and a staff of highly competent lawyers. In the course of this exhausting hunt for pieces of the puzzle, Isikoff himself became part of the story, unwittingly, since his digging actually led to establishing his own complex relationships with some of the main characters in the drama that was being played out on a national stage. Some of those involved even did and said things that directly affected the outcome of the drama. But the key to the entire scandal, it can be seen in hindsight, was Isikoff's refusal to let go of it.

Isikoff was not deterred by the fact that nobody, not even the *New York Times*, paid much attention to the charges Jones made against Clinton during her February 1994 press conference. He arranged to interview her and, in fact, got the full, unedited version of what allegedly took place during Jones's encounter with Clinton. "The truth was," he wrote,

> I wasn't entirely sure at that point what I made of Jones' account. My instincts told me she was describing *something* that was real. Liars generally get fuzzy and dodgy when you press for details. Jones didn't; her account was studded with particulars that would have taken considerable rehearsal had it been concocted.[17]

Even so, Isikoff admitted he started off with a bias against Clinton. "He had a history—and that unquestionably influenced how I approached the story."[18]

In other words, Isikoff operated under the age-old premise that where there's smoke, there's fire. This kind of digging is his signature modus operandi. When I asked him what the characteristics of an exceptional investigative reporter are, Isikoff replied: "There's no magic here. A lot of it is determination to pursue a story—combined with creativity in going about it. The best stories I've gotten are inevitably because I stayed late to make that extra call, to think of documents to look up or sources to contact that weren't the obvious ones, and to not take no for an answer—to keep going back to people, usually with little nuggets of extra information that might get them to open up. All that—and luck, which usually comes eventually."[19] He provided a detailed overview of his strenuous pursuit of this story, in which he became enmeshed with numerous contacts, including some other women who claimed they had been harassed by Bill Clinton.

Isikoff summarized his story in an interview with TV host Charlie Rose on April 8, 1999, after his book *Uncovering Clinton* was published.[20] Rose started off this way: "When Michael Isikoff first decided to check out the story of an unknown Arkansas state employee by the name of Paula Jones, he had no idea this story would lead him to the next impeachment of the President of the United States. Along the way, his friends would say, he pursued this story like a heat-seeking missile. His persistence resulted in the revelation of the biggest political scandal since Watergate."

In response to questions from Rose, Isikoff said: "I don't think anybody will look back fondly on the Lewinsky matter. But, you know, it's part of our history now and people will be talking about it in the historical context for years to come. It will leave a lot of bitterness on all sides. On the one hand, that the President, ought to have been removed from office, that his conduct was terrible and that his contrition was phony and contrived. That's one segment. And then there is a substantial segment of people who think it is a real attack on the Constitution, that the real outrage is that it ever got that far. There's an element that believes these sort of political cataclysms take place every generation or two, and for this generation this will be somewhat analogous to the Vietnam War."

Asked by his TV host how he got involved, Isikoff talked about how it unfolded for him: "It took amazing twists and turns; it led from one thing to 125 other things that ended up resulting in the impeachment process." He then referred to the press conference in 1994 where he heard Paula Jones, whom he described as "a rather obscure Arkansas state employee," make charges of sexual harassment against Bill Clinton. "I just said, well, I'd like to know a little bit more about this."

The Clinton campaign denied any charges, but Isikoff was not satisfied with that—certainly not with the rumors about Clinton that were swirling around for quite some time about his womanizing in Arkansas. "I felt there was more to this than was commonly understood, that there was perhaps a pattern of behavior here that was potentially troubling," Isikoff told me.[21] He said that's what made him think he would like to know more about the Jones allegations. Although his paper decided not to run the story of her press conference—which had been sponsored by admitted political enemies of Clinton—the executive editor, Len Downie, who had succeeded Ben Bradlee—gave him a green light to continue to investigate the story. In fact, Isikoff recalled, Downie told him: "I want you to fly out to Arkansas, I want you to talk to people, and I want you to look into it, see what you find out."

Isikoff told me that he was already armed with the knowledge of a previous lengthy affair Clinton had had with Gennifer Flowers, a Little Rock nightclub singer, when Clinton was governor. Clinton had successfully denied this rumor.

"When you went back to Little Rock, what else did you find?" I asked.

"It was complicated," replied Isikoff. "There were legitimate journalistic issues to debate. I thought it was worth reporting in the context of all other rumors about women and Clinton. It told you something about what I was coming to believe was a pattern of potentially reckless conduct that, if true, would affect the course of his presidency. I think in retrospect I was right about that. I think that enough of the allegations came to be troubling to enough people that it was inevitable this was going to get him into political trouble."

Isikoff said there was "no consensus" about where his trip would lead except that his paper wanted to know more. "And that's what I proceeded to do." Other reporters, he noted, had recollections of being near Jones that day, watching as a state trooper came over and told Jones that "the governor wants to see you upstairs, watching Jones being escorted, watching her come back and being highly upset and highly agitated."

Isikoff said he phoned Clinton confidant George Stephanopoulos, who told him it was all made up and that Clinton was not even there that afternoon, "He steered me to a former aide who attended the conference with Clinton, and the aide said he was not there," Isikoff reported. "The implication being it was completely concocted. I checked that out, but I finally found the afternoon speaker and asked him if he remembered Bill Clinton speaking. He said he was there and he was wandering around in the hallways after Clinton's speech. That's what upset me, it was clear that they were trying to mislead me. Stephanopoulos confessed years later that Clinton *was* there. The standard spin in all this is, if you do this kind of stuff it will be sleazy. . . . I think George had been told a cover story by Clinton."

"It got me upset when I found out that I was being spun and I didn't like that," Isikoff told me. "That's the kind of thing that gets my reportorial juices flowing. Perhaps the most significant thing about the Paula Jones incident was the timing. This was the day Clinton had flown back from Cleveland, Ohio, after addressing the Democratic Leadership Conference and had given a speech which effectively launched his Presidential campaign for 1992. He knew after he got a rousing reception that he had a damn good chance of being the Democratic nominee for President. Stephanopoulos told me, Who would be so foolish and so reckless to do something like that the day after he got back from Cleveland? It doesn't make any sense. Therefore it cannot be true."

"Regardless of whether you believe what Paula Jones said actually took place," he continued, "it is pretty much beyond dispute that Clinton asked a state trooper to speak to Jones. All the testimony was consistent. Clinton said go fetch her and bring her upstairs to his hotel room for purposes that we may assume were probably not innocent. Her version of events was ultimately more credible than his. Will we ever know precisely what happened in that hotel room? Well, of course not."

Isikoff revealed in our interview that in the Lewinsky case, the story he had was solid because he learned that Kenneth Starr, the special prosecutor, had launched a secret investigation of the president about allegations of perjury and obstruction of justice relating to the Lewinsky matter. "That seemed to be a no-brainer because it was in its core about sex and allegations of a sexual relationship."

Anxious to see his story go to press, Isikoff disclosed during our conversation that he told Starr: "I've got a deadline coming up and I am going to go with the story. I told him nobody else knew about his criminal investigation. So they were pretty much forced to confront Lewinsky. People thought I was working hand in glove with Starr. In fact, Starr's people were quite upset about my pursuit of this story because I upset their timetable. They might have been able to gather a lot more evidence had it not been the mere fact that Starr's investigation was explosive news that said as much about Ken Starr as about Bill Clinton. I said I had an obligation to report it."

Isikoff went on to say that he learned that Linda Tripp, a friend of Lewinsky's who also worked for the government, had taped Lewinsky's "confession" to her that she was having a sexual encounter with the president. He learned from Tripp that she had pressured Lewinsky to lie to avoid possible charges against her of perjury and obstruction of justice. "Tripp was primarily concerned that she has made all these tapes which she learned were illegal. And she was going to be exposed for her own illegal conduct for secretly taping Lewinsky. She wants to protect herself."

When I asked Isikoff about First Lady Hillary Clinton's charge that there was a "vast right-wing conspiracy" out to get her husband, Isikoff replied: "There was an element of truth to the charge. But at the end of the day, Bill Clinton did what he did and knew the risks that he was running."

Isikoff went on to say that Tripp "was unquestionably the source that led me to Monica Lewinsky. She is the one who told me about her. I came to learn a lot more that was not known to others at the time. I was caught up in it myself—as a player in the drama—which had a lot of twists and turns. It was not a comfortable place for a reporter to be. I had hoped *Newsweek* would publish it sooner rather than later, but I understand the reluctance. I knew that if you are a good reporter, you don't write a story before you do all of the reporting. The best stories, the most fascinating stories, unfold through the process of reporting, and that is clearly what happened here. This is not a hugely ennobling experience. There are a lot of problematic issues of dealing with sources and being misled by sources, pursuing one story and then discovering the sources are manipulating you, that you are being lied to."

I asked Isikoff what kind of reaction he got after his stories finally began to run in *Newsweek*. "I heard from a lot of people on both sides because there is ammunition on both sides," he replied. "I'm getting ammunition from everybody. I am getting as much of a positive feedback from people who think there was a vicious right-wing conspiracy against Clinton as I am getting from people who think that Clinton was a disgraceful individual and should have been removed from office."

The overall political drama first known as "Whitewater" had been launched in January 1994 by Attorney General Janet Reno when she picked U.S. Attorney Robert B. Fiske Jr. as a special counsel to investigate the involvement of President and Mrs. Clinton in an earlier speculative land deal with the failed Madison Guarantee Bank in Arkansas. After 29 Clinton administration officials were subpoenaed to testify at congressional hearings, all were cleared of any wrongdoing.

Nonetheless, bowing to pressure by a Republican Congress, Reno appointed Kenneth W. Starr, a former federal appeals judge and U.S. solicitor general, to succeed Fiske. He continued the probe, which was also being addressed by the House Banking Committee for nearly a year, culminating in a finding in August 1995 of no illegalities on the part of the Clintons, although others were implicated, indicted, and jailed in a series of legal decisions. Overall, the Whitewater investigation cost the taxpayers $25 million.

Despite months of repeated denials, President Clinton was called to testify before a grand jury (the first sitting president to do so), and he finally admitted in taped testimony on August 17, 1998, that he had had an "improper physical relationship" with Lewinsky. On September 9, 1998, Starr delivered his report to Congress. The House Judiciary Committee voted to begin impeachment hearings, and in December, Republicans on the Judiciary Committee made public four articles of impeachment against the president, alleging that he had lied, obstructed justice, and abused his power. Independent Counsel Starr, who had been investigating Whitewater without success, made the case for impeachment before the U.S. House of Representatives, which formally impeached the president on December 19, 1998.

Polls at the time showed that the American public supported Clinton, with 60 percent opposing impeachment. He was subsequently acquitted by the U.S. Senate on February 12, 1999, with the necessary two-thirds majority not having been achieved for conviction. The president was thus acquitted on two charges—perjury and obstruction of justice—stemming from the Lewinsky scandal. In the end, Clinton admitted to "giving false testimony" in the Jones case and said he would accept a five-year suspension of his law license and a $25,000 fine in return for an agreement by the independent counsel, Robert W. Ray (Starr's successor), to end the investigation and not prosecute him. He served out the remainder of his term through January 20, 2001.

Putting the entire journalistic milestone in perspective, the *American Journalism Review* summed up Isikoff's crucial role in the whole affair:

> Michael Isikoff was the first journalist to learn of the liaison between President Clinton and former White House intern Monica Lewinsky—long before Matt Drudge revealed online in January that *Newsweek* had held up Isikoff's initial story on the saga. . . .
>
> In fact, not only did he know about the romance, it's clear from grand jury testimony [released in the fall of 1998] that Isikoff's tireless reporting was often a significant factor in decisions made by the major players: Clinton, Lewinsky, Betty Currie, Linda Tripp, Kathleen Willey, Vernon Jordan, Lucianne Goldberg, the Paula Jones legal team and Kenneth Starr.[22]

ABOUT MICHAEL ISIKOFF

Michael Isikoff is one of the premier investigative reporters in the United States. He is best known for his stories in *Newsweek* that led to the impeachment of President Bill Clinton. He became a member of the staff of that magazine in June 1994. For Isikoff's reporting on the Monica Lewinsky scandal, along with other stories written by his colleagues on the magazine, *Newsweek* was awarded the National Magazine Award in the Reporting category in 1999 for "its extraordinary year-long coverage of the entire scandal." *Newsweek* was called "a model of reporting excellence" for its continuing, in-depth coverage of the scandal. In 2001, *Washington* magazine included Isikoff's name on a list of the most influential journalists in Washington, D.C.

Isikoff is the author of the book *Uncovering Clinton: A Reporter's Story*, which spells out how he went about his own reporting of the Lewinsky scandal. The book was praised by the *Washington Post–Los Angeles Times* news service as "the absolutely essential narrative of the scandal with revelations that no one would have thought possible." The book was a *New York Times* best-seller and received the accolade of being named the Best Non-Fiction Book of 1999 by the Book of the Month Club.

Isikoff came to *Newsweek* in 1981 from the *Washington Post*, where he had specialized in covering the Justice Department and the Persian Gulf War. Isikoff graduated from Washington University with a B.A. in 1974 and received a master's degree in journalism from Northwestern University's Medill School of Journalism in 1976.

NOTES

1. Two U.S. presidents have been impeached: The 17th president, Andrew Johnson, was impeached by the House of Representatives in 1868 for violation of the Tenure in Office Act of 1867, a dispute with Congress about the president's legal powers over the defeated South. Johnson was acquitted by one vote in the impeachment trial before the Senate. The 42nd president, William J. Clinton, was impeached in 1998 by the House for perjury and obstruction of justice. As with Johnson, the Senate could not come up with the required two-thirds majority to convict Clinton. President Richard Nixon was not impeached. While the House issued articles of impeachment for obstruction of justice, illegal wiretapping, and bribery, Nixon resigned the presidency in 1974 before the House voted on impeachment. Most historians believe that had he not resigned he would have been impeached.

2. Tom Rosenstiel and Amy Mitchell, eds., *Thinking Clearly* (New York: Columbia University Press, 2003).

3. Transcript of *This Week with Sam Donaldson and Cokie Roberts*, ABC-TV, January 18, 1998.

4. Author's interview with Michael Isikoff, July 8, 2009.

5. Brett Sokol, *Miami News*, June 28, 2001.

6. Ethan Porter, "Drudge Has Lost His Touch: Technology, the Competition, and the Times Passed Him," *Columbia Journalism Review*, September/October 2009, 14–16.

7. Author's interview with Isikoff.

8. Howard Kurtz, *Washington Post*, January 24, 1998.

9. The reporters included Jonathan Alter, Martha Brant, Karen Breslau, Lynette Clemetson, Matthew Cooper, Evan Halper, Joshua Hammer, Thomas Hayden, Mark Hosenball, Barbara Kantrowitz, Daniel Klaidman, John Leland, Dianne Hemphill McDonald, Daniel McGinn, Avani Metita, Debra Rosenberg, Allan Sloan, Deborah Tannen, Pat Wigert, and Kenneth L. Woodward. Isikoff wrote many stories under a double byline with Thomas; in addition, Isikoff, Hosenball, Klaidman, Fineman, and Alter offered readers political analysis. The *Newsweek* Washington bureau chief, Managing Editor Ann McDaniel, oversaw the reporting effort. Each week, the team spent many hours in discussions in McDaniel's office, reviewing its work for accuracy and fairness. In New York, *Newsweek* editor Mark Whitaker and Managing Editor Jon Meacham shaped the overall coverage.

10. Topics included were the roles of Clinton's trusted secretary, Betty Currie, and his longtime friend, attorney Vernon Jordan; the part played by Tripp, who emerged as one of the central characters in the Lewinsky investigation; the testimony of various witnesses in the Starr depositions; Clinton friend Kathleen Willey's 1998 allegations on CBS-TV's *60 Minutes* about Clinton making unwanted sexual advances to her in the White House in 1993; the role of the Secret Service; how the deals made with Lewinsky and Clinton to secure their testimony on their relationship changed the nature of Starr's investigation; and speculation that, if impeached, Clinton could face the "trial of the century."

11. "Tabloid Journalism," *American Decades* (2001), http://www.encyclopedia .com/doc/1G2-3468303499.html.

12. *American Journalism Review*, March 1998, 20.

13. Ibid., 21.

14. Michael Isikoff, *Uncovering Clinton: A Reporter's Story* (New York: Three Rivers Press, 1999), 8.

15. Elisabeth Bumiller, *New York Times*, January 23, 1998.

16. Frank Rich, *New York Times*, August 15, 1999.

17. Isikoff, *Uncovering Clinton*, 24; emphasis in original.

18. Ibid., 25.

19. Author's interview with Isikoff.

20. *Charlie Rose*, syndicated, April 8, 1999.

21. Author's interview with Isikoff.

22. Alicia C. Shepard, "The Isikoff Factor," *American Journalism Review*, December 1998, 22.

CHAPTER 5

THE COLLAPSE
OF ENRON

Reported by Bethany McLean, Fortune, 2001

They didn't see it coming. They were deluded partly because they were making so much money. Greed plays an important role in self-delusion. But people don't see. It's not like they are making a conscious choice.

—Bethany McLean

Bethany Mclean, a talented young writer, is credited with producing the first story that touched off the eventual fall of the multibillion-dollar Enron Corporation—one of America's premier financial giants—in an article in *Fortune* in 2001. The scandal would also prove be a major embarrassment for President George W. Bush, whose friendship with the top brass of Enron, especially its founder, Kenneth Lay—whom the president affectionately called "Kenny Boy"—was well known. The collapse of the supergiant company was perceived by Bush's political detractors and the media to have had a negative impact on the White House in terms of Bush mingling with businessmen of questionable character.

Born in the heart of America on December 12, 1970, in the town of Hibbing, Minnesota (pop. 17,000), McLean was a vivacious, fresh-faced 31-year-old journeyman who had majored in English and math at Williams College. She came to New York to make her mark, first joining the brokerage firm of Goldman Sachs, and then *Fortune* magazine, even though she had no background in journalism.

Her role in uncovering the scandal started out routinely enough. "At that stage I was hired as a fact-checker," she said in an interview.[1] "We were called reporters. So they didn't really care if we had actual writing experience. They thought it was valuable that I understood how to read a balance sheet and could calculate annual growth rate. I got the job purely on my ability to check facts."

Like many other eager, bright newcomers to the Big Leagues of journalism, McLean worked hard and got ahead, but by her own admission, it was more serendipity than anything else—as is sometimes the case—that enabled her to break loose from the pack and shoot right to the top of her field in just a few years. In the course of her work, she came across some documents about Enron that aroused her suspicion: she could not find proof of exactly how Enron was able to maintain a profitable bottom line. So she drafted an article for the magazine that raised questions about the immense profitability of Enron, then a darling of the stock market. "In fact," she told me, "when I wrote my first story, headlined 'Is Enron Overpriced?' [*Fortune*, March 5, 2001], I wrote that it's in a bunch of complex businesses. Its financial statements were nearly impenetrable."

The story did not make a big splash immediately after it was published. "At the time," she said, "it was not like there was a rush of follow-on news coverage from people saying, 'Maybe Enron really is in trouble.' My story didn't change anything immediately." She continued: "But I guess people did care, because Enron stock started to decline after that. I believe my story expressed people's feelings about Enron. I was just lucky as a journalist to write that story at a time where the perception of Enron was changing. It was only after Enron declared bankruptcy later on that people looked back and pointed to my story as a warning sign that there were problems there."

Indeed, when McLean broke her story raising some questions about Enron's runaway profits, she was far ahead of the business and journalistic curve. At the time, Enron was an international behemoth—seventh on the *Fortune* 500 list of companies—having risen spectacularly from $31 billion in 1998 to $100 billion only two years later. For six years running, it was voted "America's Most Innovative Company" among *Fortune's* "Most Admired Companies." Led by Chief Operating Officer Jeffrey Skilling, who had joined the company in 1990 from a consulting firm, McKinsey, it had a worldwide reputation for excellence. Luminaries such as James Baker and Henry Kissinger were on its lobbying payroll, and Nobel Laureate Nelson Mandela flew to its superbly designed $200 million 40-story skyscraper in Houston headquarters to receive the Enron Prize for Distinguished Public Service, an award also bestowed on Colin

Powell and Mikhail Gorbachev. Enron was recognized as a beacon of excellence and a sound company that had "transformed the way gas and electricity flowed across the United States."[2]

McLean opened her March 5, 2001, piece in *Fortune* with this imaginative lead-in:

> In Hollywood parlance, the "It Girl" is someone who com-
> mands the spotlight at any given moment—you know, like
> Jennifer Lopez or Kate Hudson. Wall Street is a far less glitzy
> place, but there's still such a thing as an "It Stock." Right now,
> that title belongs to Enron, the Houston energy giant. While
> tech stocks were bombing at the box office last year, fans
> couldn't get enough of Enron, whose shares returned 89%. By
> almost every measure, the company turned in a virtuoso per-
> formance: Earnings increased 25%, and revenues more than
> doubled, to over $100 billion. Not surprisingly, the critics are
> gushing. "Enron has built unique and, in our view, extraordi-
> nary franchises in several business units in very large markets,"
> says Goldman Sachs analyst David Fleischer.[3]

McLean went on to write that, despite all the attention Enron was receiving, the company remained "largely impenetrable to outsiders, as even some of its admirers are quick to admit." It seemed that McLean could not uncover how Enron was making its money, and all of the Enron executives she talked to told her she did not know what she was talking about. She became skeptical and, after a while, realized that her story would not supply answers. Instead, it would simply raise uncomfortable questions about one of the mightiest companies on earth. Her management agreed.

Did McLean sense that Enron may have had a possible soft underbelly in the first place? As she told me in our interview: "I had been in touch with Doug Millett, who worked for James Chanos [founder of Kynikos Associates, a New York City investment com-pany]." She reported that Millett suggested she look at Enron's finan-cial figures. Since she had a background in the world of finance, she first went to the Securities and Exchange Commission, but her inquiry raised more questions than it answered.

Where did she go from there? I asked her. Considering that her investigative reporting involved one of the foremost corporations in the world and she had no evidence—thus far—why did she think Enron was doing anything wrong? "When you start out reading a company's financial statements, particularly one that is complicated, it sort of looks like gibberish at first," she explained. "Then you read through it again, and you read through it again, and you read everything that's been written about the company, and you see how they think about their business and how they divide up the various segments and the terminology that they use. It's one of those things— I'm probably slow—but it did take me a long time, multiple times of reading it, before it begins to make sense."

With a hunch that something was amiss, I inquired, did she then call Enron for comment? "No, I didn't," she replied quietly. "You can debate the best way of doing things. I believe that it's better to work from the outside in, because if you go to a company before you understand things, you wind up being seduced by their point of view more easily. Whereas, if you have your own point of view and you understand what they are talking about, you can ask much better questions. You could definitely turn that around from a company's perspective: [They could say] you, as a journalist, are doing your work without involving the company, but they should have the opportunity to be involved from the beginning. I can hear either side of that argument, but I generally do believe it's better to do your homework first."

Still uncertain about where to get additional information, McLean said she discarded the idea of talking with Wall Street analysts "because all the analysts were very bullish on the company. You have to have a good deal of skepticism about 'buy' ratings from Wall Street analysts." So she started nibbling around the edges of Enron by talking to Enron's competitors, including money managers whom she knew well. She added: "Very few people were willing to criticize a corporation on the record, but people who know you, they might be willing to say, 'Yeah, I'm really scared of Enron, I have to own it because I run an energy index fund and that's one of the biggest energy companies, but I don't understand how they make money, either.' Or, I raised my concerns about Enron's accounting and people would say, 'You can't quote me on this, but I've been thinking about that, too.' It's that sort of thing. As a journalist, if you are ever looking to do a critical piece about a company, you are not going to find somebody on the record to say, 'Yeah, this is a problem. What a great story!' It doesn't work that way.

Nonetheless, I quickly realized there was a story here. Nobody understood how the company made money. Nobody could explain. When I talked to people who were bullish and owned a ton of Enron stock, they'd say things like, 'Well, we know Enron is going to grow its earnings in double digits and that makes the stock a buy.' And you say, 'Well how do you know they are going to grow their earnings at double digits?' And they say, 'It's because they tell us that's what they've done in the past and that's what they tell us they're going to continue to do in the future.' They say things like, 'Their management team is so incredibly good, so of course it's a great stock.' It was that sort of thing.

I could not get any answers to the deeper questions I was asking Wall Street analysts about why is the cash flow so negative. They'd say it is *not* negative, and I'd say, yes, it is. I'd ask about these weird off-balance-sheet partnerships that were disclosed in Enron's financial statements and they would not know what I was talking about. I didn't get answers to my questions, and the issues were clear in terms of their low return on capital and their negative cash flow and the rapid rise in their debt.

But, that was the time that the Internet bubble was just beginning to crack, and so the idea that a company's unsustainable financials was a problem did not occur to anyone. You could point that out until you were blue in the face and it didn't matter. Kind of like the current mess we're in now [the Wall Street crisis of 2008–2009]. For years, this practice of lending money to people with no income and no assets was not a problem. It was not like I wrote the Enron story and thought, 'Wow, I just revealed this and the whole thing is going to come down!' I never had the feeling that, 'Man, I am on to a big story!'

I think part of that was my fault. I was too naïve at the time. This was early 2001, before the wave of dot-com bankruptcies and World-Com. That was really the first time in a long time we had a major company [that got into trouble]. So the idea that a major company could go under or that there would be the sort of fraud that there turned out to be—I was too naïve to ever have thought that."

After spending many months gathering background information—mostly unanswered questions—McLean overcame her reservations and decided to call Enron. She told me she started at the top—a journalistic technique that sometimes works, she said, if you know you have some information or questions that will get a CEO's attention. "I talked to Jeff Skilling. He was very upset and said that people had raised these kinds of questions before who wanted to throw rocks at the company. He said I had not done enough homework, that I did not know what I was talking about, and [for me] to raise these kinds of questions without understanding what I was talking about, I was 'unethical,' and he hung up."

Enron founder Kenneth Lay promptly called *Fortune*'s editors complaining that McLean had her facts wrong and demanded a meeting at *Fortune*, according to McLean. Lay was a hard-driving, name-dropping Houston businessman who had been a fund-raiser for George W. Bush earlier in his political career. Bush considered him one of his political cronies.

Despite the Enron executives' rude behavior, McLean was willing to concede that they were right "in the broader sense." She explained: "As a journalist, no matter how much homework you have done, it's always possible that you're wrong. I didn't involve Enron in my story until the end—until I had already done a great deal of homework and come to, if not conclusions, then questions. So, as I said earlier, you can spin that both ways. I believe that from a journalist's perspective that's a better way to operate [to do your research thoroughly first], because you are forced to arrive at independent conclusions. But I can certainly see from a company's perspective that it feels unfair to have somebody call you up and ask you these types of questions when the story is just about going to print. Still, I viewed Skilling's comments at the time as an intimidation technique—I was terrified. Nevertheless, in many ways, I actually understood his point, which I know sounds a little bit strange."

The Enron executives, she reported, demanded a meeting with her and her editors before any story was published. *Fortune* agreed to one with Andrew Fastow, the chief financial officer of Enron; Mark Koenig, head of investor relations; and Mark Palmer, head of public relations. "I was concerned because Skilling had flown three men to *Fortune*. Skilling had told me on the telephone that I was so far off base and that I needed to understand how Enron works." McLean said she vividly recalled that she was apprehensive. "It was totally nerve-racking," she said. "I still remember crystal clear the Enron executives coming up the elevator and greeting them at the door. I would have done anything at that point to go back into my office and forget the whole thing, I have never enjoyed the moment of confrontation, and sometimes I wonder about why I tend to write very tough stories, because I don't enjoy that. I'm from Minnesota. We're supposed to be nice."

"We sat there in this windowless conference room for about three hours," she continued. "They talked through their view of the world. I asked questions, and at the end of it my editors, Joe Nocera and

Jim Impoco, told me, 'They didn't answer a single question you asked them.'" McLean said she was relieved and happy that it was over with.

When I asked her if she felt her editors were with her from the outset, she replied: "You know, I don't think they were necessarily with me from the get-go. But they were very supportive of the story; I think that meeting was a key event. If the Enron people had been able to come up with good answers to the questions I was asking them, I don't think *Fortune* would have published the story. It's interesting, I recall, that on his way out Fastow turned to me and said: 'I don't care what you write about the company, just don't make me look bad.'"

The remainder of the shocking story of Enron is now consigned to history. Trouble in the form of reduced quarterly earnings first arrived at Enron's doorstep in August 2001 when Lay gave a cheer-leading speech to an all-employee meeting, insisting that the company was doing well, despite a few obstacles in the way. The majority of the more than 12,000 employees, who had saved 60 percent of their retirement savings in Enron stock, accepted Lay's words in good faith.

Within weeks, however, the company announced a third-quarter loss of $618 million and revealed that it had overstated its profits since 1997 by $580 million. It had also hidden $500 million worth of debts from its public accounts. Moody's, a credit-rating agency, then cut Enron's rating, which set off a series of mandatory repayments to creditors. This caused Enron's share price to decline precipitously. A "rescue merger" with a rival firm then fell through, leading to the company's inevitable bankruptcy filing on December 2, 2001, after a series of management failures that cost hundreds of thousands of employees their pensions and their livelihoods. Just as shocking perhaps was the fact that Arthur Anderson—one of the most widely respected accounting firms in the world for decades—was also toppled by the Enron scandal.

On May 25, 2006, Ken Lay and Jeff Skilling were found guilty of numerous counts of accounting fraud, conspiracy, and dozens of other charges. Enron is remembered by most business and journalistic observers as perhaps the biggest symbol of overwhelming greed in corporate history. Skilling was sentenced to 24 years in prison. A U.S. appeals court subsequently upheld 19 criminal convictions against the former Enron executive, but ruled that his prison sentence was too harsh. The 55-year-old Skilling, serving time in a

Colorado jail, secured a minor concession in 2009 on a technicality as the court found that his original trial judge had applied flawed guidelines in sentencing him. Skilling was scheduled to be resentenced. Lay, 64, while awaiting sentencing after being found guilty of conspiracy and fraud, had a heart attack and died while vacationing in Colorado in 2006. His conviction was vacated in federal court because he hadn't been sentenced.[4]

Despite her bitter personal experience with Skilling, it is instructive to note that McLean, while unearthing the scandal at the outset, had mixed feelings about the entire story—and especially about Skilling himself. Long after Skilling went to prison, McLean commented on his role in the scandal in response to a question I raised about whether or not she realized at the time that she had a right—indeed, an obligation—to ask Skilling tough questions. "Yes, I do—but I don't," she answered. "You know, when Jeff Skilling said he was innocent, I think he meant it. I think there's a level of cross-delusion that goes into any kind of white-collar crime, and something that may be short of white-collar crime, where senior management has put so much of themselves into building this business that they've done something wrong and can't even see it anymore." Asked if she felt compassion for him, she replied: "I always have."

The Enron scandal did more than make business news. It also made political news on the front pages of the nation's newspapers and on television because of the long-established personal friendship between Kenneth Lay and George W. Bush, beginning when the latter had served as governor of Texas and then as President. Howard Kurtz, who covers the media for the *Washington Post*, wrote in a story on January 18, 2002, in the immediate aftermath of Enron's demise, that Lay had made a foray into Vice President Dick Cheney's office in May 2002 for a half-hour meeting on energy. Kurtz pointed out that the *Wall Street Journal* noted "there were a few critical pieces [in the press] but they mostly focused on politics."

"Over the years," Kurtz added, "Enron had donated nearly $2 million to President Bush and that some top administration officials had worked for Enron." He also commented that other newspapers— including the *Los Angeles Times*—were critical of the link between Bush and Enron. The Los Angeles daily, Kurtz said, reported on the close ties between Lay and the president, noting that "Bush had flown on Enron jets during the campaign." Kurtz also reported that the *Washington Post* ran a story on Lay's growing influence in the administration.[5]

In 2004, the link between Bush and Lay was addressed in an editorial in the *New York Times*, which stated flatly: "When President Bush was elected, there was much speculation about whether his top corporate sponsor, Kenneth Lay of Enron, would end up as secretary of the Treasury or the Department of Energy."[6]

In a TV interview in 2005, McLean herself commented on the connection between Lay and Bush. She was asked: "What was the relationship between Ken Lay and both Bush presidents?" She replied: "They were buddies, although Ken Lay was closer with George Bush senior than he was with George Bush junior. But Enron was very close to the Bush administration." The interviewer asked her if Enron's association with the Bushes adversely affected George W. Bush's image in the country. McLean replied: "I think it did initially. There was a lot of furor about this, and a lot of, I think, sort of the notion that this could be 'Enrongate.' However, I think some of that has been diffused by the undeniable fact that the Bush administration didn't save Enron as it was going down."[7]

A year later, in 2006, the *Washington Post* reported:

> In the 1980s, when Bush was working in the Texas oil industry, his firm invested in a drilling partnership with Lay's company, a predecessor to Enron. In 1992, Lay was co-chairman of the Republican National Convention in Houston that re-nominated President George H. W. Bush. Later, Lay was a major fundraiser for George W. Bush's political career. He delivered more than $300,000 for his two gubernatorial campaigns, according to Texans for Public Justice. In 1997, Bush wrote to Lay: "Dear Ken, One of the sad things about old friends is that they seem to be getting older—just like you! 55 years old. Wow.... Laura and I value our friendship with you.... Your younger friend, George W. Bush."[8]

Kurtz included a note of praise for McLean in his 2002 article: "Now that Enron's stock has been booted off the New York Stock Exchange, *Fortune* staffers can't say enough about the way McLean defied both Enron executives and conventional wisdom." He reported that *Fortune*'s managing editor, Rik Kirkland—who had previously said Enron did not like McLean's story—had told him: "It was a gutsy thing to do. We trusted her. When you look back, it's obvious: Why weren't we all asking the questions?"[9]

That is high praise from a boss for anyone, but McLean had earned it, putting so much effort into translating all the gobbledygook in Wall

Street and SEC terminologies into a memorable story that will stand for many years to come as one of the finest examples of investigative journalism in America. She had plenty of follow-up competition—most importantly from the *Wall Street Journal* and a book that told the story of the company from an insider's viewpoint, coauthored by Sherron Watkins, an Enron vice president[10]—but it was McLean whose initial story kicked off the entire scandal.

McLean's original *Fortune* story had been approved by Joe Nocera, who has since left for the *New York Times*, where he writes business stories. Nocera called McLean and told her: "You should write a book," McLean recalled in our interview. "I was 31 at the time. I had been at *Fortune* five or six years, but I had not done very many long pieces. The idea of writing a book on my own—I'm smart enough to know when I am in over my head—I knew I was not at a stage in my career where I could pull it off. Joe suggested I get in touch with Peter Elkind, who was also at *Fortune* at that time. We worked out a unique deal in terms of my understanding of how this stuff usually works. *Fortune* took part of our advance and in exchange, we got to stay on staff, although we didn't write for the magazine during that period. We only worked on the book. It took about two years."

When there is a great best-selling book about a national scandal, a movie often follows. Such was the case for McLean who said that Carrie Welch, who used to run the media effort for *Fortune*, suggested the idea of a film to Alex Gibney, a documentary filmmaker. Recalls McLean: "He came to us and said he wanted to make a documentary out of the book. I didn't see how you could take this story and show it in movie format. But I was thrilled that somebody was interested in it. And I was stunned by how successful it was. I actually had a role in it [playing herself]. When Alex came to film me in my apartment in Manhattan, I had just come from yoga practice and had my hair pulled back into a ponytail and I had no makeup on. The movie was accepted in Sundance and it got a distribution deal, and the movie, *Enron: The Smartest Guys in the Room*, got nominated for an Academy Award. I said, 'My gosh!' I came away with such respect for Alex's ability to make movies. That was not an easy undertaking."[11] It is worth noting that her book was recommended by none other than financier Warren Buffet in a list he released in 2003.[12]

I asked for her reaction to being described in the media as the person who was responsible for the collapse of Enron. McLean responded candidly: "I hate that. I don't think that's true. I think

I wrote an early story about the potential problems at Enron that hopefully—and I did hear from a bunch of people, Mom and Pop investors—caused them to take their money out of the company and saved people from losing their retirement, at least the people who read it. But I got lucky. I don't think I caused the collapse of Enron. I think I expressed a growing discontent in the market about Enron. I don't think I broke the story. To me, breaking a story would have been uncovering exactly what was going on with [chief financial officer] Andy Fastow's machinations. I didn't do any of that. I said this is risky and nobody understands how it makes money. We have problems here. I didn't say the company was going to be bankrupt in nine months."

How has all the attention, I asked, affected her in her work? "I wouldn't say it has," replied McLean. "It isn't something that affects my daily life. It's not even something that I ever anticipated happening. I frankly got lucky. I feel I got too much credit for this and, like most things in life, when you get a little too much credit for things, it has a self-perpetuating effect and it's a little easier for you to get a great job doing something else. That's the way it works." McLean, in fact, left *Fortune* to become a contributing editor with *Vanity Fair* magazine, where she has continued to write investigative journalism stories, mostly related to business.

I asked her what she learned from the entire Enron experience journalistically. "I guess I see the world in a much less black-and-white fashion than I used to," she replied. "I used to believe that if people were doing something unethical, that they knew they were doing something wrong. And that they were making a conscious choice to do that. I no longer believe that. I think that self-delusion is incredibly prevalent and incredibly dangerous. If you look at what happened at Enron, and if you look at what's happened on Wall Street since, and you ask how could so many smart people have gotten this so wrong, it's not because they were sitting there rubbing their hands together saying we can take millions of dollars out and the firm's going to go bust; they didn't see it coming. They were deluded partly because they were making so much money. Greed plays an important role in self-delusion. But people don't see. It's not like they are making a conscious choice."

When Enron finally collapsed at the end of 2001, McLean wrote an "obituary" piece for *Fortune*, titled "Why Enron Went Bust," telling the full story in detail and including all the characters who played a role in it.

McLean, as one might expect, went on a speaking tour after her book came out and amplified much of what she had already said. However, in one instance she put it all in proper perspective: "Most people at Enron had no idea. They thought they were doing a great job and being very creative. Enron is not about those bad people and how could they do this. It is really more a tale of human frailty and making human errors."[13]

At the close of 2009, Frank Rich of the *New York Times*, looking back on the first decade of the 20th century, also put the Enron story in perspective:

> If we go back to late 2001, the most revealing news story may have been unfolding not in New York but in Houston—the site of the Enron scandal. . . . That energy company convinced financial investors that it was a business deity. It did so even though very few of its worshipers knew what its business was. Enron is the template for the decade of the successful ruses that followed.[14]

ABOUT BETHANY MCLEAN

Bethany McLean, a contributing editor at *Vanity Fair*, formerly worked as an editor at large and columnist for *Fortune*. She is widely known for her exposé of Enron in an article, "Is Enron Overpriced?" which she wrote for *Fortune* and was published on March 5, 2001. She subsequently wrote, together with *Fortune* writer Peter Elkind, the best-selling book *The Smartest Guys in the Room*, describing the arrogance and manipulation by the company's top executives to manipulate the stock price. A movie came from the book, and it was nominated for an Academy Award. McLean appears regularly on television panel shows discussing business issues, and she has been on a wide-ranging tour of the nation giving speeches about corporate corruption.

NOTES

1. Author's interview with Bethany McLean, September 19, 2008.
2. Bethany McLean and Peter Elkind, *The Smartest Guys in the Room: The Amazing Rise and Scandalous Fall of Enron* (New York: Penguin Group, 2002), 240.
3. Bethany McLean, "Is Enron Overpriced?" *Fortune*, March 5, 2001.

4. Shaheen Pasha, "Enron Founder Ken Lay Dies; 64-Year-Old Former Energy Executive Was Awaiting Sentencing for Fraud," CNN, July 5, 2006.

5. Howard Kurtz, "The Enron Story That Waited to Be Told," *Washington Post*, January 18, 2002.

6. *New York Times*, editorial, July 9, 2004.

7. Bethany McLean, interview by Brian Lamb, *Book Notes*, C-SPAN, June 19, 2005.

8. Zachary A. Goldfarb, "Bush Put Lay on Layaway as Scandal Erupted," *Washington Post*, May 28, 2006. The story added: "In the 2000 Presidential race, Lay remained a steadfast ally. Lay was a Bush 'Pioneer' who raised at least $100,000, according to the Center for Responsive Politics. Enron also made its jet available and contributed to inaugural festivities. Lay later wrote to the new president and the first lady that he was 'so proud of you and look forward to seeing both of you in the White House.' But Lay also found influence in the administration. . . . Responding to public outrage, the White House promoted corporate accountability and put space between itself and Enron. Bush said only that 'Ken Lay is a supporter,' and that he 'first got to know Ken' in 1994 when 'he was a supporter of Ann Richards,' the Democratic governor Bush ousted."

9. Kurtz, *Washington Post*, January 18, 2002.

10. Mimi Swartz and Sherron Watkins, *Power Failure: The Inside Story of the Collapse of Enron* (New York: Doubleday, 2003). Following the Enron debacle, Watkins appeared before the Congressional Oversight and Investigations Subcommittee of the House Energy and Commerce Committee on the financial collapse of the Enron Corporation. Labeled a "whistle-blower" by the media, she confined her critical memorandums to within Enron, trying to call to the attention of its senior management flaws in its operations. Her testimony on February 14, 2002, was recorded by the Federal News Service.

11. The film was nominated for an Academy Award in 2005 in the Best Documentary Feature category; in 2005, it also won top honors as Best Documentary from the Los Angeles Film Critics Association, Broadcast Film Critics Association, and Chicago Film Critics Association and the Independent Spirit Award.

12. "Warren Buffett's Recommended Reading List," October 3, 2009, http://www.marketfolly.com/2009/10/warren-buffetts-recommended-reading.html.

13. Bethany McLean, remarks at "The Enron Case: What It Means for Corporate Ethics and Governance," Schimmel Center for the Arts, Pace University, Downtown New York campus, November 14, 2006.

14. Frank Rich, *New York Times*, December 20, 2009.

CHAPTER 6

ABU GHRAIB REVEALED

Reported by Seymour Hersh,
New Yorker, 2004

> The mistreatment of prisoners and the lack of due process continue today, and it is sure to be a blot for America for decades to come.
>
> —Seymour Hersh, in an interview,
> January 27, 2008

The horrific torture of Iraqi prisoners by American soldiers at the prison in Abu Ghraib in Iraq became worldwide news as a result of a conversation between two people: an Iraqi general and an American investigative reporter, Seymour Hersh, in Syria in December 2003. Hersh, who often used Syria as a meeting place for his unnamed sources,[1] was first alerted to the Abu Ghraib story by an Iraqi officer. The general, according to Hersh, told him that prison was so bad that the Iraqi women who were working there were sending messages home to their brothers and fathers to come and kill them because they had been dishonored by American soldiers. In Shiite society, Hersh explained, "shame" rather than "guilt" is the worst experience a person can suffer. Under Saddam Hussein, of course, Abu Ghraib had an equally bad reputation, but at least that was in context with the terror tactics used by the Iraqi dictator.[2]

That conversation sparked Hersh's wide-ranging series of articles in the *New Yorker* magazine, which touched off what would eventually become known as one of the worst military and political scandals in American history. It took a man almost obsessed with the truth, driven by the desire for recognition, and motivated by his complex emotional disrespect for "the Establishment" and for bureaucratic lies of any kind to uncover what actually happened in

Abu Ghraib: acts of brutal abuse that echoed around the world. The shocking photos of American GIs torturing and sexually taunting prisoners turned America's image of a nation with compassion to that of a nation that brutalizes people without regard for human rights. The photos reportedly were taken for the purpose of shaming the Iraqi prisoners by blackmailing them—threatening to show them to their families if they did not agree to be used as informants when they are sent back into the Iraqi population.[3]

Hersh, who has operated on his own for decades, had the reputation of being aggressive, fast-talking, and protective of his sources, to most of whom he promised anonymity if they talked to him. That modus operandi worked for him in Vietnam in 1969, when he uncovered the My Lai massacre of hundreds of Vietnamese civilians ordered by U.S. Army Lt. William Calley Jr. Hersh was subsequently awarded a Pulitzer Prize for the My Lai story. Restless and always on the prowl for a story, Hersh constantly receives new tips and meticulously checks out each one as if it is worthy of another Pulitzer. Hersh's history of distinguished reporting is seen as a high mark in American journalism and he has received numerous honors over the years for his hard-digging research, his dogged perseverance, and his persistence in following up on leads. In short, he is a "reporter's reporter" and one of the most highly respected journalists in America. Conversely, some high White House officials see him as a "terrorist journalist" who puts fear into the hearts of those whom he chooses to pursue.

Paradoxically, Hersh himself eschews the description of the kind of reporting he does. "I hate the phrase 'investigative reporter,'" he told me in an interview, "because I think *all* reporters should be investigative, in the sense that we have an obligation to go beyond the immediate facts of a situation or a statement and to seek the truth, or whatever approximates the truth. You can't do that, however, unless you know as much as possible about the people you are interviewing. Therefore, my essential aphorisms are two: read before you write, and get the hell out of the way of your story. In other words, let the story itself be fascinating, or spectacular, or moving, but do not characterize it; *tell* it."

That, in a few words, sums up the essence of Sy Hersh's philosophy of reporting. He expects every other journalist to, as he puts it, "go beyond the immediate facts of a situation." That's what makes him such a standout. One *New York Times* reporter once labeled him as "a sort of global cop reporter working disaffected bureaucrats, intelligence operatives, and soldiers to uncover intelligence pratfalls, foreign intrigues and administration wrongdoing."[4]

Hersh also has his critics, who see him as a belligerent, self-involved showman sometimes given to exaggeration. For his detractors, he is hardly the ideal model of an investigative reporter. According to Chris Suellentrop's profile of him in *New York* magazine:

> Seymour Hersh has always had a rather loose relationship with literal truth. He seems to share with many of the people he writes about the belief that in certain circumstances, the end justifies the means. When Hersh was pursuing the My Lai story, he tracked down the lawyer of William Calley Jr., the man later convicted of participating in the 1968 massacre of Vietnamese civilians. Hersh intentionally inflated the number of deaths for which Calley was charged, in order to get the attorney to tell him the correct number, 109. A few years ago, Hersh told a crowd at Duke [University], "a word for what I did—an actual word, it has three letters—it's called 'lie.'"[5]

On the other hand, the article also reinforced an image of Hersh as someone who would not let up until he found the story he was determined to find. Suellentrop wrote:

> Throughout his career, Hersh had a reputation as something of a journalistic pit bull, who can unsettle even his admirers with his single-minded determination to establish certain facts above others. . . . In 2004, Hersh's succession of shocking stories about abuses at Abu Ghraib prison proved that Hersh was back on top of his world—or, more precisely, underneath it, unearthing the Bush administration's trove of secure, undisclosed secrets.[6]

Hersh's editor at the *New Yorker*, David Remnick, supported him 100 percent. In an interview with the *Washington Post*'s media critic Howard Kurtz, Remnick stated: "Sy Hersh is doing what he is built to do and is obsessed with doing. He's just boiling with energy." Remnick said he enjoyed editing Hersh because "anyone that passionate about what they're doing is gold to me. . . . Even if the phone is hung up abruptly or someone shouts at someone, it's forgotten five minutes later." He added:

> There is a trust-me aspect to Hersh's reporting, given his heavy reliance on unnamed sources. His stories quoted a "senior CIA official," "former high-level intelligence official," "military analyst," "government consultant" and "Pentagon consultant." I know every source that's not named. . . . The [fact] checkers talk with those sources. Would he and I want people to be on the record? Of course. It's a trade-off we sometimes have to make.[7]

Suellentrop backed this up in his *New York* article, writing:

> The *New Yorker*'s editor-in-chief, David Remnick, looks over Hersh's copy closely and keeps himself advised of the true identities of the writer's many unnamed sources. Even so, Remnick said, "Closing is not easy. My job is to ask tough questions, and he answers them. Sometimes I say, 'We don't have enough,' and he pushes forward in his reporting."[8]

The seeds of the Abu Ghraib story had been planted long before Hersh's *New Yorker* articles were published. The eventual rogue actions at Abu Ghraib came as a result of the Allied raids in Afghanistan following the September 11, 2001, terrorist attacks and the U.S. military's failure to gather "actionable intelligence." The normal channels of intelligence communication were so bureaucratic that the Department of Defense created its own secret operation, according to Hersh, which included holding and interrogating prisoners at Abu Ghraib.

The torture at Abu Ghraib, originally reported in the press as the acts of a few errant, low-level enlisted men and women, was revealed to have been conceived by much higher levels of the military. Hersh wrote in the *New Yorker* in the spring of 2004:

> The roots of the Abu Ghraib prison scandal lie not in the criminal inclinations of a few Army reservists but in a decision, approved last year by Secretary of Defense Donald Rumsfeld, to expand a highly secret operation, which had been focused on the hunt for Al Qaeda, to the interrogation of prisoners in Iraq.

That operation, according to Hersh, "encouraged physical coercion and sexual humiliation of Iraqi prisoners in an effort to generate more intelligence about the growing insurgency in Iraq."[9]

In a subsequent keynote speech to the Annual Membership Conference of the American Civil Liberties Union (ACLU) in San Francisco on July 8, 2004, Hersh told his audience:

> Some of the worst things that happened that you don't know about. OK? Videos. There are women there. Some of you may have read that they were passing letters out, communications out to their men. This is at [Abu Ghraib], which is about 30 miles from Baghdad . . . 30 kilometers, maybe, just 20 miles, I'm not sure whether it's . . . anyway. The women were passing messages out saying please come and kill me because of what's happened. And basically what happened is that those women who were arrested with young boys, children, in cases that have been [video] recorded, watched as the boys were sodomized, with the cameras rolling, and the worst above all of them is the soundtrack of the boys shrieking. Children were sodomized in front of women in the prison, and the Pentagon has a tape of it.[10]

Hersh also said the torture at Abu Ghraib was the result of a "decision made somewhere high up in the line." As rumors of the torture began to leak out, Hersh said during a May 3, 2004, online Web site interview: "The problems began in Afghanistan. . . . What you're seeing is the result of a decision made somewhere high up in the line that we're going to turn our prisons, essentially all of them, into Guantanamo."[11]

Meanwhile, speaking for the Bush administration the next day, Deputy Secretary of Defense Paul Wolfowitz, purposely minimized the controversial issue: "It's such a disservice to everyone else, that a few bad apples can create some large problems for everybody."[12] Those words—"a few bad apples"—would come back to haunt the administration in the days and months ahead. The Pentagon immediately labeled Hersh's stories "journalist malpractice" and flatly denied the *New Yorker* article's assertion that Defense Secretary Rumsfeld had approved a clandestine unit to crack down on terrorists held at Iraq's Abu Ghraib prison, where inmates were abused. Hersh's article quoted a former intelligence official as saying the unit's instructions were: "Grab whom you must. Do what you want."[13] In response, a Defense Department spokesman called the report untrue.

Rumsfeld, according to Hersh, "reacted in his usual direct fashion: he authorized the establishment of a highly secret program that was given blanket advance approval to kill or capture and, if possible, interrogate 'high value' targets in the Bush Administration's so-called 'war on terror.' "[14]

Some of the abuses at Abu Ghraib came to light in 2003. The Army assigned Major Gen. Antonio M. Taguba to investigate these disturbing stories. Taguba, an officer whose findings Hersh valued as a key resource, was asked to look into the entire incident and to decide how it unraveled and who should be held responsible. In fact, Taguba wrote a 53-page top secret report that was not intended to be read by anyone other than his military superiors. He completed it in February 2003. Hersh, always the sleuth, obtained a copy before it was officially released, and it turned out to be an eye-opener of the first magnitude. Wrote Hersh: "Its conclusions about the failures of the Army prison system were devastating. Specifically, Taguba found that between October and December 2003 'numerous instances of "sadistic, blatant, and wanton criminal abuses" were inflicted on several detainees . . . systematic and illegal abuses.' "[15]

The abuses, according to Taguba, were perpetrated by soldiers of the 372nd Military Police Company and by members of the U.S. intelligence community. The 372nd was attached to the 320th Military Police Battalion, which reported to Brig. Gen. Janis Karpinski, an Army reservist who had been called up for duty. The military made her the scapegoat by subsequently formally admonishing her, quietly suspending her, and forcing her to return to civilian life. Taguba's report was stunning in its reporting of ugly details and reprehensible acts.

As Hersh saw it:

> Taguba's report amounts to an unsparing study of collective wrongdoing and the failure of Army leadership at the highest levels. The picture he draws of Abu Ghraib is one in which Army regulations and the Geneva conventions were routinely violated, and in which much of the day-to-day management of the prisoners was abdicated to Army military-intelligence units and civilian contract employees. . . . Interrogating prisoners and getting intelligence, including by intimidation and torture, was the priority.[16]

The photographs were taken by the GIs themselves and were not included in the report because of their sensitive nature. They showed American soldiers taunting naked Iraqis who had been forced into humiliating positions, with hoods over their heads, piled atop one another, their genitals exposed, cringing in the face of dogs on leashes. Female Army private Lynndie England was made famous by one photo of her pointing at and leashing Iraqi prisoners. "Such dehumanization is unacceptable in any culture, but it is especially so in the Arab world," Hersh explained. "Homosexual acts are against Islamic law and it is humiliating for men to be naked in front of other men."

Hersh was interviewed by Wolf Blitzer on CNN in January 16, 2007, to once again confirm what he knew about Bush's awareness of the torture tactics used in the prison at Abu Ghraib. Blitzer asked him, "It doesn't pay to do a thorough investigation for this White House as Major Gen. Antonio Taguba found out, but what about President Bush?" Hersh responded: "The President was told about Abu Ghraib in January when e-mails informed the Pentagon of the seriousness of the abuses and of the existence of photographs or in March when Taguba filed his report. Bush made no known effort to forcefully address the treatment of prisoners before the scandal became public, or to re-evaluate the training of military police and interrogators, or the practices of the task forces that he had authorized. Instead, Bush acquiesced in the prosecution of a few lower-level soldiers. The President's failure to act decisively resonated through the military chain of command: aggressive prosecution of crimes against detainees was conducive to a successful career."[17]

One former intelligence officer told Hersh that "the people assigned to the program worked by the book. . . . They created code words, and recruited . . . highly trained commandos and operatives from America's elite forces—Navy SEALs, the Army's Delta Force, and the CIA's paramilitary experts who had no traceability and no budget officially on the books." Hersh wrote that Congress was never fully briefed.[18]

According to Hersh's reporting:

> The operation enabled the Bush Administration to respond immediately to time-sensitive intelligence: commandos crossed borders without visas and could interrogate terrorism suspects deemed too important for transfer to the military's facilities at Guantánamo, Cuba. They carried out instant interrogations—using force if necessary—at secret C.I.A. detention centers scattered around the world [rendition; see chapter 8]. The

intelligence would be relayed to the SAP command center in the Pentagon.[19]

The former intelligence official told Hersh that fewer than 200 operatives and officials, including Rumsfeld and Gen. Richard Myers, chairman of the Joint Chiefs of Staff, were aware of the program. By mid-2003, Hersh learned there was a pervasive feeling inside the military hierarchy that the war was not going well. "American and Coalition forces knew little about the insurgency," he wrote, citing an internal military report. "Human intelligence is poor or lacking . . . due to the dearth of competence and expertise. . . . The intelligence effort is not coordinated since either too many groups are involved in gathering intelligence or the final product does not get to the troops in the field in a timely manner."[20]

Thus arose the need for stronger tactics to obtain intelligence. "The success of the war was at risk; something had to be done to change the dynamic," Hersh explained. "The solution, endorsed by Rumsfeld and carried out by Stephen Cambone [the undersecretary of defense for intelligence] was to get tough with those Iraqis in the Army prison system who were suspected of being insurgents."[21]

Another major player, according to Hersh, was Maj. Gen. Geoffrey Miller, "the commander of the detention and interrogation center at Guantanamo." When the conditions in the prison began to leak out, Miller told reporters in early May that "mistakes had been made," but that they had been corrected and would not happen again. However, the Army's report on the abuse charges, authored by Taguba in February, had already revealed that Miller urged that the commanders in Baghdad change policy and place military intelligence in charge of the prison. In the report, Miller recommended that "detention operations must act as an enabler for interrogation."[22] Miller's plan, Hersh reported, "was to 'Gitmoize' the prison system in Iraq—to make it more focused on interrogation." [23]

Appearing on Fox television in May 2004 with TV commentator Bill O'Reilly, Hersh responded to a question from O'Reilly about General Karpinski's lax management of the prison. Said Hersh: "I grant you, and I challenged the general. I said, 'Look, in these pictures, these soldiers didn't look like they had any fear of anybody coming down on them. I mean, they looked like they were having a rollicking good time.' And that tells me there was a problem in management, whether it's middle management or upper management, I don't know."[24]

The notion that Arabs are particularly vulnerable to sexual humiliation became a talking point among pro-war Washington conservatives in the months before the March 2003 invasion of Iraq, according to Hersh. One book that was frequently cited was *The Arab Mind*, a study of Arab culture and psychology, first published in 1973, by Israeli author Raphael Patai, a cultural anthropologist who taught at, among other universities, Columbia and Princeton and who died in 1996. The book includes a 25-page chapter on Arabs and sex—depicting sex as a taboo vested with shame and repression. "The segregation of the sexes, the veiling of the women . . . and all the other minute rules that govern and restrict contact between men and women, have the effect of making sex a prime mental preoccupation in the Arab world," Patai wrote.[25]

As it happened, the first that Americans heard and saw of the atrocities in Abu Ghraib came not in print from Hersh but in broadcast format on CBS's *60 Minutes II*. While the *New Yorker* was preparing its story, CBS obtained the photos and, with Dan Rather at the helm, broadcast a story about them on April 28, 2004, after more than a year of verbal and written notices to U.S. officials by organizations such as the International Committee of the Red Cross. There was a glaring attempt by the highest military officer in the nation to block CBS from airing the report, but it failed.[26]

Two days later, on April 30, President George W. Bush stepped into the controversy for the first time, condemning the mistreatment of some Iraqi prisoners in U.S. custody. He said he felt a "deep disgust" at pictures taken by U.S. soldiers of naked Iraqi prisoners apparently being abused. "Their treatment," said the president, "does not reflect the nature of the American people. That's not the way we do things in America. I don't like it one bit."[27]

According to Hersh, the abuses at Abu Ghraib had initially been exposed on January 13, 2004, when Joseph Darby, a young military policeman assigned to Abu Ghraib, reported the wrongdoing to the Army's Criminal Investigations Division. He also turned over a CD full of photographs. Within three days, a report made its way to Secretary of Defense Donald Rumsfeld, who informed President Bush.

The entire sordid affair was vivid and disturbing, and the media played up the story all over the world. While the television media revealed some distasteful details, it was Hersh who did the first indepth stories about how the scandal had developed and who was involved all the way up the ladder. His first story in the *New Yorker*, published on May 10, 2004, was headlined "Torture at Abu Ghraib," with a subhead that read: "American Soldiers Brutalized Iraqis. How Far Up Does the Responsibility Go?" It began:

> In the era of Saddam Hussein, Abu Ghraib, twenty miles west of Baghdad, was one of the world's most notorious prisons, with torture, weekly executions, and vile living conditions. As many as fifty thousand men and women—no accurate count is possible—were jammed into Abu Ghraib at one time, in twelve-by-twelve cells that were little more than human holding pits.
>
> In the looting that followed the regime's collapse, last April, the huge prison complex, by then deserted, was stripped of everything that could be removed, including doors, windows, and bricks. . . . Abu Ghraib was now a U.S. military prison.[28]

Hersh used anyone and everyone he could persuade to talk to him—soldiers, civilians, Americans, Iraqis, translators from different countries, even some of the youngsters whom he came across. He left nothing to the imagination. Most of his contacts were made by telephone, some in person, and others, as he explained, he met in Syria under conditions of strict confidence. So thorough was he that he could actually reconstruct what had happened at Abu Ghraib—the only journalist to do so. It was like fitting the pieces of a massive jigsaw puzzle together. But by finding all of the pieces, he was able to put down on paper the "first draft of history," as reporters call their stories, of this unforgettable breach of American morality, ethos, and national psyche.

In an interview with a business magazine in August 2007, Hersh was asked why neither Congress nor the White House had been able to crack down on Abu Ghraib. The Q&A with reporter Deborah Campbell is enlightening:

> CAMPBELL: Your recent article on the stifling of General Taguba's inquiry into the Abu Ghraib prison scandal [in which Donald Rumsfeld was accused of misleading Congress] was pretty shocking. What was the most surprising revelation for you?
>
> HERSH: I've given up being surprised by these guys. I would guess the bald effrontery of the contempt for Congress. We already know about their contempt for the press. Just going to Congress and misrepresenting what they know. And we all know they do it.[29]

Also in August 2007, in a speech at the University of California, Berkeley, Hersh theorized why the American public appeared to be lethargic about the Abu Ghraib affair: "We've adjusted. We have become inured to this reality—that the men and women at the top of our government do not share with us the values of truth and honesty. We understand that they don't tell the truth, that they lie. It's a bad deal for the commonweal. We didn't demand from the officials at the top of our government what we demand in our own lives."[30]

Hersh, though technically scooped by CBS on his own story, pointed to the network's airing of the Abu Ghraib scandal as a turning point. After that, he said, General Miller arrived in Baghdad from Guantanamo and took command of the prison.[31]

Hersh reported that he showed the photos to one retired U.S. major general, Charles Hines, a former commandant of the Army's military police school during his 28-year career in the Army. Hersh wrote: "He acted with dismay," and then quoted the general's reaction: "Turning a dog loose in a room of people? Loosing dogs on prisoners of war? I've never heard of it, and it would never have been tolerated." Hersh said that Hines observed that there had been trained dogs used on prisoners but it was for the purpose of discovering narcotics. "I would never have authorized it for interrogating prisoners," he told Hersh. "If I had, I'd have been put in jail and kicked out of the Army."[32]

Obviously frustrated by the slow response the Abu Ghraib scandal was getting from the Pentagon, and even the White House, Hersh, in his own inimitable way, painstakingly constructed a timetable based on his findings about who knew about Abu Ghraib and when, and what action was taken. He concluded that "on January 16, 2003, three days after the Army received the pictures, Central Command issued a blandly worded, five-sentence release about an investigation into the mistreatment of prisoners."[33]

Hersh found out that Rumsfeld was told about the allegations at the prison about that time. Shortly after that, Hersh wrote, Rumsfeld told President Bush what he had heard about the prison. But nothing happened—at least publicly.

On January 19, Lt. Gen. Ricardo S. Sanchez, the highest-ranking military officer in Iraq, ordered the secret probe by General Taguba, who submitted his findings on February 26. It was not until early May 2003, however, with pressure building up and the Abu Ghraib story still making headlines, that Rumsfeld, at a news conference with Marine Gen. Peter Pace, vice chairman of the Joints Chiefs of

Staff, adamantly insisted that the investigation into Abu Ghraib had "moved routinely through the chain of command." Pace, according to Hersh, stressed that investigations, as they are completed, move up the chain of command in a very orderly manner.

Hersh, challenging the entire premise, interviewed a number of high-ranking active-duty and retired military officers, guaranteeing them anonymity. These officers told him that the system had not worked. "Knowledge of the nature of the abuses—and especially the politically toxic photographs—had been severely, and unusually, restricted," Hersh concluded. "This is beyond the pale in terms of lack of command attention," one retired major general told Hersh. "Where were the flag officers? And I'm not just talking about a one-star," referring to Brigadier General Karpinski, who had been relieved of duty. "This was a huge leadership failure."[34]

Hersh wrote that a Pentagon official had specifically told him that many of the senior generals, along with civilians in the Office of the Secretary of Defense, believed that "secrecy and wishful thinking" were the "defining characteristics" of the Pentagon under Rumsfeld. Hersh wrote that, based on his informants, one high-ranking official complained that Rumsfeld's staff "always seemed to be waiting for something to turn up—for the problem to take care of itself. . . . They were hoping that they wouldn't have to make a decision."[35]

It was quite clear that Rumsfeld was Hersh's main target. With Congress members and newspaper editorials calling for his resignation, "Rumsfeld testified before House and Senate committees and apologized for what he said was 'fundamentally un-American' wrongdoing at Abu Ghraib," Hersh reported. Rumsfeld claimed he had not actually seen some of the photographs until they appeared in the press. After viewing them, Rumsfeld was quoted as saying they were "hard to believe. There are other photos that depict . . . acts that can only be described as blatantly sadistic, cruel, and inhuman." Later, Hersh reported, Rumsfeld added: "I failed to recognize how important it was."[36]

As is his custom in almost all of his articles, Hersh made his own views known: "No amount of apologetic testimony or political spin," he wrote, "could mask the fact that, since the attacks of September 11, President Bush and his top aides have seen themselves engaged in a war against terrorism in which the old rules did not apply."[37] Hersh, who obviously had collaborators inside the Pentagon, obtained copies of some of Rumsfeld's memos. Hersh wrote: "One memo spoke derisively of the generals in the Pentagon, and said, 'Our prerequisite of perfection for "actionable intelligence" has paralyzed us. We must accept that we may have to take action before every question can be answered.'"[38]

Hersh's reporting, much of which centered around General Taguba and his frank and honest report, concluded with Hersh's observation that while other generals protected themselves, Taguba did not. Hersh quoted a retired Army major general who called Taguba "the guy who blew the whistle." In fact, four years later, in the June 25, 2007, issue of the *New Yorker*, Hersh—still a thorn in the administration's side—wrote yet another red-hot piece about how General Taguba, the courageous man who investigated the Abu Ghraib scandal and had the integrity to tell the truth, was subsequently sidelined by the Army.

As one online journalistic Web site observer, a doctor, expressed it: "It makes for solemn reading as to how blatantly those in the administration, including the President himself, have lied when telling the American public time and again that they do not support torture."[39]

Apparently worried about Hersh's upcoming book, *Chain of Command: The Road from 9/11 to Abu Ghraib*, the Department of Defense issued a preemptive press release on September 10, 2004, stating, in part:

> Based on media inquiries, it appears that Mr. Seymour, Hershs [sic] upcoming book apparently contains many of the numerous unsubstantiated allegations and inaccuracies which he has made in the past based upon unnamed sources. Detainee operations in Afghanistan, Iraq, and elsewhere have been examined extensively both within the Department of Defense and by an independent panel led by former Secretary of Defense Jim Schlesinger.[40]

Hersh's first stop on his book tour was CBS's *The Early Show*, an interview during which he stated: "I have tried, in this book, to describe some of the mechanisms used by the White House—the stovepiping of intelligence . . . the refusal to hear dissenting opinions, the difficulty of getting straight talk about military operations gone bad, and the inability—or unwillingness—of the President and his senior aides to distinguish between Muslims who supported terrorism and those who abhorred it."[41]

It was Hersh's articles in the *New Yorker*, however, that caught fire and commanded the attention of the media worldwide. As one example, a review in the *New York Times* began:

> With his reports in 1969 of a massacre by young American soldiers at My Lai, Seymour M. Hersh began his run as one of journalism's best-known investigative reporters. But in spite of his longevity, none of his subsequent reportorial efforts has had the impact of his first. Until now. In less than a month, Mr. Hersh, 67, has written three articles in the *New Yorker* that have helped set the political agenda by reporting that once again American soldiers in the midst of a war where the enemy is elusive and the cause is complicated had committed atrocious acts.[42]

Asked in an interview with this writer to evaluate the impact of his *New Yorker* stories on the public, worldwide, Hersh replied: "Abu Ghraib did far less than it should have done in terms of changing government behavior, simply because the government insisted it was an isolated event perpetrated by a group of deviates. The notion that there was something systematically wrong with the prison system inside Iraq (and Afghanistan) was resisted by the President and his minions for much of 2004. Eventually, however, the U.S. military began to take a few steps to improve conditions in the U.S.-run prisons in Iraq, but much of what was done—despite some good intentions—was token. The mistreatment of prisoners and the lack of due process continue today, and it is sure to be a blot for America for decades to come."[43]

ABOUT SEYMOUR HERSH

Seymour "Sy" Hersh is arguably the most daring and independent investigative reporter of modern times. He has been both praised and criticized for his body of work as a newspaper reporter, author, and magazine writer. In recent years, his most famous exposé was of the horrendous conditions at the Abu Ghraib prison in Iraq and the torture inflicted by the American military forces there, first published in 2004 in the *New Yorker*. Hersh maintained that the abuses, carried out by low-ranking troops, could be attributed to high Bush administration officials, including Secretary of Defense

Donald Rumsfeld. Hersh also charged publicly that President George W. Bush had been informed ahead of time. Although spokespersons for the White House vehemently denied the charge, Hersh himself became a topic of controversy because of his stories, on which he based a book in September 2004, *Chain of Command: The Road from 9/11 to Abu Ghraib*. Hersh's magazine articles on Abu Ghraib were strongly defended by his editors at the *New Yorker*.

Hersh, a longtime investigative reporter who sometimes rubbed people the wrong way with his gruff manner, became famous for his extraordinary reporting in 1969 of what was then known as the "My Lai massacre" in Vietnam. It involved the court-martial of Lt. William Calley, the commanding officer of the unit involved at My Lai. This exposé of the willful killing by U.S. soldiers of nearly 500 civilians won Hersh a Pulitzer Prize. Reporting for the *New York Times* in the 1970s, Hersh touched off another major controversy by writing stories about the Central Intelligence Agency's covert operations in Vietnam.

NOTES

1. Author's interview with Seymour Hersh, January 27, 2008.

2. The prison was built in the 1960s and occupied approximately 280 acres of land.

3. Rosemary Ruether, "Sexual Abuse at Abu Ghraib Stemmed from Pentagon Policy: Photos Were Part of Plan to Blackmail Prisoners," *National Catholic Reporter*, October 15, 2004. Ruether wrote: "The idea behind these photos was not only that sexual humiliation would break the prisoners and cause them to tell what they knew, but also would be a tool for ongoing blackmail. Fear of exposure of their humiliating treatment would cause the released prisoners to inform on their neighbors. According to Hersh's informant, 'I was told that the purpose of the photographs was to create an army of informants, people who you could insert back into the population.'"

4. David Carr, "Dogged Reporter's Impact, from My Lai to Abu Ghraib," *New York Times*, May 20, 2004. Carr's article also stated: "'There is a sense of outrage at this story for him,' said Tom Goldstein, a professor of business and journalism at Arizona State University who was a colleague of Mr. Hersh at the *New York Times* (and his tenant) in the 1970s. 'He has a sense of outrage unlike anyone I have ever known, and it remains undiminished over a career.'"

5. Chris Suellentrop, *New York*, April 11, 2005, 15.

6. Ibid., 16.

7. Howard Kurtz, *Washington Post*, May 19, 2004.

8. Suellentrop, *New York*, 16.

9. Seymour Hersh, "The Gray Zone," *New Yorker*, May 24, 2004, 38.

10. *Sacramento Bee*, July 25, 2004.

11. Maureen Farrell, BuzzFlash.com.

12. *Daily Kos*, March 7, 2009.

13. Hersh, "Gray Zone," 38.

14. *New Yorker*, June 25, 2007, 58.

15. Seymour Hersh, *Chain of Command: The Road from 9/11 to Abu Ghraib* (New York: HarperCollins, 2004), 46.

16. Hersh, "Gray Zone," 39.

17. CNN January 16, 2007. Five months later, on June 18, the Associated Press ran a story stating that the White House denied any prior knowledge of the Abu Ghraib abuse. It read: "The White House has insisted that President George W. Bush first learned about abuse at Iraq's Abu Ghraib prison from media reports. This is contrary to assertions by General Antonio Taguba that Mr. Bush likely knew about the scandal before it broke. 'The President said over three years ago that he first saw the pictures of the abuse on television,' White House spokesman Scott Stanzel said. Mr. Stanzel was responding to questions about a *New Yorker* magazine report quoting the top military investigator of the Abu Ghraib scandal, retired Army Major General Antonio Taguba, as saying 'the President had to be aware of the abuse of prisoners by US military guards at the facility.'"

18. Hersh, "Gray Zone," 41.

19. Ibid., 43.

20. Ibid., 44.

21. Ibid., 46.

22. Ibid., 47.

23. Ibid., 48

24. Seymour Hersh, interview by Bill O'Reilly, *The O'Reilly Factor*, Fox-TV, May 3, 2004.

25. Raphael Patai, *The Arab Mind* (New York: Hatherleigh Press, 2002), 118. Patai made references in the book to shame, particularly through sexual humiliation, in Arab culture.

26. An attempt was made by Defense Department officials to thwart the CBS broadcast under the heading of "protecting national security interests," but it was rebuffed.

27. *New York Times*, May 1, 2004.

28. Seymour Hersh, "Torture at Abu Ghraib," *New Yorker*, May 10, 2004, 42.

29. "It Will All Fall Down: A Conversation with Seymour Hersh," *Adbusters*, August 22, 2007, https://www.adbusters.org/magazine/73/It_Will_All_Fall_Down_A_Conversation_with_Seymour_Hersh.html.

30. 9th Annual Mario Savio Memorial Lecture, University of California, Berkeley, August 21, 2007. The Mario Savio Memorial Lecture and Young Activist Award are presented annually to honor the memory of Mario Savio (1942–1996), spokesperson for the University of California's free speech movement.

31. Seymour Hersh, "Chain of Command," *New Yorker*, May 17, 2004, 39.

32. Ibid.

33. Ibid., 37.

34. Ibid., 40.

35. Ibid., 41.

36. Ibid.

37. Ibid.

38. Ibid., 58.

39. Todd Huffman, "Taguba, Torture and Abu Ghraib," OpEdNews.com, June 19, 2007.

40. http://www.defense.gov/releases/release.aspx?releaseid=7724.

41. *The Early Show*, CBS-TV, September 14, 2004.

42. David Carr, *New York Times*, May 20, 2004.

43. Author's interview with Seymour Hersh.

CHAPTER 7

DOMESTIC EAVESDROPPING: "THE BIGGEST SECRET"

Reported by Eric Lichtblau and James Risen,
New York Times, 2005

The sources of information that we got for our story felt compelled to make the public aware of the government's illegal wiretapping of American citizens because they believed that it was either unconstitutional or illegal. They were classic whistleblowers.

—James Risen

Two enterprising *New York Times* reporters shook up the nation's capital and the very foundation of America's faith in their government just before Christmas in 2005 when they broke a major exposé of how the National Security Agency (NSA) was eavesdropping on Americans inside the country, seeking evidence of terrorist activities without obtaining court-approved warrants. It was clearly the worst assault on the U.S. Constitution since the Watergate scandal when a president was toppled for covering up abuses of power. The *Times*'s series was so sensitive that the paper withheld publishing it for 14 months until the controversy had escalated to the point where the publisher of the *Times*, Arthur Ochs Sulzberger, was summoned to the Oval Office. President George W. Bush was desperately concerned that publication would "endanger national security."

Indeed, the *New York Review of Books* headlined its review of *New York Times* reporter James Risen's book *State of War: The Secret History of the CIA and the Bush Administration* "The Biggest Secret."[1] This was the terminology used by the *Times*'s main government source, who told Risen: "This [wiretapping] is the biggest secret I know about." This was a remarkable admission for a career intelligence official who had access to virtually all of the government's top secret material at the time and who must have known about the possibility of violating an individual's right to privacy.

In an interview with me, Risen disclosed that this one phrase—"the biggest secret"—propelled him into high gear. "It began to freak me out," he admitted in an interview. "I remember telling my editors that when we were deciding whether or not to print the series. I said, 'This is the kind of story that made Sy Hersh in the 1970s.' Not to be immodest. That was what happened to me. When you have sources like we had, it really triggered things for me."[2] Risen and Eric Lichtblau were awarded a Pulitzer Prize the following year "for their carefully sourced stories on secret domestic eavesdropping that stirred a national debate."[3]

The *New York Times*'s investigation led to the discovery of what the NSA innocuously called a "special collection program." Risen traced its origins back to the first Allied attacks against the Taliban in Afghanistan in 2003, when al Qaeda suspects were captured with high-tech equipment such as cell phones and computers that carried data linking the suspects to people in the United States. But that was only the beginning. The NSA, according to Risen, soon widened the scope of its eavesdropping to many thousands of U.S. citizens.

Risen's book came out immediately after he and his colleague Lichtblau wrote a series of stories published by the *New York Times* in December 2005 about the government's illegal eavesdropping program. The articles revealed that the NSA not only wiretapped Americans without court orders but also "mined" the data for anything "suspicious" that could offer evidence of terrorist activities. While digging into this story, Risen painstakingly cultivated a number of reliable intelligence sources, promising them complete anonymity.

Lichtblau also wrote a book, *Bush's Law: The Remaking of American Justice*, published in 2008, in which he offered his inside perspective on how the intelligence system changed markedly under President Bush. In a TV interview about the book, he said: "What we've seen since 9/11 is really a historic shift, as I try and lay out in the book, the way we look at intelligence and law enforcement and the role of the federal government. You know, it's akin to what Hoover did at the FBI in going after organized crime in the '50s and '60s or against Communists. It's just a remaking of the sense of what the federal government's purpose is. After 9/11, Bush and his top advisers—[Defense Secretary Donald] Rumsfeld, [Attorney General John] Ashcroft, [Ashcroft's successor, Attorney General Alberto] Gonzales, [Vice President Dick] Cheney certainly—said this will not happen again, and they made clear that every branch of the federal government would be tasked to remake itself within the Pentagon, within the Justice Department, within the CIA, within the NSA, to ensure that every possible lead, every possible tension that could lead back to al Qaeda would be checked, would be scrubbed before another attack could happen. Now, what was lacking in that pursuit was really the checks and balances that we've taken for granted in terms of constitutional principles, and that's the story that I try and lay out in the book."[4]

Asked by the interviewer how the *Times* discovered the NSA story in the first place, Lichtblau answered: "Well, what I lay out in the book is that in the chapter that discusses the back story, if you will, the story of how the *New York Times* came to publish the story, was that there was an intense nervousness over this program from the very beginning, literally from the first hours and days that it began in October 2001. There were people within the government, within the FBI, within the Justice Department, who were worried that the NSA was doing something illegal. Remarkably, they kept a bottle on that for the better part of two-and-a-half years."[5]

So, there was a story in hand as the congressional elections of 2004 approached. Nonetheless, the *Times*'s editors decided just before the election to go to the White House with their findings. But, as Lichtblau has pointed out on numerous occasions, the timing was "somewhat coincidental; that couldn't be removed from the debate about whether to publish it entirely, but it was really a matter of happenstance that we happened to be debating this right before the election. [We] decided before the election that the editors felt we did not quite have enough to go . . . given the administration's insistence about the national security concerns."[6]

Had the story run, it might well have changed the outcome of the close race between Bush and Massachusetts Democratic senator John Kerry. One can speculate that, in addition to saying the story was not ready, the *Times* may well have leaned over backwards not to publish it just before such an important election. This already "left-leaning" newspaper could easily have been accused not only of threatening the national security but also of purposely trying to influence an election.

The *Times*'s stories had taken more than a year to research and write at a time when a majority of people in the government feared talking to news reporters on the record. Risen and Lichtblau did learn, however, that shortly after the September 11, 2001, terrorist attacks, President Bush had secretly authorized the NSA to listen in on conversations of Americans in the states. The NSA was told to track e-mail messages in an illegal effort to find suspected al Qaeda terrorists in the country's midst without the consent or knowledge of the American citizenry.

Not since the Watergate scandal in 1972 (see chapter 3), which involved sensitive but not classified information, had the presidency been exposed so boldly for wrongdoing. But this time, it involved a national security issue that could affect the outcome of a nation at war. *Washington Post* reporters Bob Woodward and Carl Bernstein "had plenty of problems dealing with an illegal cover-up," said James Risen in an interview with me, "but we had a different kind of problem—gathering secret intelligence."[7]

Lichtblau told me in a separate interview that it all started in the city room of the *Times* in 2004 when he was assigned to cover the Department of Justice because he had just about run out of stories about the U.S. Patriot Act. But, as Lichtblau tells it, one of his best sources encouraged him to keep looking. "'There's more there.' What did this mean? The source, a government official, was unwilling to say. The tip, if it could even be called that, was beguilingly vague. This was one of the lesser known by-products of the *All the President's Men* phenomenon. Just as Bob Woodward and Carl Bernstein had inspired a generation of young journalists like myself to become government watchdog sleuths, they had also given rise to armies of self-styled Deep Throats. Sources who had seen Hal Holbrook utter 'Follow the money' a few too many times now felt emboldened, with a simple but maddeningly vague command, to send reporters on their way in search of scandal and journalistic riches."[8]

Lichtblau's source had played a similar game, not revealing his real name at first, and using an intermediary to arrange meetings at bookstores. About all he could glean after repeated attempts was a rumor that Attorney General John Ashcroft might be indicted. After a number of conversations, he learned there was anxiety about what might or might not be happening in the Foreign Intelligence Surveillance Court [known as the FISA Court because it was established under the Foreign Intelligence Surveillance Act (FISA)], a place where the Department of Justice could offer secret evidence as to why a specific American should be wiretapped. He continued to poke around, but, as Lichtblau wrote, "It was, at best, half of a lead desperately in search of two thousand words or so to follow it."[9]

At that point, good fortune shone on Lichtblau in the person of Jim Risen, whom he knew from past experiences with him at the *Los Angeles Times*. "We literally sat next to each other, so there was a lot of back-and-forth talk," Lichtblau explained to me, "especially as we got close to publication. Ultimately there were a lot of sessions between us both in the office and outside of the office."[10]

Risen said he had left the *Los Angeles Times* because "I wanted a new challenge, covering things hard to find out. I thought the CIA would be an interesting challenge. It turned out to be the hardest reporting challenge there is, because there is no front door to cover the CIA through. They don't have press conferences very often, and when they do, they don't say anything. They don't put out reports that are very interesting—the interesting ones are all classified. And they don't really tell you what they are doing very often. In the '90s, they would talk a little bit, but never very much. I saw it as a great opportunity."[11] Risen's beat, simply put, was uncovering government secrets in the intelligence community.

Risen described to me how he went about learning investigative reporting at the *Los Angeles Times*. "Basically, you can't rely on the conventional way that a beat reporter goes about his business—showing up at a press conference or going to a building every day. You got to think creatively. How to get access to people and develop relationships. It's a different kind of reporting. You meet people, but you must be careful. I know for a fact that the government has subpoenaed people whom I know to try and find out how I meet people, so I can't tell you that. That's part of an ongoing leak investigation [as of June 2009]."

I posed this question to Risen: "Is part of the investigation process as simple as looking at records that are public?"

"In the intelligence world, no," he answered. "I wish it was. That's not how we could have found out about the NSA story. There was nothing public whatsoever about it. What we had to do is wait for people to come to us. Over time, Eric and I had been around and gotten to know people who knew what we were working on. Those who came to us wanted to talk to us; these were people who were troubled by things inside the government."

I asked Risen if either he or Lichtblau had had any "Deep Throat" type meetings, alluding to the clandestine meetings *Washington Post* reporter Bob Woodward had with his Watergate source in a Washington, D.C., garage.

"Yes," he replied. "But I can't give you any names or places. We had intermediaries who would tell us where and when to meet someone we had not met before. At first, we did not know their names, but after a while they confided in us, as long as we promised to keep their names anonymous. One of the difficulties was that there were so few people who knew about the existence of this program to begin with."

The two men shared tidbits of information from time to time, but neither was too willing to tell the other too much. As Lichtblau explained in his book:

> It would be many weeks before we realized that we had been tugging on different strands of the same ball of yarn. Whatever I was pursuing seemed to be causing agitation focused at least in part on the FISA court; what Jim was chasing was an intelligence program that appeared to be focused overseas. The twain, at first blush, did not meet.[12]

Lichtblau credits Risen for putting the pieces of the puzzle together. While Lichtblau had been looking into possible FBI involvement, Risen suggested that the place he should be looking was Fort Meade, Maryland, where the NSA resided. The NSA had been created by President Harry S Truman in 1952 to consolidate the federal government's code-making and code-breaking operations.[13] Risen, following leads in the intelligence community, clued Lichtblau in on the fact that the NSA had quietly assumed the capability of wiretapping U.S. citizens in their own homeland without their knowledge in the "war on terrorism." But nailing down concrete information involved some heavy lifting by both reporters. It was a brand-new discovery—and illegal at that. Wrote Lichtblau:

> Even senior government officials who normally had access to the most highly classified operations in the executive branch were shut out. And the ramifications for domestic policy, it became clear, were equally dramatic. The idea that the NSA was running the operation was a seismic shift in how domestic surveillance was carried out.[14]

Lichtblau said that one former official "who had heard whispers about the program told me early on: 'This is a sea change. It's almost a mainstay of this country that the NSA only does foreign searches.'"[15]

At this point, in the summer of 2004, Risen called Gen. Michael Hayden, head of the NSA, in person and read to him the first paragraph of a draft story stating that the NSA was eavesdropping on Americans without warrants. As Lichtblau told this story:

> The usually unflappable Hayden was clearly jolted, and a bit flustered. An Air Force general, accustomed to carefully scripted briefings on classified material in bug-free, secure facilities, was now being asked on an open phone line about perhaps the most classified program in the government. Whatever the NSA was doing, Hayden told Jim, was "intensely operational." And, he added quickly, it was "legal, appropriate, and effective." Jim tried to ask him a few more questions. Hayden refused to say anything more. But he didn't deny anything either.[16]

The reporters then briefed the *New York Times* Washington bureau chief, Phil Taubman, who would soon receive a call from General Hayden asserting that the *Times* should not be writing this story in the interest of national security. That was just the beginning of a series of escalations that left the *Times* with a powerful plea from the White House not to run the story. There had been precedents for such a request coming from the White House. For example, in 1963 John F. Kennedy had asked the *Times* to withhold a story on the impending Bay of Pigs attack (see chapter 2). And there had been the battle with President Richard M. Nixon over publishing the famous "Pentagon Papers," revealing the secret history of the Vietnam War.

Risen and Lichtblau continued pressuring their editors to go to press. But the Bush administration's insistence on holding the story came from the president as well as at least 10 of his senior advisors, who kept up their own pressure on Sulzberger and the *Times*' management. Beginning in October 2004—only weeks before the presidential election—the dialogue with the administration went on for 14 months, much to the disappointment of Risen and Lichtblau. Lichtblau quotes Bill Keller, the paper's top editor, as later telling him: "I've never had a case where the government raised such strident alarms, at such a high level, as the NSA eavesdropping program. This was, at least in recent times, an unprecedented show of official alarm."[17]

The Bush administration's case was based on its contention that, if the *Times* printed the story, it would aid and abet al Qaeda. Neither

Risen nor Lichtblau bought that argument. Realizing that reporters and editors do not always agree on when a story should be published, the reporters were advised by Keller during this protracted period of waiting that the story was not ready. His fundamental question was whether or not the story would be harmful to national security. But White House officials kept insisting that publishing the series would actually put American lives at risk. Risen expressed mixed feelings. "As disappointed as I was at the time, I am not sure in hindsight that there are any editors in the country who would have come to a different decision, just three years after the 9/11 attacks."[18]

It was a real challenge—and a very frustrating one indeed—for the two reporters to continue writing stories about the U.S. Patriot Act and the president's wartime powers under discussion in Congress, knowing all the while that the NSA had already violated some of the provisions of that Act.

During this period, Risen took a leave of absence to write his book *State of War*, and he confided to Lichtblau that he was considering including a chapter about what the NSA had been doing illegally— the very same story that his newspaper was sitting on. Finally, after meeting with his editors in September 2005, Risen persuaded them to run the newspaper series before his book came out. But first, the reporters were asked to check with their sources and make the case—once again—that there was more reason to run the series than to keep it secret.

The second time around, Risen and Lichtblau found clear evidence that the administration had lied to them. By this time, they had persuaded another editor, Rebecca Corbett, an investigative editor in Washington who monitored the story, to support them. But she, too, wanted to eliminate anything in it that they could not prove. So they met with her day after day in her office, refusing to tell their inquisitive colleagues what they were doing. "We need to be bulletproof on this," Risen repeated from time to time during those sessions.[19]

Finally, in early December 2005, Risen said, a meeting was arranged for Keller, Taubman, and Lichtblau to go to the White House once again and explain their case for publishing the series. The principal White House officials this time were Condoleezza Rice, the new secretary of state; Stephen Hadley, the national security adviser; Harriet Miers, the White House counsel; and the NSA's General Hayden. (Vice President Cheney, the reporters said, chose not to be present because of the high tensions that already existed between him and the *Times*.) The Bush officials told them it would be a calamity. One official told them the story would "shut down the game." A second said, "It's all the marbles."[20] In effect, according to Lichtblau's account of the meeting,

> The message was clear from the long, grave faces around the room and the stern words of warning: if the story was published and the United States were attacked again, the *New York Times* would share in the blame for the next attack.[21]

Despite these strong statements, the *Times* delegation left the meeting the same way they had entered it—leaning towards publishing. But the back-and-forth was not over yet. Shortly after the meeting, after Bush was briefed, he said he wanted to meet personally with the publisher, Sulzberger, who would bring Keller and Taubman with him. According to Keller's account of the second meeting, Bush warned the newspaper executives that if there was a second attack, they, too, would be sitting in a hearing room explaining to Congress why they ran the story. "Bush's message, as Keller said later in recounting the episode, was clear: If there's another attack 'there'll be blood on our hands.'"[22]

Following that tense meeting, according to Lichtblau's account, Keller told Sulzberger that nothing he had heard from Bush changed his mind. He wanted to publish. Sulzberger gave him the go-ahead.

But it still was not over. In an apparent effort to stall longer so that Congress could pass the Patriot Act, the White House strung the editors along for 12 more days. The reporters found themselves continuing to ride an emotional roller coaster of uncertainties. Risen, whose book was still waiting in the wings, felt it was time to push for publication of the series again. He conferred with Jill Abramson, the managing editor, for whom they had worked in Washington. Risen sent her an e-mail from home, reading:

> I am not a religious person, but I have prayed about this. I believe that there are a few times in our lives when we must make moral choices. Sometimes, we don't recognize those moments until they have passed. To me, this story has been like a stone in my shoe. I can't walk away from it. . . . But all I want is this story to be told, so the American people can decide what they think about it.[23]

Still, the White House continued to delay for four more days. Then Lichtblau learned that the administration was considering seeking an injunction against the paper, as the Nixon administration once did with the Pentagon Papers, but had not yet moved on it. Before any legal action could be taken, the *Times* editors, using a new technology that had not been available in the 1970s—the Internet— decided to put out the story online on the *Times* Web site the night before it was actually to appear in print in the paper.

"So we put it on the Web site early," Risen recalled in his interview with me, "and Keller called Steve Hadley, the national security advisor and Andy Card, on the White House staff, and he told them we were running it. They got furious."[24]

At last, Risen and Lichtblau were able to breathe a collective sigh of relief. They had done it—finally. As Lichtblau put it half-jokingly in his book: "After all this time, we were just relieved to see the story in the newspaper at all; in the back of the paper among the bra ads would have been fine."[25]

During the 14 months they were researching this story, Lichtblau and Risen had written five carefully sourced articles on secret domestic eavesdropping that would stir national debate on the boundary line between fighting terrorism and protecting the individual civil liberties of U.S. citizens. Their stories were published between December 16 and December 28, 2005.

On Friday morning, December 16, 2005, the first story in the series hit the newsstands under the headline "Bush Lets U.S. Spy on Callers without Courts; Secret Order to Widen Domestic Monitoring." The article began:

> WASHINGTON, Dec. 15—Months after the Sept. 11 attacks, President Bush secretly authorized the National Security Agency to eavesdrop on Americans and others inside the United States to search for evidence of terrorist activity without the court-approved warrants ordinarily required for domestic spying, according to government officials.
>
> Under a Presidential order signed in 2002, the intelligence agency has monitored the international telephone calls and international e-mail messages of hundreds, perhaps thousands, of people inside the United States without warrants over the past three years in an effort to track possible "dirty numbers" linked to Al Qaeda, the officials said. The agency, they said, still seeks warrants to monitor entirely domestic communications.[26]

The story reported that nearly a dozen current and former government officials, all of whom were granted anonymity because of the sensitive nature of the program, had discussed the program with the reporters. It also pointed out that the Bush administration had asked the *New York Times* not to publish the articles for one year because it would alert would-be terrorists that they might be under scrutiny. Accordingly, the articles told readers that some information that administration officials believed to be useful to terrorists was omitted.

By law, the NSA is prohibited from monitoring the telephone calls of anyone domestically, but the article explained that if the federal government wanted an exception to that rule, it could go to a secret court, the Foreign Intelligence Surveillance Court, in Washington that deals with national security issues.

The story noted that the NSA, based at Fort Meade, Maryland, was the government's largest and most secretive intelligence operations organization. Its purpose, the article said, was to break codes and maintain "listening posts" around the world, from which it could eavesdrop on foreign governments, diplomats, and trade negotiators, as well as drug lords and terrorists. But it had operated under tight restrictions—up until the Bush administration changed that—against spying on Americans. That activity had previously been done only under the purview of the Federal Bureau of Investigation.

Risen and Lichtblau informed readers that the Bush administration had initiated "a special collection program" after it began capturing top al Qaeda operatives in Afghanistan; its purpose was to obtain the names and addresses of anyone in the United States who had been in contact with al Qaeda terrorists. The breach in constitutionality, the *Times* article stated, came when the NSA began to conduct warrantless eavesdropping on people in the United States who were linked, even indirectly, to suspected terrorists through telephone numbers and/or e-mail addresses. When the program first started, the article said, congressional leaders, including the ranking members of the Senate and House intelligence committees, were briefed by Vice President Cheney's office in the White House.

When Risen and Lichtblau's first article in the *Times* appeared, Congress was in the midst of discussing provisions of the U.S. Patriot Act, which also dealt with methods of increasing the government's ability to gather intelligence in what was being called the "war on terror." Opponents of the Act had called parts of it an intrusion on the civil liberties of U.S. citizens, and the topic had been under heated debate for some time.

The first article in the series immediately drew blood from the Bush administration when a story on CNN the next day, December 17, in effect confirmed the *New York Times* story. It read:

> WASHINGTON (CNN)—In acknowledging the message was true, President Bush took aim at the messenger Saturday, saying that a newspaper jeopardized national security by revealing that he authorized wiretaps on U.S. citizens after September 11.
>
> After the *New York Times* reported, and CNN confirmed, a claim that Bush gave the National Security Agency license to eavesdrop on Americans communicating with people overseas, the President said that his actions were permissible, but that leaking the revelation to the media was illegal.
>
> During an unusual live, on-camera version of his weekly radio address, Bush said such authorization is "fully consistent" with his "constitutional responsibilities and authorities."
>
> Bush added: "Yesterday the existence of this secret program was revealed in media reports, after being improperly provided to news organizations. As a result, our enemies have learned information they should not have, and the unauthorized disclosure of this effort damages our national security and puts our citizens at risk."[27]

It is both amusing and instructive to learn exactly how Risen and Lichtblau reacted when they heard the news. Lichtblau's account tells it all:

> Jim [Risen] is a notorious night owl, and a Saturday morning call signaled that something was up. "Turn on CNN," he said. "Why, what's going on?" I asked. "Just turn on the TV," he repeated. "Bush just confirmed the program." "Holy shit" was all I could think to say.
>
> I scrambled to find the remote for the TV. It was true. The president, at the last minute, had scrapped the canned Saturday morning radio address that he had taped a few days earlier. In its place, he was delivering a live talk about the NSA on national television. . . . Now, after arguing for a year that our story should not be published, a grim-faced Bush sat in the Roosevelt Room next to the Oval Office, confirming the

existence of perhaps his administration's most tightly held secret. "This is a highly classified program that is crucial to our
national security," said Bush. Now I could see why Jim was so
excited. I'd had big breaks before as a reporter. But in the journalistic coarseness made famous by *The Washington Post's* Ben
Bradlee during Watergate, this qualified as a true "holy shit"
moment for me.[28]

"How did you feel at that very moment?" I asked Risen. "Well, to
tell you the truth," he said, "that was the most intense period of my
life. I don't really remember what other members of the press were
doing. I was trying to get my book out. It came out about 10 days
after the story broke." He continued: "The day the story ran I told
somebody, 'This took five years off of my life.' I was just totally ex-
hausted. It was the most intense thing I've ever done. Just going
through everything, it took me a year to recuperate. It took a lot out
of me. But it was worth the effort."

What legacy would he like to leave as a result of winning the Pulitzer
Prize for this story? "I'd like to see this as part of a journalism textbook.
I'd like students to know about how we did this," said Risen.[29]

Risen and Lichtblau could not have been more pleased. Nixon
had attacked the paper's decision to publish the highly secret story
about the Pentagon Papers, but in doing so he had confirmed its
truthfulness. They were glad that they had been forced to double-
and triple-check their facts. Nonetheless, they admitted to insiders
who knew them well that they had doubts until the very end.
"Now, on live TV, the President himself was providing about as
good an answer as we ever could have envisioned. The President
was confirming our story," wrote Lichtblau.[30]

The fallout, as Lichtblau put it, was "fierce." In *Bush's Law*, he
wrote that he figured that the story would cause "major reverbera-
tions" inside Washington, but that he was "unprepared" for the upheaval it triggered throughout the country. The first major impact,
Lichtblau wrote, was that the Senate—which had been arguing over
reauthorization of the U.S. Patriot Act for months—blocked a vote
on the measure only hours after the story was out. Some Congress
members, he said, called for a complete cessation of the Act; others
called for a censure measure against the president—or even
impeachment. One senator, Russ Feingold (D-WI), was quoted as
saying: Bush "doesn't need the Patriot Act because he can just make
it up as he goes along."[31]

On the subject of the Bush administration's abuses of the Constitution, Risen had kept his opinions to himself during the course of his investigative series. After the stories were published, however, he allowed himself to speak out publicly in his book on the lessons he had learned and, indeed, why he felt it was important to write the history of the CIA and the Bush administration. At long last, a journalist had been able to breach the previously impenetrable walls of that mysterious institution. Risen wrote in his prologue:

> There is a secret history of the CIA and the Bush administration both before and especially after 9/11. It is a cautionary tale, one that shows how the most covert tools of American national security policy have been misused. It involved domestic spying, abuse of power, and outrageous operations. It is a tale that can only now begin to be told.[32]

That first article sent shock waves far and wide. For example, the *Kuwait Times* ran a headline "Bush in 'Eye' of Storm." Talking heads on TV discussed the scandal 24/7. The reporters received e-mails from all over the world expressing suspicion that the government might have been playing "Big Brother" for generations. Some people even complained that they might unknowingly have had microchips planted in their heads by the government. As Lichtblau expressed it: "We became the dumping ground for the distressed."[33] Lichtblau wrote about conservative analysts calling him and Risen "traitors," and of hate mail that arrived by the boxful; one blogger posted a note titled "High Treason and the *New York Times*" and another called them "21st Century Julius Rosenbergs," who should be hanged. They were, in Lichtblau's words, "lionized by the left and vilified by the right."[34]

Even as they were surrounded by sound and fury, they continued to have their articles published. On December 18, the second article in the series appeared, under the headline "Eavesdropping Effort Began Soon after Sept. Attacks; Operation Started in Secret, Officials Say." This story revealed that the warrantless eavesdropping effort began soon after the 9/11 attacks by the Bush administration in an effort to detect "sleeper cells" in the United States that might be planning future attacks. The December 18 article also reported that there were few, if any, controls placed on the warrantless operations that swept up the communications of hundreds of Americans on their own soil.

The third article, published on December 21, reported that government officials had spied on as many as 500 people at any one time, with the total number of intercepts mounting into the thousands from 2002 to 2005. The readers were told that two high government officials had both previously denied any connection to domestic spying in the overall effort to find terrorists. Here's how the article quoted officials, who were later proven to be untruthful:

> Gen. Michael V. Hayden, the former N.S.A. director who is now the second-ranking intelligence official in the country, was asked at a White House briefing this week whether there had been any "purely domestic" intercepts under the program.
>
> "The authorization given to N.S.A. by the President requires that one end of these communications has to be outside the United States," General Hayden answered. "I can assure you, by the physics of the intercept, by how we actually conduct our activities, that one end of these communications are always outside the United States."
>
> Attorney General Alberto R. Gonzales also emphasized that the order only applied to international communications. "People are running around saying that the United States is somehow spying on American citizens calling their neighbors," he said. "Very, very important to understand that one party to the communication has to be outside the United States."[35]

The fourth article in the series, published on December 24, carried the headline "Spy Agency Mined Vast Data Trove, Officials Report; Link to Phone Networks; Action without Warrants Are Called Wider than Yet Acknowledged." This piece reported that the intercepts of phone calls involved obtaining access to data by tapping directly into some of the major U.S. private telecommunications companies to obtain streams of domestic and international data. It said some officials were calling it "mining" operations and involved large volumes of phone and Internet traffic patterns that might lead to terrorism suspects. The two reporters skillfully got executives from a few of the private telecommunications companies to confirm the allegations. They quoted one executive as saying: "If they get content, that's useful to them too, but the real plum is going to be the transaction data and the traffic analysis," he said. "Massive amounts of traffic analysis information—who is calling whom, who is in Osama Bin Laden's circle of family and friends—is used to identify lines of communication that are then given closer scrutiny."[36]

The fifth and last story, "Defense Lawyers in Terror Cases Plan Challenges over Spy Efforts," appeared on December 28, 2005. It began this way:

> WASHINGTON, Dec. 27—Defense lawyers in some of the country's biggest terrorism cases say they plan to bring legal challenges to determine whether the National Security Agency used illegal wiretaps against several dozen Muslim men tied to Al Qaeda.
>
> The lawyers said in interviews that they wanted to learn whether the men were monitored by the agency and, if so, whether the government withheld critical information or misled judges and defense lawyers about how and why the men were singled out.
>
> The expected legal challenges, in cases from Florida, Ohio, Oregon and Virginia, add another dimension to the growing controversy over the agency's domestic surveillance program and could jeopardize some of the Bush administration's most important courtroom victories in terror cases, legal analysts say.

There followed a battle royal between advocates of civil liberties and members of Congress on the right over whether or not the stories compromised national security. The president used strong language at a White House news conference on December 19 to denounce the leaking of information, stating: "My personal opinion is, it was a shameful act for someone to disclose this very important program in time of war. The fact that we're discussing this program is helping the enemy."

The following are excerpts of Bush's news conference at the White House with reporters on December 19, 2005:

> PRESIDENT BUSH: You've got to understand—and I hope the American people understand—there is still an enemy that would like to strike the United States of America, and they're very dangerous. And the discussion about how we try to find them will enable them to adjust. Now, I can understand you asking these questions, and if I were you, I'd be asking me these questions too. But it is a shameful act by somebody who has got secrets of the United States Government and feels like

they need to disclose them publicly. Let me give you an example about my concerns about letting the enemy know what may or may not be happening. In the late 1990s, our Government was following Osama bin Laden because he was using a certain type of telephone. And then the fact that we were following Osama bin Laden because he was using a certain type of telephone made it into the press as the result of a leak. And guess what happened? Osama bin Laden changed his behavior. He began to change how he communicated. We're at war, and we must protect America's secrets. And so the Justice Department, I presume, will proceed forward with a full investigation. I haven't ordered one, because I understand there's kind of a natural progression that will take place when this kind of leak emerges. . . .

REPORTER: . . . Why did you skip the basic safeguards of asking courts for permission for the intercepts?

PRESIDENT BUSH: First of all, right after September the 11th, I knew we were fighting a different kind of war. And so I asked people in my administration to analyze how best for me and our Government to do the job people expect us to do, which is to detect and prevent a possible attack. That's what the American people want. We looked at the possible scenarios. And the people responsible for helping us protect and defend came forth with the current program, because it enables us to move faster and quicker. And that's important. We've got to be fast on our feet, quick to detect and prevent. We use FISA still—you're referring to the FISA court in your question—of course, we use FISA. But FISA is for long-term monitoring. What is needed in order to protect the American people is the ability to move quickly to detect. Now, having suggested this idea, I then, obviously, went to the question, is it legal to do so? I am—I swore to uphold the laws. Do I have the legal authority to do this? And the answer is, absolutely. As I mentioned in my remarks, the legal authority is derived from the Constitution as well as the authorization of force by the United States Congress.

The *Times* story continued:

But defense lawyers say they are eager to find out whether prosecutors—intentionally or not—misled the courts about the origins of their investigations and whether the government may have held on to N.S.A. wiretaps that could point to their clients' innocence. . . .

But some Justice Department prosecutors, speaking on condition of anonymity because the program remains classified, said they were concerned that the agency's wiretaps without warrants could create problems for the department in terrorism prosecutions both past and future.

"If I'm a defense attorney," one prosecutor said, "the first thing I'm going to say in court is, 'this was an illegal wiretap.'"[37]

By late January 2006, Risen and Lichtblau had finally achieved what they were after: a direct confirmation by the president that he had, in fact, given the order for the eavesdropping in the States. Pressure on the White House had built to the point where it had come time for President Bush to come clean. In an interview with *CBS Evening News*, on January 27, 2006, despite the fact that the administration had up to then insisted that the NSA wiretapping program was strictly international, Bush replied in answer to a direct question about the legality of the program: "I made the decision to listen to phone calls of al Qaeda or suspected al Qaeda from outside the country coming in, or inside the country going out because the people, our operators, told me this is one of the best ways to protect American people." He quickly added that he intended to impose limited checks on his broad powers by having the Justice Department constantly review and recertify the legality of the program.[38]

Bush had the last word, however. A *New York Times* story published on December 31, 2005, reported that the Justice Department had opened a formal criminal investigation into the disclosure or "leak" of classified information about the NSA program under which Bush had authorized eavesdropping on people in America without court warrants. The article stated that the program, "whose existence was revealed in the *New York Times* on December 16," has provoked sharp criticism from civil libertarians and others who believe it circumvented the law governing national security wiretapping.[39]

As this book went to press, the inquiry had not been closed, according to Risen. The aftereffects of the series were still with both men.

Had they been threatened at all? I asked. Risen said they had. "They [the Department of Justice] tried to prosecute me for espionage.

The Bush administration—Attorney General Alberto Gonzalez went on TV and said he was thinking of prosecuting us for espionage. We caught a lot of highly organized hate mail campaigns from right-wing groups for months and months, e-mails and phone calls. We had protestors outside of our office in Washington. Our editors said we should stay away from the office for a day or two after the story broke. They protested outside the New York office, too. There was one blog that recommended people find out where Eric and I lived so they could come after us. For the past two years [2006–2008], they [the government] had agents running all over Washington trying to find out who our sources were."

Asked if any of their sources tried to call them, Risen replied: "I really can't go into that. The investigation is still going on."

After listening to his story, I asked Risen what lessons he and Lichtblau had learned from this landmark investigation. Risen answered: "The best way that we can promote ourselves as a country in the Middle East and around the world is to know that we are a real democracy, and a real democracy has a vigorous and aggressive press."

Another widely misunderstood lesson, Risen added, was the use of anonymous sources. "Anyone who tries to tell the truth and to get the story out can get into trouble if they're identified, and yet there is a public need to get those stories out. I think that is where the public misunderstands the role of anonymous sources. There's a sense that, oh, these are made-up people or the reporter is fabricating or these are people with an ax to grind when in fact it's quite the opposite: It's people who are really determined patriots, I believe, to get the truth out with reporters who they trust, in a way that they believe will help the country. That may be a leap of faith, in this environment, where there is so much of a culture of secrecy in Washington today—I think as a reader you have to take that leap. And the only way over time to determine that this source—meaning me—is credible is if the stories hold up. You have to determine what the track record of the reporter is.

The people and the sources of information that Eric Lichtblau and I got for our story were people who were in some cases tortured by their knowledge of this information. They felt compelled to make the public aware of the government's illegal wiretapping of American citizens because they believed that it was either unconstitutional or illegal. They were classic whistle-blowers. I know that the 'classified' stamp is there. But they say—and apparently some members of Congress agree—that they were briefed and this was a very valuable program. Yeah, I know what their arguments are. But I also think that there was a First Amendment in the Bill of Rights long before there was a CIA or an NSA, before there was classification."[40]

Most legal scholars say that there is no explicit right to privacy in the Constitution. It derives from a penumbra (a word of legal art in the context of privacy) of legal rights protecting the individual laid out in the First, Fourth, Fifth, Sixth, Eighth, and Ninth Amendments in the Constitution's Bill of Rights. This principle was laid out in detail in the course of Justice William O. Douglas's opinion for the Supreme Court in *Griswold v. Connecticut* (1965) and has since been accepted and expanded to include various kinds of intrusions by the state such as illegal surveillance and its attendant abuses.

In a televised interview in 2006, Risen was asked about how they decided what to print and what not to print. He commented: "I think that if someone's life is in danger, that you as a reporter have a moral obligation not to print that kind of information. But I think that it's up to the news organization and reporters to make the decision in the end, because it's not the government's role to edit newspapers." How does he feel about violating national security? "You can always raise the issue of national security," he replied. "There's always a spectrum between the rights of the American people to know something and national security. It's something that we'll always debate. In the end, it's the right of the editors and the publishers under the First Amendment, to make the final decision. And until the Bill of Rights is changed, that will be what will happen. . . . The job of a reporter is to be the curmudgeon who raises the questions that nobody else wants to raise, and that's what the best reporters try to do."[41]

In a separate TV interview in 2006,[42] Lichtblau put the topic of using anonymous sources in perspective by stressing that the *New York Times* editors insist on knowing who they are before any story goes to press. "The paper has now a set policy whereby at least one editor is aware of who the sources are. All newspapers in the last few years have gotten more stringent about that as a result of problems that came up elsewhere."

The interviewer asked: "Is your relationship to a source sort of the way it was portrayed in *All the President's Men*?—somebody writes a little note on our newspaper; you see that, and then you should be in the parking garage?" Lichtblau answered: "We're not usually that clever. I wish we were, but it's oftentimes a lot more run-of-the-mill. But no real spy craft."

Asked how it felt to be a part of a story, Lichtblau replied: "I'd just as soon not be. I like reporting the news; I don't like being in it.

Reporters want to be the fly on the wall. You don't want to be in the center of the story." Had his notoriety as a result of his series on the NSA gotten him more sources? "Yeah, I suppose at times," he said. "Some people might pick up the phone a little quicker; other people may not. It cuts both ways."

About Eric Lichtblau

Eric Lichtblau became a member of the staff of the *New York Times* in 2002, starting with the Washington bureau of the newspaper, where he was assigned to report stories on the Department of Justice. Lichtblau came to the *New York Times* from the *Los Angeles Times*, where he worked as an investigative reporter assigned to stories on law enforcement and crime. He is a graduate of Cornell University.

About James Risen

James E. Risen became a member of the *New York Times* staff in 1998 in the Washington bureau. His beat was national security and intelligence. He came to the *New York Times* from the *Los Angeles Times*, where he served as chief economic correspondent in Washington. Prior to that, from 1984 to 1990, Risen obtained an undergraduate degree in history from Brown University and a master's degree in journalism from Northwestern University. He is the recipient of a Pulitzer Prize, along with Eric Lichtblau, for their groundbreaking reporting on eavesdropping in the United States.

Notes

1. Thomas Powers, review of *The State of War: The Secret History of the CIA and the Bush Administration* by James Risen, *New York Review of Books*, February 23, 2006, 9.
2. Author's interview with James Risen, December 3, 2008.
3. Quoted from the Pulitzer Prize Board, Columbia University, 2006.
4. Eric Lichtblau, interview by Amy Goodman, *Democracy Now*, syndicated, April 1, 2009.
5. Ibid.
6. Ibid.
7. Author's interview with Risen.
8. Author's interview with Eric Lichtblau, December 2, 2008.

9. Eric Lichtblau, *Bush's Law: The Remaking of American Justice* (New York: Pantheon Books, 2008), 186–89.

10. Author's interview with Lichtblau.

11. Author's interview with Risen.

12. Lichtblau, *Bush's Law*, 191.

13. James Risen, *State of War: The Secret History of the CIA and the Bush Administration* (New York: Free Press, 2006), 42.

14. Lichtblau, *Bush's Law*, 192.

15. Ibid.

16. Ibid., 193.

17. Ibid., 194.

18. Ibid., 198.

19. Ibid., 204.

20. Ibid., 207.

21. Ibid.

22. Ibid., 208.

23. Ibid., 210.

24. Author's interview with Risen.

25. Lichtblau, *Bush's Law*, 211.

26. James Risen and Eric Lichtblau, "Bush Lets U.S. Spy on Callers without Courts; Secret Order to Widen Domestic Monitoring," *New York Times*, December 16, 2005.

27. "Bush Says He Signed NSA Wiretap Order," CNN, December 17, 2005, available at http://www.cnn.com/2005/POLITICS/12/17/bush.nsa/index.html.

28. Lichtblau, *Bush's Law*, 212.

29. Author's interview with Risen.

30. Lichtblau, *Bush's Law*, 213.

31. Ibid., 214.

32. Risen, *State of War*, 10.

33. Lichtblau, *Bush's Law*, 215.

34. Ibid., 218.

35. James Risen and Eric Lichtblau, "Spying Program Snared U.S. Calls," *New York Times*, December 21, 2005.

36. Eric Lichtblau and James Risen, "Spy Agency Mined Vast Data Trove, Officials Report," *New York Times*, December 24, 2005.

37. Eric Lichtblau and James Risen, "Defense Lawyers in Terror Cases Plan Challenges over Spy Efforts," *New York Times*, December 28, 2005.

38. Lichtblau, *Bush's Law*, 154.

39. Scott Shane, "Criminal Inquiry Opens into Spying Leak," *New York Times*, December 31, 2005.

40. Author's interview with Risen.

41. James Risen, interview, *Frontline*, PBS, March 28, 2006.

42. Eric Lichtblau, interview, *Frontline*, PBS, July 14, 2006.

CHAPTER 8

RENDITION EXPOSED

Reported by Dana Priest,
Washington Post, *2005*

I found people in the CIA who had questions about what they were doing, who thought the CIA was going to be left holding the bag when things came out, that rendition and interrogation was off the rail and should never have been done in the first place.

—Dana Priest

The *Washington Post* on Sunday, January 2, 2005, carried some disturbing news. The story blew the lid off what would eventually be labeled as abuse and degradation of prisoners—"renditions"—the transporting of prisoners to foreign countries for the purpose of interrogating and torturing them on an outsourcing basis. The series of stories by investigative reporter Dana Priest that followed both shocked and dismayed millions of U.S. citizens who, although fearful of additional terrorist attacks, found it repugnant that their government was in such flagrant violation of international law.

It would soon become a worldwide scandal, forming a dark cloud over the Bush administration's no-holds-barred strategy for protecting the U.S. homeland. It was severely criticized by the president's political opponents for violating the Geneva Conventions and international human rights—a charge that would remain in the news until President Barack Obama took the oath of office on January 20, 2009. The very next day, January 21, Obama announced that America would no longer rely on torture in the gathering of intelligence.

The plan, in effect, appeared to violate the rights and freedoms of foreigners. Longtime observers of the Washington political scene were asked questions that until now would have seemed preposterous: Did this mean America could do whatever it wanted with terrorist suspects? Could the suspects be sent to foreign prisons where they could be tortured? Had the U.S. Constitution suddenly gone by the boards? What about the Geneva Conventions—were there not limits to what a country could do with captured prisoners? These and many more questions caught everyone by surprise. The series of stories set off a firestorm of reaction from across the nation—everything from complete and total support for *anything* done in the name of national security, to strong protests from liberal groups such as the American Civil Liberties Union that the new policy violated the Constitution.

Clearly, it was a new ball game.

The groundbreaking series of nine stories published in 2005 earned Priest a Pulitzer Prize in 2006 "for her persistent, painstaking reports on secret 'black site' prisons and other controversial features of the government's counterterrorism campaign." The Pulitzer Committee at the Graduate School of Journalism, Columbia University, called the series "a distinguished example of beat reporting that characterized sustained and knowledgeable coverage of a particular subject or activity."

Priest, a brilliant and tireless journalist, spent three years investigating the sensational stories about rendition. When she broke her series, it immediately rekindled memories of another history-making scandal unearthed by *Washington Post* reporters: Bob Woodward and Carl Bernstein's Watergate cover-up stories that drove President Richard M. Nixon from office in 1974 (see chapter 3). Not since "Deep Throat" was used as a prime source for the Watergate exposé had a *Washington Post* reporter delved so deeply, using mostly anonymous sources, into the intelligence apparatus of the United States, an always mysterious facet of American government.

The rendition scandal broke in the *Washington Post* on January 2, 2005, in an article headlined "Long-Term Plan Sought for Terror Suspects." Priest reported in this initial story that the idea of transferring some of the 500 prisoners then being held in Guantanamo Bay—Afghans, Saudis, and Yemenis—to new U.S.-built prisons operated in foreign countries around the world was under way. She quoted Bryan Whitman, deputy assistant secretary of defense for public affairs, justifying the idea by stating: "Since global war on terror is a long-term effort, it makes sense for us to be looking at solutions for long-term problems," he said. And, Priest added:

> The administration considers its toughest detention problem to involve the prisoners held by the CIA. The CIA has been

scurrying since Sept. 11, 2001, to find secure locations abroad where it could detain and interrogate captives without risk of discovery, and without having to give them access to legal proceedings.[1]

At the same time, she wrote that no public hearings in Congress had taken place on the controversial CIA detention methods. Congressional officials had complained that CIA briefings on the subject had been too superficial and were limited to only a handful of Congress members. Her first article also pointed out that the CIA was transferring prisoners it picked up abroad "to third countries willing to hold them indefinitely and without public trials." Priest explained that such transfers were referred to as "renditions," a practice that she traced back to covert actions shrouded in the deepest secrecy that were first authorized by President Ronald Reagan in 1986 and later also used by the Clinton administration to pick up criminals abroad, such as drug kingpins, and deliver them to other countries.

Priest wrote that such a concept would call for cooperation between the United States and other countries such as Afghanistan, Egypt, and Jordan, each of which would have to "agree to have their own local security services hold terror suspects in their facilities for interrogation by CIA and foreign liaison officers." Still, she quoted one CIA official, who told her, quite bluntly: "The whole idea has become a corruption of renditions. It's not rendering to justice—it's kidnapping."

Nonetheless, in fairness, she pointed out to her readers that high U.S. intelligence officers and other experts—including former CIA director George J. Tenet in his testimony before Congress—had commented that, in his view, renditions were an effective method of disrupting terrorist cells and persuading detainees to reveal information.

I conducted a lengthy in-depth interview with Dana Priest in 2008, in which she talked about how she went about gathering information for her stories and double-checking the facts.[2] She explained: "I guess when we started to write stories about so-called high-value terrorists being picked up, we knew we were really on the track of catching the 9/11 terrorists. Once you got on the idea that they were being picked up, there were a bunch of logical questions to ask: *Who* is picking up them up? The FBI, the CIA, the military? Why? And how was it being handled? What are the rules for this? It's sort of like the basic things you would ask about any police raid."

She continued: "Then the questions gave me answers I just never thought of, because it had never happened in my lifetime. I learned which agency was involved [the CIA], then I knew not only does it become much harder because of the nature of what they do, but you cannot reach them. The agency works in a way that nobody else can. So you ask what their rules are and where are they keeping people and what are they doing with them? It's just a whole series of questions I set out to answer with regard to the 9/11 suspects and their cohorts. And then I got a little bit of a sense of what officials were slightly willing to talk about, and that's when it became clear they were holding prisoners in separate areas with separate rules.

What was really hard to figure out is how they were different from the military. I had a frame of reference, having been a reporter at the Pentagon for seven years, so in a war I wanted to know the basic thing I would ask about the military: Who's fighting it? Where are the weapons? How successful are they? What's the collateral damage? Were their tactics getting to the strategic goal? That was always my simple frame of reference: How was the war being fought? That led me to all those other questions."

I asked her if anyone was answering her questions at the CIA. "Obviously, a lot of people were answering them in a way, but not in a way I had experienced before," she replied. "Everything took 10 times or more as long to ferret out. Every little story took so much longer because of the nature of intelligence reporting. People [government officials] got polygraphed every six months; they were asked if they have had any contact with the media, which makes it a lot more difficult. So it took me some time to realize the CIA was not going to help me like the Defense Department helped reporters cover wars. So I spent a fair number of months—maybe more, a year and half—banging my head against the wall, thinking if only I could say this in the right way with the right people I could somehow go through the front door. I wrote a book[3] and all of that came from going through the front door of the Pentagon. If you stay there long enough they don't follow you around. But you can't do that at the CIA. I had to wean myself away from any kind of official channels."

When I asked her if she had ever talked to Tenet when he was CIA director, she told me that first she had to develop her own sources, other than "officialdom," and get them to trust her. "I had people talking to me anonymously who were knowledgeable about what was going on." Pressed about whether she talked directly with Tenet, she replied: "I can't answer the question except to point out that if George Tenet is quoted on the record, it was very seldom. Like I said, I learned to wean myself way from official sources."

Did the CIA simply ignore her questions? I inquired. "I would say the agency shut almost every door there was," she said. "I had very little official contact with the agency, and when they heard about the secret prison story, they certainly wanted to shut that story down. The President of the United States asked the executive editor of the *Washington Post* [Leonard Downie] not to run that story in the form that it was in so, yes, they did try and stop us. But they did it in a legal way. A decision was made to run the story without the names of the countries. That was Len Downie's decision, not George Bush's or anybody else's."

I asked Priest if there were some people in the government anxious to get this story out. "I did find people who had questions about what they were doing," she explained, "people who thought the Agency was going to be left holding the bag when things came out, that this whole rendition and interrogation process was off the rail, really, and it should never have been done in the first place. So there were people who were uncomfortable with it, and over time, they were part of the reason I could get a hold of some information."

Priest began to think about the rendition story in 2002, she recalled in the interview with me. "That's when I first wrote about stress techniques and the idea that somebody other than the military was questioning people that they picked up on the battlefield." She continued: "Once I started to think that way, it caused a whole bunch of questions to come into my mind, like who else is out there on the battlefield? I had to really roll back my thinking on this and remembered that it wasn't until an article by Peter Finn in 2002,[4] which reported there were Special Ops and CIA people on the ground hunting people, and then that raised the question, well, what do you do with them? And then over a period of nearly three years, those questions got to be answered. We didn't even have all the questions at first."

I asked Priest how she gathered the pieces of the puzzle. "Well, it really started as what I think of as a classic investigative project," she explained. "We had one little teeny corner of information and we really dove it into what it became. There were a lot of stories about interrogation being done in a segregated area of Bagram Air Base in Afghanistan."

Following her first story, the series continued on March 3, 2005. Priest's second story, "CIA Avoids Scrutiny of Detainee Treatment; Afghan's Death Took Two Years to Come to Light; Agency Says Abuses Are Probed Fully," revealed that, in November 2002,

> a newly minted CIA case officer in charge of a secret prison just north of Kabul allegedly ordered guards to strip naked an uncooperative young Afghan detainee, chain him to the concrete floor and leave him there overnight without blankets, according to four U.S. government officials aware of the case.
> The Afghan guards—paid by the CIA and working under CIA supervision in an abandoned warehouse code-named the "Salt Pit"—dragged their captive around on the concrete floor, bruising and scraping his skin, before putting him in his cell, two of the officials said.
> As night fell, so, predictably, did the temperature.
> By morning, the Afghan man had frozen to death.[5]

The man's death was reported to be caused by hypothermia, she wrote, and he was buried in "an unmarked, unacknowledged cemetery used by Afghan forces. . . . The captive's family has never been notified; his remains have never been returned for burial." She reported that the man

> is on no one's registry of captives, not even as a "ghost detainee," the term for CIA captives held in military prisons but not registered on the books. . . . "He just disappeared from the face of the earth," said one government official with knowledge of the case.

Priest went on to report that the patience of many members of Congress was severely tested. Testimony before Congress did elicit the fact, however, that the CIA had developed "recommendations for improving administrative procedures for holding, moving and interrogating prisoners," including "more detailed reporting requirements from the field, increased safeguards against abuse and including more CIA officials in decisions affecting interrogation tactics." Only two were fully adopted and the name and manner in which the prisoner died was never fully explained by the CIA for two years, Priest wrote.

During my interview with Priest, she told me that she had found out about at least a half dozen cases of such abuse. I asked her how she discovered this. "Well," she replied, "part of being a beat reporter, which I was, you keep developing and deepening your relationship with an ever-expanding group of people who are really knowledgeable about things that are going on; you want to keep your ear to the ground all the time. Nobody was going to sit down and tell you a short story. That would be breaking too many rules. This was the case where somebody along the way through a network of sources hinted at something that had gone wrong somewhere—it was that vague—and like a lot of things you go to someone else. You are partly guessing and you are putting things together and you say, 'I hear that something went wrong,' and you ask, 'Did someone die?' You might get something more out of that—you have to find the location. That particular story probably took me six months to do."

I asked her whether she felt fully supported by her editors at the *Washington Post.* "People were very interested and they did not want to get anything wrong, and especially not me, because I would have had a credibility problem after that. That's why I took so long to do a story. At times I asked myself, 'Why am I doing this story?' I know his name. His family probably does not know he is dead. We're in Afghanistan, and the CIA is going to bury the story. But there was some gut-level feeling on my part, you know, that what I do gives voice to the most voiceless person."

The third story, on March 17, 2005, was co-bylined with R. Jeffrey Smith, another *Post* reporter. It was headlined "CIA's Assurances on Transferred Suspects Doubted." In the article, Priest reported that U.S. officials had found that the system of transferring suspects was not being monitored, and she said she had gotten confirmation that prisoners were being tortured in contravention of verbal pledges made by countries accepting the detainees not to torture them.

Priest noted that at a press conference the day before, President George W. Bush had "weighed in" on the topic, declaring that rendition was an important part of the nation's defense. Bush was quoted as saying: "In the post-9/11 world, the United States must make sure we protect our people and our friends from attack. That was the charge we have been given. And one way to do so is to arrest people and send them back to their country of origin with the promise that they won't be tortured. That's the promise we receive. This country does not believe in torture. We do believe in protecting ourselves. We don't believe in torture."[6]

One CIA officer involved with renditions, however, called the assurances from other countries "a farce," according to Priest's story. She quoted one official anonymously who said: "It's beyond that. It's widely understood that interrogation practices that would be illegal in the U.S. are being used."

At the time this story came out, the U.S. House of Representatives had just voted 420 to 2 "to prohibit the use of supplemental appropriations to support actions that contravene anti-torture statutes." Priest wrote:

> Attorney General Alberto R. Gonzales said in an interview that, once a transfer occurs, "we can't fully control what that country might do. We obviously expect a country to which we have rendered a detainee to comply with their representations to us. If you're asking me 'Does a country always comply?' I don't have an answer to that."

But Priest pointed out to the reader that the countries to which detainees were being sent were "sovereign" and do not necessarily have to agree to U.S. terms.

When I subsequently asked her about the difficulty of cultivating sources, Priest explained: "There was nobody telling you officially that these interrogation practices would be illegal in the U.S.— namely, torture. I can't remember what the attribution was, but people would talk to me 'on background.'[7] When they talked to me, I would identify them as 'a government official' or 'a defense department official'; there was a debate over what you could call them and I was always pushing. But on the other hand, I was definitely sympathetic to them for not being fingered in any way. I didn't want anyone clamped down or to be investigated. The Bush administration broadened the CIA's authority after 9/11."

I asked if she talked directly with Attorney General Gonzales. "I can't recall," she replied vaguely. "But the thing I was most proud of," she quickly added, "is that I was the first person to get a copy of the so-called Bush Torture Memo put out by the administration on August 1, 2002, based on a memorandum from his Office of the Legal Counsel."

At the White House press conference the day before Priest's article, March 16, Bush unapologetically defended his decision to expand the practice of turning over alleged terrorists to governments that are notorious for torturing prisoners.[8] Toward the beginning of the news conference, a reporter asked: "Mr. President, can you explain why you approved of and expanded the practice of what's called 'rendition'—of transferring individuals out of U.S. custody to countries where human rights groups and your own State Department say torture is common for people in custody?"

Bush replied by citing his directive with the standard administration spin, justifying the use of "enhanced techniques" of interrogation on the grounds of "national security." He said: "In the post-9/11 world the United States must make sure we protect our people and our friends from attack." He then added, lamely, that the U.S. received "promises" from countries that they would not torture those rendered to them by the American authorities. "We seek assurances nobody will be tortured when we render a person back to their home country," Bush said. This de facto defense of torture did not prevent Bush, at a later point in the new conference in reply to a query about "antipathy to America around the world," from declaring: "People need to understand we're a compassionate nation that we care deeply about suffering."[9]

Seven days later, on March 23, the president once again articulated the White House position on torture in an order outlining the treatment of al Qaeda and Taliban detainees. It was based on the August 1, 2002, findings supplied by the Department of Defense and the recommendation of the Department of Justice. The order stated that the Geneva Conventions did not apply to the detainees captured by the CIA because the Taliban detainees were "unlawful combatants" and therefore did not qualify as prisoners of war under Article 4 of the Conventions.[10]

The following June, in an interview on *Frontline*, Priest said that Bush's August 1, 2002, statement on torture was amazing in what it said. It basically said the commander-in-chief can disregard any law during time of war. "That really broke things loose," she continued. "People involved in investigations, began telling the government: 'Wait a minute!' People inside the government were also upset about being cut out of the decision-making and not knowing what the legal background and framework was."[11]

The next story in the series, "Italy Knew about Plan to Grab Suspect," followed on June 30, 2005. "Before a CIA paramilitary team was deployed to kidnap a radical Islamic cleric off the streets of Milan in February 2003, the CIA station chief in Rome briefed and sought approval from his counterpart in Italy," wrote Priest, attributing this information to "three CIA veterans with knowledge of the operation and a fourth who reviewed the matter after it took place." The CIA, Priest said, told only a small number of people about the action, noting that it was not clear how high up in the Italian intelligence service the information was shared or whether Prime Minister Silvio Berlusconi was aware of the situation.[12]

Priest revealed that the CIA had rounded up more than a hundred suspects, using "extraordinary renditions," since 9/11, according to "intelligence officials." Priest took pains, like any good investigative reporter, to try to obtain comments from Italy and the United States, but reported that "the CIA and a spokesman for the Italian Embassy in Washington yesterday declined to comment on the Milan case or this article."

When I interviewed Priest, I asked her whether she had had her own Deep Throat–type sources in the course of the investigation, providing information that could not be attributed to anyone. She replied, succinctly: "Yes." But when I asked her to elaborate on her answer, she demurred: "I don't think I am going to answer that question. There might have been."

She told me she was able to solicit some candid quotes from French officials for her fifth story, which came out on July 3, 2005, and was headlined "Help from France Key in Covert Operations; Paris Alliance Base Targets Terrorists." "I think that most reporters sequence their reporting at some point. When they want to get to the middle of their target they know the story already. There are sources who know the story and it makes it a little bit easier for those sources to help them. By letting them know what I knew, and not having them contradict me—that served as a signal my information was correct."[13]

In her fifth article, Priest wrote her piece from Paris starting out with an interview with a German convert to Islam, a man who had traveled from Paris back to Germany. When he arrived in France, officials picked him up and took him into custody, where he remained until the day Priest wrote her article. He was captured in a secret center in a Paris Operation under the code name of Alliance Base, a joint venture set up by the French intelligence and the CIA. "The rarely discussed Langley-Paris connection also belies the public portrayal of acrimony between the two countries," Priest reported. She explained that a French general headed the Alliance Base. She also described the base as "unique in the world because it's multinational and actually plans operations instead of sharing information among countries. It has case officers from Britain, France, Germany, Canada, Australia, and the United States."

On November 2, 2005, the *Washington Post* published the sixth story in this series: "CIA Holds Terror Suspects in Secret Prisons; Debate Is Growing within Agency about Legality and Morality of Overseas System Set Up after 9/11." Priest began this article with the revelation that "the CIA has been hiding and interrogating some of its most important al Qaeda captives at a Soviet-era compound in Eastern Europe, according to U.S. and foreign officials familiar with the arrangement." She added that only "a handful of officials" in the U.S. government and a few top intelligence officers in each host country were aware of the locations.

> Virtually nothing is known about who is kept in the facilities, what interrogation methods are employed with them, or how decisions are made about whether they should be detained or for how long. . . . The CIA has not even acknowledged the existence of its black sites. To do so . . . could open the U.S. government to legal challenges, particularly in foreign courts, and increase the risk of political condemnation at home and abroad.

"At the request of U.S. senior officials," she wrote, her paper would not publish the names of the Eastern European countries involved in the covert program. "The officials argued that the disclosure might disrupt counterterrorism efforts in those countries and elsewhere and could make them targets of possible terrorist retaliation."[14]

Priest quoted one former senior intelligence officer talking about how the program developed: "We never sat down, as far as I know, and came up with a grand strategy. Everything was very reactive. That's how you get to a situation where you pick people up, send them into a netherworld and don't say, 'What are we going to do with them afterwards?'"

"Waterboarding" became a term that would attract considerable attention in the media and in Congress in the coming months and years. Referring to waterboarding, which many deemed to be an illegal way to get prisoners to talk, Priest wrote: "The interpretation by the agency [CIA] was that waterboarding was *not* illegal. I don't think it was until several years later that anybody acknowledged publicly that they did that. It was used but not used widely."[15]

She said details of the CIA's detention program have emerged in "bits and pieces."

> The idea of holding terrorists outside the U.S. legal system was not under consideration before Sept. 11, 2001, not even for Osama bin Laden, according to former government officials. . . . "The issue of detaining and interrogating people was never, ever discussed," said a former senior intelligence officer who worked in the CIA's Counterterrorist Center, or CTC, during that period. "It was against the culture and they believed information was best gleaned by other means."

The article also stated that six days after 9/11, President Bush signed a "sweeping finding that gave the CIA broad authorization to disrupt terrorist activity, including permission to kill, capture and detain members of al Qaeda anywhere in the world." The "black-site" program, she said, "was approved by a small circle of White House and Justice Department lawyers and officials, according to several former and current U.S. government and intelligence officials."

"Meanwhile," wrote Priest, "The debate over the wisdom of the program continues among CIA officers, some of whom also argue that the secrecy surrounding the program is not sustainable." When I asked her about this during our interview, Priest observed: "It's kind of an ironic quote, don't you think? Especially when you hear qualms about its effectiveness. I think there was no one looking at the whole operation. The congressional part of this was broken for a while and their oversight was lacking." Priest said that she learned about the debate among officials at the CIA on the rendition program itself. "You learned from one or two people about debate on the rendition program in the CIA whether or not to use rendition," she told me.

I asked her how she went about gathering information that made sense. She replied: "It was about just putting the jigsaw puzzle together, but every part of the puzzle has 10 parts. Just pieces of little scraps and eventually you can begin to see a picture. That was the culmination of two years of reporting about rendition. Where do the people go? It was an obvious question to ask. The hard part was finding the answer. Once you knew there were places not in the U.S. and not in Guantanamo, they had to be somewhere."[16]

On the same day this article by Priest appeared—November 2, 2005—National Security Advisor Stephen Hadley, at a White House press conference, defended the Bush administration's policies on gathering intelligence. Asked by a reporter, "Why does the administration feel it's necessary to maintain a network of secret detention centers around the world, out of sight of the Congress and the American people, and out of reach of American law and values?" Hadley replied: "There have been some press reports this morning that have touched on that subject. And as you can appreciate, they raise some issues about possible intelligence operations. And as you know, we don't talk about intelligence operations from this podium." But the reporter then followed up: "Don't they also raise the issue of our values and our reputation in the world?" Hadley responded: "I think the President has been pretty clear on that, that while we have to do what is necessary to defend the country against terrorists' attacks and to win the war on terror, the President has been very clear that we're going to do that in a way that is consistent with our values. And that is why he's been very clear that the United States will not torture. The United States will conduct its activities in compliance with law and international obligations. And in some of the issues involving detainees and the like, as you know, where there have been allegations that people have not met the standard the President has set. More than a dozen investigations have been done in the Department of Defense to find out what has been going on. Two things have happened as a result. There have been revisions of procedures and practices to ensure that the standard the President set is met; and then there have been investigations, prosecutions, and people punished for the failure to meet those standards. So we think that, in line with the President's guidance, we are both protecting the country against the terrorists and doing it in a way that is consistent with our values and principles."[17]

Story number seven had this headline on November 18, 2005: "Foreign Network at Front of CIA's Terror Fight; Joint Facilities in Two Dozen Countries Account for Bulk of Agency's 9/11 Successes." The story began:

> The CIA has established joint operation centers in more than two dozen countries where U.S. and foreign intelligence officers work side by side to track and capture suspected terrorists and to destroy or penetrate their networks, according to current and former American and foreign intelligence officials.[18]

It then explained that "the secret Counterterrorist Intelligence Centers [CTICs] are financed mostly by the agency and employ some of the best espionage technology the CIA has to offer."

"Today's CIA," wrote Priest, "is desperately seeking ways to join forces with other governments it once reproached or ignored to undo a common enemy." She reported that CIA Director George Tenet "orchestrated the shift during his tenure, working with the agency's station chiefs abroad and officers in the Counterterrorist Center at headquarters to bring about an exponential deepening of intelligence ties worldwide after Sept. 11."

The CIA, Priest said, was operating "joint intelligence centers in Europe, the Middle East and Asia, according to current and former intelligence officials. In addition, the multinational center in Paris, codenamed Alliance Base, includes representatives from Britain, France, Germany, Canada and Australia." The agency recruited many foreign services after Congress allocated funds. Priest wrote: "'The money was just flowing,' said one CIA case officer. In fact, the budget for the CIA's operations increased in the first two years by 2½ times what it had been before Sept. 11, according to two government experts."

The determined reporter she was, Priest told me she asked the CIA numerous times to comment, but it refused. To gather her information, she said she talked to more than two dozen former and present intelligence officials, as well as State Department employees and sources in Congress. They talked to her anonymously because they were not authorized to speak publicly. However, she wrote that legal experts and intelligence officials have said that the prisons—which had been mentioned in her previous articles—would be categorized as illegal under the laws of a few host countries.[19]

In her November 18 article, Priest shared with her readers that one of the reasons it was extremely difficult to get officials—on any level—to talk to her was that officers from the host nations serving in the newer detention centers were "usually supervised," she wrote, "by the CIA's chief of station and augmented by officers sent from the Counterterrorist Center at Langley. Such daily interaction with U.S. personnel, say intelligence officials, helps keep the foreign service focused."[20]

Priest noted that Tenet reached out to other countries, both friendly and hostile, seeking cooperation. She wrote:

> He was a natural at bonding with foreign chiefs of service, current and former intelligence officials said. Once, during a dinner for a foreign service chief, the guests asked Tenet about Bush, whom Tenet briefed every morning. "He would tell them what time he gets up. He'd say, 'The President calls me Jorge.'

It was really human-being-to-human-being," said a former intelligence official. "He didn't give away anything classified, but they felt important and could go back to their President and say, 'The President calls him Jorge.'"

I asked Priest about her reporting, which appeared to give credit to Tenet and, indeed, made him out to be an attractive figure creating the worldwide attack matrix. Asked if she spoke to him about this, she replied: "If I could answer without answering, I'd say what I was trying to do was to describe if the terrorists are being taken down, and get one question answered: How are they doing that? It's a simple question and I think we know now that Tenet, in all sorts of ways, was up front in trying to figure out how to take down the al Qaeda network. I was just trying to describe what those were. I wasn't trying to pass any judgment as to whether they were right or wrong; I just wanted to talk about the situation. When you say I gave Tenet credit, I think it was just reporting that his plan was X, it was global in its efforts, and he was good at deepening the relationships with foreign agencies, which was really key to all of this. He was a great schmoozer."[21]

The eighth story in Dana Priest's rendition series, on December 4, 2005, detailed a most unusual happening. Entitled "Wrongful Imprisonment: Anatomy of a CIA Mistake; German Citizen Released after Months in 'Rendition,'" this story described what happened when the White House learned that the CIA had wrongfully imprisoned a German citizen, Khaled Masri. "Masri was held for five months largely because the head of the CIA's Counterterrorist Center's al Qaeda unit 'believed he was someone else,' one former CIA official said. 'She didn't really know. She just had a hunch,'" reported Priest.[22] The U.S. government then requested that the Germans not disclose what had happened even if Masri went public. Priest noted that "U.S. officials feared exposure of a covert action program designed to capture terrorism suspects abroad and transfer them among countries."

The ninth and final story in Priest's 2005 series, on December 30, carried this headline: "Covert CIA Program Withstands New Furor; Anti-Terror Effort Continues to Grow." This article summed up the previous eight, starting with the fact that shortly after President Bush authorized the fight against al Qaeda, it rapidly grew into "the largest CIA covert action program since the height of the Cold War."[23] It was growing larger and larger—despite an increasing number of complaints in the United States from Congress and from the public over its clandestine tactics. Priest summed up the frustration of both government officials and average citizens that revelations of the rendition program raised questions about its legality and its morality. She even sought out a former CIA official for comments and reported:

> "In the past, Presidents set up buffers to distance themselves from covert action," said A. John Radsan, assistant general counsel at the CIA from 2002 to 2004. "But this President, who is breaking down the boundaries between covert action and conventional war, seems to relish the secret findings and the dirty details of operations."

Priest pointed out that Bush had "signed and issued a secret Presidential finding authorizing the C.I.A. to create paramilitary teams to hunt, capture, detain, or even to kill designated terrorists by name almost anywhere in the world," according to one reliable magazine account, titled "The Black Sites" by writer Jane Mayer. She added: "Critics, including military historians, have described it as a program of state-sanctioned torture and murder."[24]

Describing that "finding," Priest wrote:

> Bush delegated much of the day-to-day decision-making and the creation of individual components to CIA Director George J. Tenet, according to Congressional and intelligence officials who were briefed on the finding at the time.
>
> "George could decide, even on killings," one of these officials said, referring to Tenet. "That was pushed down to him. George had the authority on who was going to get it."
>
> Tenet, according to half a dozen former intelligence officials, delegated most of the decision making on lethal action to the CIA's Counterterrorist Center. Killing an al Qaeda leader with a Hellfire missile fired from a remote-controlled drone might have been considered assassination in a prior era and therefore banned by law.

"When the CIA wanted new rules for interrogating important terrorism suspects," Priest pointed out,

> the White House gave the task to a small group of lawyers within the Justice Department's Office of Legal Counsel who believed in an aggressive interpretation of presidential power.

   The White House tightened the circle of participants involved in these most sensitive new areas. It initially cut out the State Department's general counsel, most of the judge advocates general of the military services, and the Justice Department's criminal division, which traditionally dealt with international terrorism.

Focusing on the volume of data she was compiling, I asked Priest during our interview how she kept track of all the information. She replied: "It was painstakingly slow. I just saved all the data I gathered. It was exciting to be able to finally put something on paper. If you compare it to what the military [Department of Defense] people were doing, it was so much shorter; the stories were relatively easy. But on the intelligence beat, you had to be satisfied with less detail, but even that was something illuminating. During that period from '02 to '06, it was the media who uncovered and wrote about the whole intelligence part of the war on terror. It wasn't interest groups or human rights groups; it really was a handful of reporters with whom I was proud to be associated. That's the way it was. There wasn't any congressional subcommittee looking into this in any way that the public could know about. There was nothing but dead, cold silence."[25]

   Looking back on her unique experience compiling her stories, I asked Priest what could she tell a young investigative reporter she learned from this experience. "Patience, persistence, a lot of listening," she answered. "Finding people who are not at the top of an organization who will help explain how things really work on the ground, weaning yourself away from the large public affairs apparatus, whose job is to sometimes help, but oftentimes deflect reporters' inquiries. I was a daily 'get the scoop before the other guy' and I am still that way. But taking on a beat like this [intelligence], you had to learn to be patient and you had to learn perseverance on a different level.

   The last thing is to listen more carefully than you were listening before because people, especially when they are talking about sensitive subjects, give you things, little hints, that if I had not picked up some of those I could not have started some of these stories. The people were constrained in not telling me a large chunk of any story, but they might give me hints of places and of things that bothered them. That was the beginning of some of my stories. It's really to listen—to listen carefully—to what people are saying and to take notes so you process all of their words."

What did Priest think her stories accomplished in terms of changes in policies in U.S. Armed Forces wartime intelligence practices? I asked. "Mainly, all of it. But not immediately," she replied. "Immediately, the Bush people criticized the *Washington Post* series, saying it damaged national security. There were human rights groups that applauded them and there were some readers who were thankful that they had been published. But the biggest group was the voices that wanted to silence the whole thing.

"It became easier to write my stories a year or two later. I don't know exactly why; maybe it's because the Democrats took over the Congress and they felt more confident. The fact is that rendition has become a topic of great national scrutiny. I'm thinking that's why they shut down the black sites [and] they transferred the prisoners out and stopped, as far as we can tell, waterboarding and similar techniques. I don't think they are doing renditions anymore. If they are, they might be doing them in a different way. All of this became a topic of public discussion, and I think that's what our role is—to highlight things the government is doing, and if the public wants to discuss it, then that is their business."

In a TV interview on PBS's *Frontline* in 2008, Priest expressed some of her concerns about what she called the "militarization" of U.S. foreign policy after her series on renditions was published. "It is clear that the shift that is occurring at the Department of Defense is trying to create their own intelligence apparatus," she told the interviewer. "They have a lot of resources already. I think they're trying to take those and they would say make them more efficient, make them more aggressive, make them more operational, so they won't have to rely solely on the CIA, and they will have that ability to prosecute the war on terror themselves. So I think you see a consolidation of power within the military."[26]

On the topic of the press often being accused of giving away state secrets when reporting on intelligence matters, Priest told me she believes that the government cries wolf too often. "Every time there's a national security story they don't want published, they say it will damage national security. But they've never given us any proof. They say it will stop cooperation, but the fact is that the countries of the world understand that they have to cooperate on counterterrorism. It's not a crime to publish classified information. In fact, there are some narrow categories of information you can't publish, certain signals, communications, intelligence, the names of covert operatives and nuclear secrets.

"Why is it not a crime? Because the framers of the Constitution wanted to protect the press so that they could perform a basic role in government oversight, and you can't do that. Look at the criticism that the press got after Iraq that we did not do our job on WMDs [weapons of mass destruction]. And that was all in a classified arena. To do a better job—and I believe that we should've done a better job—we would've again found ourselves in the arena of trying to acquire classified information. The point is the tension between the media and the government is long-standing. And that's to be expected."[27]

Priest stressed during her interview with me that the *Washington Post* took her stories to the White House before going to press and, as a result, withheld the names of the black sites in the interest of national security. "In the prison [rendition] stories, we talked with the administration. In fact, people said, 'We know you have your job to do, but please don't publish the names of the countries where the prisons are located.' So a reasoned dialogue often goes on between the media and the government."

As for the total impact of her stories, Priest commented in an interview on *Hardball with Chris Matthews*: "Some people told us the administration has gone too far in some of the counterterrorism measures they've taken but, on the other hand, others said the stories created a debate that could not have happened before." For example, she cited the case of Guantanamo, among other issues that her series focused on. "The impact was huge," she said. "You know, we are covering the war on terror. It's a classified war. Why are we covering it? Because we want to figure out whether the government is going to achieve its strategic goals, which is to defeat terrorism and to compete in the realm of ideology. It's not just the tactical questions. And on Guantanamo, this has cost us a lot internationally as a defender—a primary defender—of human rights. And you have to take those things into consideration when you're trying to win a war."[28]

Yet another issue Priest addressed in our conversation was the relationship between reporters and their government sources: I asked her if the two parties have become too close. "It's complicated," she answered. "It's easier to maintain a distance. I think you should maintain a distance. I mean, people talk about Washington and people who are very close and socialize. That's OK, but you really need to keep your head about you when you do. You can be friendly with people, and I think the reason that I'm successful in getting information out of a largely all-male military or people in the intelligence community is that I really do come to empathize with their mission and their view of themselves and what they are doing.

"The war on terror is the centerpiece of what the United States is all about these days. We have to look at it in the same way that I looked at wars when I was a military correspondent: 'What are the tactics? Are they effective? And, ultimately, are those things going to achieve your strategic goal?' I'm always trying to give even the most controversial stories the fullest context, which means asking: Why did they choose to do something? Why did they set this up the way that it is? Why are they acting in a particular way? That's how I found out about the worldwide system of detention that has several different layers and components to it, but also the logistics mechanism to bring people around. In fact, most of my work concentrated on the relationships that were built up between the CIA and their foreign counterparts overseas. The whole reason for having the detention sites was so that the CIA could interrogate the people in them. And nobody else—not the host nation, not the Pentagon, not the FBI. Nobody. Just the CIA."[29]

Priest indicated to me that some conversations were so far off the record that she did not even attempt to give a source. "Eventually," she explained, "the administration—as I wrote in my stories—asked us not to publish the names of the countries. They cited at least two reasons, both of which we put in the paper. One was that those particular countries might be subject to terrorist retaliation, and the second was that those particular countries might decide to stop their cooperation on other productive counterterrorism cooperation."

"We kind of cut it in half," she continued. "We didn't name the countries, but we've named the region, and most important to me is that we've said 'Eastern European democracies' because the existence of the prisons and the places that they're in, are illegal in the places where they are. And it just so happens those countries used to be under the thumb of the Soviet Union and their pseudo, fake legal system. Now they are all trying to live under the rule of law, except they have made an exception—when we ask them not to. And the rest of the network was in Thailand or Jordan or Egypt or other countries."

Also in our interview, she emphasized that her paper took great care in not damaging the United States. "It's the nature of national security secrets. We don't do this frivolously. And as much as I hate having information myself that I am not going to publish—because that is so antithetical to how I've thought of myself since I became a journalist—that's life.

"I've been asked about President Bush's admonition to the media that it is 'not in the interest of the national security' of the United States to have detention centers revealed. Well, the Constitution does not make the President of the United States 'the decider' when it comes to the flow of information. That's so fundamental to who we are as a country, that we have a press that is independent of the government. It's not a perfect system in that we could make mistakes, but the alternative is that the government does decide what gets in print, and that would be revolutionary. That would make it impossible to do accountability stories. Every administration has wanted to control the flow of information.

There is no way that you could do this sort of reporting without anonymity. And it's not just the 'no-name' faction—it's the no-name, no-job-description, and no-agency sometimes. It's the journalistic equivalent of deep cover. You have to give readers something, but there were times when I could only say 'according to a U.S. government official.' That's because, depending on what it was that I was saying, very few people would know it, or it was so sensitive that you couldn't get a particular agency to confirm it. I've gotten a lot of support from people within the government bureaucracies who keep secrets, who are supportive of the idea that we wrote this story. And I'm not talking about the CIA. I'm talking about the military. I'm talking about the Justice Department; not members of Congress, but the congressional branch."

In another TV interview on *Meet the Press* in April 2006, Priest further detailed her philosophy about protecting her sources. She said she felt so strongly about this process that she would "willingly go to jail, if pressed to the limit. I try not to spend much time thinking about things that I really can't game out what's going to happen. I've traveled with troops around the world. I've been in situations that other people might think are dangerous. But I'm not somebody who's going to dwell on a future potential bad thing that might happen."[30]

I asked Priest about the government's policy of releasing information in the immediate aftermath of 9/11. Priest said that President Bush "started to put in place a new capability that was not yet fully developed. We needed to figure out how to gather more intelligence ourselves from the military, not rely so much on the CIA." She said this was the result of expansion of executive power. "It basically means that the commander in chief can disregard any other law during time of war."[31]

This posed an entirely new challenge for the media, Priest said in that earlier interview on *Meet the Press.* "The dark side after 9/11 had to do with [our government finding and] killing [terrorists]. And then you have to keep up with them. And they had nothing set up with that in mind. [Secretary of State Colin] Powell's vision of the world was not, as we saw, the one shared by the other alpha males in the Cabinet. And there are a group of them that are formidable—George Tenet, Paul Wolfowitz, Dick Cheney, Don Rumsfeld. They're all such dominant characters."[32]

Indeed, there were a great many "dominant characters" in the life of an investigative reporter trying to unearth the hidden secrets of what the CIA was doing with its newly created rendition program. Dana Priest managed to unlock the government's secrets and shed some light on a part of American history that historians will have to think about long and hard before they bring in a verdict about the whole issue.

Meanwhile, a movie, *Rendition,* came out in 2007 based, in large part, on her series in the *Washington Post.*[33] That undoubtedly gave her and those who believe in her cause some satisfaction. She had, after all, uncovered one of the most flagrant violations by the government of the nation's Constitution in generations.

ABOUT DANA PRIEST

Dana Priest is one of Washington's outstanding investigative reporters. She spent nearly two decades at the *Washington Post* prior to investigating and writing her award-winning articles on rendition. Before that, she wrote stories about the poor intelligence of the United States government prior to the 9/11 attacks. Priest also filed reports on the nation's covert operations against men suspected of terrorism. Included in her background experience are her stories on the Pentagon beat about the U.S. military. She accompanied the Army's Special Forces in a number of strife-torn regions around the world, including Asia, Africa, and the Middle East. Priest is a graduate of the University of California at Santa Cruz, where she received a bachelor's degree in political science. She has been recognized for her book, *The Mission: Waging War and Keeping Peace with American Military,* which earned her recognition as a finalist for a Pulitzer Prize in the category of books.

Notes

1. Dana Priest, "Long-Term Plan Sought for Terror Suspects," *Washington Post*, January 2, 2005. Additional quotes follow from this article.

2. Author's interview with Dana Priest, September 30, 2008.

3. Dana Priest, *The Mission: Waging War and Keeping Peace with America's Military* (New York: Norton, 2003).

4. Peter Finn, *Washington Post*, June 16, 2002.

5. Dana Priest, "CIA Avoids Scrutiny of Detainee Treatment," *Washington Post*, March 3, 2005. Additional quotes follow from this article.

6. Dana Priest and R. Jeffrey Smith, "CIA's Assurances on Transferred Suspects Doubted," *Washington Post*, March 17, 2005.

7. Providing information to a reporter that can be used—but not attributed to the name of the source—and can be used as quotes. An example would be, "According to a high administration official," or "a senior administration official."

8. White House, transcript of presidential press conference, March 16, 2005.

9. Ibid.

10. Bush's order stated, in section (2)c: "I accept the legal conclusion of the Department of Justice and determine that common Article 3 of Geneva does not apply to either al Qaeda or Taliban detainees, because, among other reasons, the relevant conflicts are international in scope and common Article 3 applies only to 'armed conflict not of an international character.'"

11. Dana Priest, interview, "The Dark Side," *Frontline*, PBS, June 20, 2006.

12. Dana Priest, "Italy Knew about Plan to Grab Suspect," *Washington Post*, June 30, 2005. Additional quotes follow from this article.

13. Author's interview with Priest.

14. Dana Priest, "CIA Holds Terror Suspects in Secret Prisons," *Washington Post*, November 2, 2005. Additional quotes follow from this article.

15. Emphasis added.

16. Author's interview with Priest.

17. White House briefing by Steven J. Hadley, November 2, 2005.

18. Dana Priest, "Foreign Network at Front of CIA's Terror Fight," *Washington Post*, November 18, 2005. Additional quotes follow from this article.

19. Author's interview with Priest.

20. Priest, "Foreign Network at Front." Additional quotes follow from this article.

21. Author's interview with Priest.

22. Dana Priest, "Wrongful Imprisonment: Anatomy of a CIA Mistake," *Washington Post*, December 4, 2005. Additional quotes follow from this article.

23. Dana Priest, "Covert CIA Program Withstands New Furor," *Washington Post*, December 30, 2005. Additional quotes follow from this article.

24. Jane Mayer, "The Black Sites," *New Yorker*, August 13, 2007.

25. Author's interview with Priest.

26. Dana Priest, interview, "Bush's War," *Frontline*, PBS, March 24, 2008.

27. Author's interview with Priest.

28. Dana Priest, interview, *Hardball with Chris Matthews*, MSNBC, November 17, 2004.

29. Author's interview with Priest.

30. Dana Priest, interview, *Meet the Press*, NBC-TV, April 27, 2006.

31. Author's interview with Priest.

32. Priest, *Meet the Press*.

33. *Rendition* was released on October 19, 2007. It was about an American family torn apart by an "extraordinary rendition" and was based on some of the information that had been published in Priest's dispatches.

CHAPTER 9

WALTER REED VETERANS ADMINISTRATION SCANDAL

Reported by Anne Hull and Dana Priest,
Washington Post, 2007

We've been given so many awards for these stories, but the real reward has come when individual soldiers and parents write us letters because their kid is in Iraq and is coming home. That kind of gratification you can never find.

—Anne Hull

One of America's most honored traditions is the care and treatment of its military men and women on the battlefield and after they return from war. For that reason alone, the story that hit the front page of the Sunday, February 18, 2007, issue of the *Washington Post* describing the neglect at America's premier Veterans Administration (VA) hospital—the Walter Reed Army Medical Center in Washington, D.C.—hit like a bolt of lightning. It described in detail the incredibly bad conditions in which veterans were living there: rotting floors, black mold in the rooms, mouse droppings, cockroaches, stained mattresses, urine- and feces-stained carpeting, and other horrifying conditions. The story shook the very foundations of America's faith in the institution that was supposed to care for those who put their lives on the line to protect the country. The conditions at Walter Reed were seen as symptomatic of how the war in Iraq was being managed by the Bush administration.

The story, the first of 10 in a series that was recognized with the highest possible honor journalists can receive—a Pulitzer Prize—was researched and written by Anne Hull and Dana Priest, reporters for the *Washington Post*, after an intensive, year-and-a-half investigation during which they literally embedded themselves and went entirely unnoticed by hospital officials. Their photographer, Michel Du Cille, also was awarded a Pulitzer. Their stories starkly pointed out that many wounded veterans were being totally neglected and, unable to manage their own medical care, elected to return to their families rather than remain trapped in what one observer described as "medical limbo."

In that first article, Hull and Priest emphasized the sorry conditions in Building 18, a converted lodge just outside the gates of the hospital nearby (and only a few miles from the White House, the reporters pointed out). It housed hundreds of maimed soldiers recuperating from injuries suffered in the wars in Iraq and Afghanistan.

"We used Building 18 as our lead story because the physical neglect of that building symbolized the larger neglect of the wounded soldiers," Anne Hull explained in a 2008 interview with me.[1] "The poor state of the building was a paperwork story—failure to process repair orders. Building 18 was something readers could understand immediately. They could see it."

I asked Hull how they got into the hospital, and she said: "We simply went onto post on our own. We bypassed the normal protocol of requesting permission to visit Walter Reed and be accompanied by an escort. We never lied about our identities. We presented our driver's licenses at the guard gates as all visitors do. Once on the post, we made sure to not bring attention to ourselves while reporting. We tried to never put ourselves in the position where [an official] might ask, 'Who are you?' As with any reporting, you try not to stand out from your subjects."

In their February 18 story, under the eye-opening headline "Soldiers Face Neglect, Frustration at Army's Top Medical Facility," Priest and Hull wrote:

> The common perception of Walter Reed is of a surgical hospital that shines as the crown jewel of military medicine. But 5 1/2 years of sustained combat have transformed the venerable 113-acre institution into something else entirely—a holding ground for physically and psychologically damaged outpatients. Almost 700 of them—the majority soldiers, with some Marines—have been released from hospital beds but still need treatment or are awaiting bureaucratic decisions before being discharged or returned to active duty.

They suffer from brain injuries, severed arms and legs, organ and back damage, and various degrees of post-traumatic stress. Their legions have grown so exponentially—they outnumber hospital patients at Walter Reed 17 to 1—that they take up every available bed on post and spill into dozens of nearby hotels and apartments leased by the Army. The average stay is 10 months, but some have been stuck there for as long as two years. . . .

On the worst days, soldiers say they feel like they are living a chapter of "Catch-22." The wounded manage other wounded. Soldiers dealing with psychological disorders of their own have been put in charge of others at risk of suicide. . . .

"We've done our duty. We fought the war. We came home wounded. Fine. But whoever the people are back here who are supposed to give us the easy transition should be doing it," said Marine Sgt. Ryan Groves, 26, an amputee who lived at Walter Reed for 16 months. "We don't know what to do. The people who are supposed to know don't have the answers. It's a nonstop process of stalling."[2]

Priest, an experienced reporter who had previously covered the Pentagon, had been tipped off in 2006 about the wretched conditions at Walter Reed. "I got a call from an acquaintance of mine," she said in an interview with me, "who said she had a friend who wanted to talk to me about bad conditions at Walter Reed and asked me if we could go to lunch. Her story was jaw-dropping. Too good not to check out. She had a couple of names, and both led me to some other people [related to soldiers in the hospital] and I started developing a network of sources. I asked my colleague at my paper, Anne Hull, to join me because she is such a great writer. I thought this was a real human story."[3]

This raised the question of how the two reporters remained in the hospital, unnoticed, and interviewed as many soldiers as they eventually did. "I know the military pretty well," Priest explained. "Anne had gone to Walter Reed through the front door [with prior approval of the Army] doing a story on Walter Reed in 2003 on the orthopedic ward.[4] She knew her away around.

We decided that, given the nature of the military, this was not going to be a story in which the Army would cooperate. So we just went in through the front door as Anne had done before and neither asked any questions nor were we stopped. We didn't have to lie about who we are. The people whom we quoted we had spent many hours with and we got to know them over long periods of time. And we said we were going to quote them, and they said okay. It was completely different from the officials involved in the rendition series (see chapter 8) that I had reported on previously [when no military official would cooperate]."

I asked Hull: "When you both finally went to the Army to tell them about your reporting and get some answers to your questions, how did that go?" "We confronted them with everything we'd found out during the previous four months," she replied. "Since we were off the radar, they didn't know we'd spent time on post. With Dana understanding the culture of the Pentagon, and wanting to give them ample time, we called on a Monday before their Sunday publication."

The two reporters submitted 30 questions, but purposely withheld any names; nor did they say how they did the story. They also did not specifically tell the Army about what they had found in Building 18. Walter Reed's commander, Army Maj. Gen. George W. Weightman, responded by asking them to come to his office. "It was all very nice. They realized we really knew what we were talking about," said Priest. "General Weightman was a complete professional. He didn't get angry. He tried to put the best face on it without lying."

When Hull and Priest were leaving, Priest said she told the general—because she had covered the military for so long she knew that what they hated more than bad news was not knowing that the bad news is coming—"I just want you to know that we have been up here [at Walter Reed] and you will see that in the story." He said, "Okay," and then added, "I suppose you're not coming to the press conference tomorrow?" Priest was stunned. "What press conference?"

"It turned out that he put on a preemptive press conference Friday," Priest explained, "which ended up kind of backfiring, because the other reporters couldn't figure out why they were there. Eventually they got the military to admit that there was a *Washington Post* story coming out. So all these Pentagon reporters were now really upset. Then on Saturday—the day before we went to press—we told the Army about Building 18. Meanwhile, the other reporters boycotted doing stories until the *Post*'s story came out."

Why did they wait until the last minute to get the answers to their questions? Hull answered this at a Nieman Foundation–sponsored journalism conference in 2008: "We wanted the full weight of what had been going on in that building to be in the paper. And we didn't want to give them a chance to clean it up and say, you know, 'Well, it's been cleaned up.' We'd been there four months; we thought, for sure, they would clean it up, because it wasn't that hard to do. But they never did. We felt it was fair in telling them at the last minute. We still got a 'I'll go right over there, ma'am.' And they went over there, and they came back, and that Saturday afternoon, we got a statement that included the fact that their roach and rodent abatement program had started several weeks ago, and they believed that it was making great progress."[5]

"It caused me to think less of the Army," Priest observed when I asked her about her reaction to the hasty press conference. "At that point, we had our stories written and there really was no way that the Army could have preempted us because they didn't have a clue as to how deeply we had reported on the conditions and the soldiers at Walter Reed."[6]

In their second story, the two reporters boldly stated:

> The conflict in Iraq has hatched a virtual town of desperation and dysfunction, clinging to the pilings of Walter Reed. The wounded are socked away for months and years in random buildings and barracks around this military post.
>
> The luckiest stay at Mologne House, a four-story hotel on a grassy slope behind the hospital.[7]

The duo said that after looking at the regular patients, they "discovered" soldiers in outpatient care. "That is where we literally stumbled into a civilization of 800 wounded soldiers who were at Walter Reed for as long as two or three years." Hull said. "The wounded soldiers were just being parked there and not being attended to. The amputees got the greatest care, because they had physical injuries, and they were also used [by the Army's public relations apparatus] as powerful symbols of American bravery.

The bulk of the soldiers were dealing with less physical injuries like traumatic brain injuries or psychological injuries. They were truly the hidden wounded population. They could not get anyone to pay attention to them. They were psychologically wounded. The ones with post-traumatic stress syndrome or other psychiatric issues truly had second-class status and were not given the attention they needed. Nor did Walter Reed in any way have enough psychologists and mental health care workers trained in combat trauma to give these soldiers any treatment. They were watching movies much of the time, even though they needed treatment for people who had been traumatized in battle."[8]

These were only the first barrages. The reporters told readers in their stories that they had spent hundreds of hours in Mologne House documenting the intimate struggles of the wounded who lived there. The reporting was done, they clearly stated, without either the knowledge or permission of Walter Reed officials, but those soldiers directly quoted—many had been there for 18 months or longer—agreed to be interviewed and were aware that Hull and Priest were *Washington Post* reporters.

At the 2008 journalism conference, Hull spoke about what she saw in Building 18: "When you contrast the picture of that cruddy room where a soldier who'd been blown up by an IED [improvised explosive device] is living under this mold with the shining promise the country has given these soldiers, it makes all the difference in the world. One way we knew that the story would come to life is by describing these moments in vivid detail and not just having a source describe them for us. We needed to see as much of it as possible, which is why we asked to sleep in the rooms of [different] soldiers. And what do you get from one night? It yields a whole bunch of stuff that ends up in a story," she replied. We had to see it with our own eyes; we can't have someone tell it to us. And that's one reason why the story was time-consuming, but it's also a reason that we hoped it popped to life in ways that traditional investigative reports often don't.

"In my usual narrative reporting, I'm used to submerging in a particular subculture, and the rest of the world kind of falls away. But in this story, we really needed to be conscious of building sources and fostering relationships with people who are going to pick up the phone and call and tell us something. So, by the end of the process, we probably had 10 subcontractor reporters at work for us, and they were soldiers and Marines. And it's because we kept greasing those relationships, which is traditional in Dana's world but less so in mine. For every one name that appeared in a story, there were 10 soldiers talking to us whose name never appeared in a story. We had this whole network of soldiers and Marines calling us all the time, and we babysat them, checked on them, and it was just a really intense relationship all that time."[9]

The second story, which appeared on February 19, headlined "The Hotel Aftermath; Inside Mologne House, the Survivors of War

Wrestle with Military Bureaucracy and Personal Demons," began: "The guests at Mologne House have been blown up, shot, crushed and shaken, and now their convalescence takes place among the chandeliers and wingback chairs of the 200-room hotel on the grounds of Walter Reed Army Medical Center."[10]

In a series of vignettes, the reporters told the whole, painful story. One 41-year-old soldier who had been there for a year and took 23 pills a day was in a constant panic, they wrote, despite comforting from his wife, who was with him. Another scrawny soldier sat alone in a wheelchair, his eyes closed, his chin dropped to his chest. Many soldiers, they observed, wandered the hallways trying to remember their room numbers because they were suffering from traumatic brain injuries; others took pills for depression or insomnia to stop nightmares and calm the nerves.

The third article, published on February 20, was subtitled "Walter Reed Official Had Own Charity." This was about corruption. It disclosed that, for years, Michael J. Wagner, director of "the Army's largest effort to help the most vulnerable soldiers" at the Army's Family Medical Assistance Center there, was misusing funds. Instead of funneling donors' money to help wounded soldiers who could not feed their children, pay mortgages, or buy plane tickets home, he allegedly used his position to solicit more than $200,000 in funds for his own private veterans' assistance charity organization in Texas—a clear conflict-of-interest, at the very least. The *Post* learned that he had resigned and that the hospital had already launched its own investigation through the Criminal Investigation Command.[11]

The first three articles drew an immediate and dramatic response from the government. On February 21, the *Post*'s headline summed it up: "Swift Action Promised at Walter Reed; Investigations Urged as Army Moves to Make Repairs, Improve Staffing." The story reported that both

> White House and congressional leaders called yesterday for swift investigation and repair of the problems plaguing outpatient care at Walter Reed, as veterans groups and members of Congress in both parties expressed outrage over substandard housing and the slow, dysfunctional bureaucracy there.[12]

Within 48 hours, they reported, Army Secretary Francis Harvey and Vice Chief of Staff Richard Cody toured Building 18 and spoke to soldiers as workers in protective masks stripped mold from the walls and tore up soiled carpets. At the White House, Press Secretary Tony Snow said that he had spoken with President Bush about Walter Reed and that the president had told him: "Find out what the problem is and fix it." Tellingly, Priest and Hull's article continued, Snow conceded that Bush "first learned of the troubling allegations regarding Walter Reed from the stories this weekend in the *Washington Post*. He is deeply concerned and wants any problems identified and fixed."

The fourth article of the series came out two weeks later on March 5, headlined "'It's Just Not Walter Reed'; Soldiers Share Troubling Stories of Military Health Care across U.S." After quoting the angry comments of some of the soldiers and their spouses at Walter Reed, Priest and Hull reported that

> the official reaction to the revelations at Walter Reed has been swift, and it has exposed the potential political costs of ignoring [the soldiers'] 24.3 million comrades—America's veterans—many of whom are among the last standing supporters of the Iraq war. In just two weeks, the Army secretary has been fired, a two-star general relieved of command and two special commissions appointed; congressional subcommittees are lining up for hearings . . . ; and the president, in his weekly radio address, redoubled promises to do right by the all-volunteer force.[13]

The story also focused on complaints from soldiers trapped in a place within the VA hospitals across the country referred to as "Medhold"—Medical Holding or Medical Holdover companies, which housed some 4,000 outpatients still suffering from physical or psychological wounds. At Walter Reed, the reporters wrote, the facility was in "bureaucratic disarray," the staff was "indifferent, untrained," and there were extraordinarily long waits for medical attention. The *Post* story also revealed that "nearly 64,000 of the more than 184,000 Iraq and Afghanistan war veterans who have sought VA health care had been diagnosed with potential symptoms of post-traumatic stress, drug abuse or other mental disorders."

This story again prompted immediate reactions from politicians on both sides of the aisle, especially the Democrats. On March 6, the day after this article appeared, Sen. Chuck Schumer (D-NY) charged at a press conference: "This is the Katrina of 2007," comparing the hospital scandal to the 2005 hurricane that left Gulf Coast residents stranded for days without federal assistance. There was no doubt that Priest and Hull had succeeded in arousing the enmity of the soldiers, Congress, the military establishment, and indeed the White House, including the president. All were forced into action as a direct result of the *Post*'s articles.

On March 6, in a speech to the American Legion in Washington, Bush named Democrat Donna Shalala, a former secretary of health and human services in the Clinton administration, and Republican Bob Dole, a former Republican presidential nominee, to head a commission to investigate problems at Walter Reed. "It's unacceptable to me, it's unacceptable to you, it's unacceptable to our country, and it's not going to continue," Bush said to anxious members of the Legion. And, in a rare moment of candor, he added: "My decisions have put our kids in harm's way. And I'm concerned about the fact that when they come back they don't get the full treatment they deserve."[14]

It was not until March 30—41 days after the *Post* broke the Walter Reed story—that the president visited the hospital. The *Post* reported that the president made

> a two-hour tour to publicly apologize for the physical and bureaucratic conditions inflicted upon soldiers recovering from injuries on faraway battlefields.
>
> The president inspected new accommodations for patients who had been living in squalid quarters and visited a physical therapy room to talk with soldiers who lost arms or legs in Iraq only to find them lost in a broken system back home. The stories they told him about their frustrations at Walter Reed, he said later, left him troubled and determined to resolve the soldiers' grievances.
>
> "I was disturbed by their [the soldiers'] accounts of what went wrong," he said in a speech to hospital staff members after the tour. "It is not right to have someone volunteer to wear our uniform and not get the best possible care. I apologize for what they went through, and we're going to fix the problem."[15]

That same night of March 30, Bush responded to a question on PBS's *NewsHour* about why the conditions at Walter Reed were allowed to occur. "The problems at Walter Reed were caused by bureaucratic and administrative failures," Bush said. "The system failed you, and it failed our troops, and we're going to fix it. I met some of the soldiers who had been housed in Building 18. I was disturbed by their accounts of what went wrong. It is not right to have someone volunteer to wear a uniform and not get the best possible care. I apologize for what they went through, and we're going to fix the problem."[16]

Article number 5, "The War Inside," published on June 17, 2007, continued to focus on getting the story across through interviews with individuals—perhaps the most effective journalistic technique available to investigative reporters, especially if it is filled out with a description of the individual and an empathetic picture of his or her dilemma. Priest and Hull were successful on both counts. In this article, they led off with the story of Army Spec. Jeans Cruz, one of the men who had helped capture Saddam Hussein—for which he had been honored upon his return home by the mayor of New York, officials for his hometown in Puerto Rico, and other dignitaries who heaped awards upon him, handed him their business cards, and urged him to call them.

What more could a soldier ask for?

Unfortunately, as the *Post*'s story continued, it was all downhill from there. "A 'black shadow' had followed Cruz home from Iraq, he confided to an Army counselor," Priest and Hull wrote. "He was hounded by recurring images of how war really was for him; not the triumphant scene of Hussein in handcuffs, but visions of dead Iraqi children."[17] The story continued:

> In public, the former Army scout stood tall for the cameras and marched in the parades. In private, he slashed his forearms to provoke the pain and adrenaline of combat. He heard voices and smelled stale blood. Soon the offers of help evaporated and he found himself estranged and alone, struggling with financial collapse and a darkening depression.

"None of that seemed to matter when his case reached VA disability evaluators," the reporters wrote.

> They turned him down flat, ruling that he deserved no compensation because his psychological problems existed before he joined the Army. They also said that Cruz had not proved he was ever in combat. "The available evidence is insufficient to confirm that you actually engaged in combat," his rejection letter stated.

The article reported that the VA would spend $2.8 billion in 2008 on mental health, "but the best it could offer Cruz was group therapy at the Bronx VA medical center." No sessions were "held on the weekends or late enough at night for him to attend," the reporters wrote.

"My experience so far is, you ask for something and they deny, deny, deny. After a while you just give up," the reporters quoted Cruz as telling them. In the end, Cruz was unable to get help from anyone. "Why can't I have a counselor with a phone number? I'd like someone to call," they quoted him as saying in desperation. "I have plaques on my wall—but nothing more than that."

The sixth story also ran on June 17, 2007, under the headline "Soldier Finds Comfort at Dark Journey's End." To balance their series—which is a "must" when doing investigative reporting—the *Post* reporters featured a soldier whose story had an upbeat ending. The article was about a female officer, Lt. Sylvia Blackwood, who, having "survived two tours in Iraq, first as a military journalist and then as a State Department spokeswoman," checked herself into Walter Reed's psychiatric ward after her second tour of duty because of extreme emotional problems she was having. "I don't have one event," she told the *Post* reporters, "I have a gazillion events. I have Iraqis pleading with me to get them out of the country. I have friends who turned up dead."[18]

According to this account, Blackwood took a job in media relations with the special inspector general for Iraq reconstruction, based in nearby Crystal City, Virginia. She did not tell anybody—except the *Post* reporters—that she could not sleep or eat, and that she was "clawing her forearms so fiercely the blood sometimes soaked through her sleeves." One day in the spring of 2007, the story went on, she panicked while on the Metro and decided not to return to work, triggering an overwhelming anxiety that she would not be able to support her son and that she might be sent back to Iraq.

When she finally got home, Blackwood told the reporters, she went to her bedroom and took out her Leatherman knife. With almost clinical detachment, they wrote, "she debated how to slash her wrists," but decided at 4 A.M. that she could not leave her son. By 7 A.M. she walked into a VA Medical Center in Washington, D.C., "crying so hard that her shoulders shook."

She was admitted to a "mixed-gender" ward with 26 men and three other women. The ward had "no exercise equipment. No indoor courtyard. No treatment either, other than prescription medication. The linoleum corridor was 39 paces long, and Black-wood walked it many times a day." She told the *Post* reporters, "There's nothing to do all day . . . and there's no air."

After talking with five different psychologists in her first few days, she said nobody offered any therapy. Fortunately, a friend of Blackwood's who was a military and VA surgeon told her: "We've got to get you out of here," according to the *Post* account. Sub-sequently she was moved to New York and then to Fort Thomas residential women's clinic in Kentucky, where she received person-alized mental health care. "It saved my life," she told the reporters. Were it not for her friend, the surgeon, however, there is no telling what might have happened to her.

On June 18, the seventh story by the two reporters was published, headlined "Little Relief on Ward 53." Once again the reporters offered insight into what was happening at Walter Reed through an individual soldier, PFC Joshua Calloway, 20, who was in the "locked-down psychiatric ward," a victim of PTSD—a condition that, according to the article, "in the Army alone outnumber[s] all of the war's amputees by 43 to 1."[19] Calloway had lasted for nine months in Iraq, the story related.

The first night in Walter Reed, the reporters wrote, "his dreams were infected by corpses. He tasted blood in his mouth. He was par-anoid and jumpy. He couldn't stop the movie inside his head of Sgt. Matthew Vosbein stepping on the bomb. His memory was shot. His insides burned."

The young soldier was still in a confused state. "I can't remember who I was before I went into the Army," he told the reporters. "Put me in a war for a year, my brain becomes a certain way. My brain is a big, black ball of crap with this brick wall in front of it." It took a week before he was stabilized and released, the reporters point out, "without a scratch."

The *Washington Post* reporters followed Calloway every step of the way from his arrival until his departure. "His physical metamorpho-sis was rapid," they wrote. "The burnished soldier turned soft and fat, gaining 20 pounds the first month from tranquilizers and micro-waved Chef Boyardee." After being sent to Mologne House, the hotel on the grounds, he gradually became angry. He left one day to ven-ture outside of the hospital to nearby Silver Spring, Maryland, the story reported, where he "became enraged" by the sight of young people laughing in a Starbucks. "Don't they know there is a war going on?" he said.

Anne Hull told me that she literally shadowed Calloway. "I spent hundreds of hours with Josh at Walter Reed, in his room where he was living in the barracks. I went out to eat with him. I went with him when he got tattoos. I went to movies with him," Hull said. "I continued to report on Josh at Walter Reed for the next three months. I continued going on to the post undetected. You would think the Army would have been more on their toes."[20]

Assigned to an Indian psychiatrist, Calloway—who was on a total of seven medications and had gained 30 pounds—exhibited a negative reaction, the story said, "to anyone he thought looked Iraqi, a paranoia shared by many of Walter Reed's wounded." Calloway told the doctor: "I want to kill Arabs."[21]

By his fourth month, his anger level had increased and he grew more hostile to therapy. He was allowed to leave the hospital to attend a VFW brunch in nearby Arlington, Virginia, but it didn't help. He remained in the hospital. One night he got drunk and wound up in the emergency room. "I'm losing my mind more and more while I'm here," he was quoted as saying.

Meanwhile, according to Priest and Hull, his relationship with his psychiatrist deteriorated, so the hospital provided him with another doctor, Lt. Col. Robert Forsten, who had been in combat in Iraq. Forsten agreed with Calloway that violence in Iraq was

> transforming and harrowing but said it should not define the rest of Calloway's life. The doctor also tried to reframe the experience. "You're a soldier," he said, according to Calloway. "You went to Iraq. You did your job."
>
> Something clicked for Calloway. . . . His physical evaluation board process was nearly complete, and he would be going home soon. His worries turned to what diagnosis the Army would give him and how he would be rated for disability pay.

Calloway was diagnosed with depression and chronic PTSD, which "had a 'definite impact' on his work and social capabilities." He was sent home to Cincinnati, receiving $815 a month and told to report to the VA hospital there for treatment. After eight months, however, Calloway's step-grandfather, Greg Albright, interviewed by the reporters, described him as "a grenade with the pin half-out."

That was a typical example of how the *Post* reporters not only embedded themselves inside the hospital but also followed the soldiers home after they were released to find out how they were doing. Never before had two reporters from a metropolitan Washington, D.C. newspaper involved themselves so deeply and intensely into the lives of the soldiers inside of Walter Reed.

When I interviewed Dana Priest, I asked her if she derived satisfaction from talking with the soldiers and their families for the series. She replied: "You know, I did. It was a unique experience . . . just gaining their confidence, understanding the depths of their problems and then watching some of them get their problems resolved. . . . For the first time in my life, I realized the true power we have, as journalists, to create change. As a journalist you go about your daily work life trying to get a story out or make someone's life better or shine a light on wrongdoing. Most of us don't seek to entertain, we seek to illuminate. Still, the chances to play a role in creating reform are rare. The Walter Reed stuff landed with a ferocious wallop. Washington— Congress, the Pentagon, the White House—all reacted in dramatic fashion. It was a reminder to everyone in the *Post* newsroom that journalism is still this mighty tool for good. You always think you know this basic fact but seeing it unfold so viscerally is a powerful reminder."[22]

Did any of the soldiers stay in touch with either of the reporters? I asked. "Yes, some of them do. We worked with them for a while," said Priest.

I followed up by inquiring about how long it took the two reporters to research and write all of their stories. "The first two stories took us six months," Priest responded. "Then we did about eight other stories, none of which took us six months, but we did spend a lot of time on them. We did it all in a year and a half."

How could they avoid getting emotionally involved with the soldiers in such trying circumstances? "I felt for them," Priest answered, "but in our stories, we retained our objectivity even though you are sitting there listening to this incredible injustice that could not be happening. It was an emotional experience sometimes. But when it came to actually writing this in your newspaper, you have to ask yourself: Is this true? Is every part of it true? And that's where the old journalist's brain is working away, saying, 'You know, I don't want to have anything overblown or any part of this be wrong.' Even though some of the interviews ended up being emotional experiences, when it came to putting the stories together we only wrote what we could be absolutely 100 percent certain of."

Did the two reporters double-check the stories they heard from the soldiers with other sources? "Yes, absolutely," said Priest. "We were doing that as we went along. We had many other sources. You know if a guy tells you he had his eye blown out in a sniper attack, we would confirm that by reading the official report."

Despite trying their best to retain their objectivity, Hull disclosed that there were a few times when she could not remain neutral and became emotional. Priest, too, admitted she was moved to tears once or twice. In one online interview, Priest recalled: "The depth of the injuries and the road to repair seemed so overwhelming for some of these soldiers and their families. Each story was the same, yet it was completely different; a different body part gone, a different, awful nightmare, and a different set of burdensome family or financial problems. The fact that they were living in such silence in the midst of all the thunderous clapping on their behalf was so powerful. . . . Even though some of these people may have brought me to tears and to the point of red-faced anger, when it came to writing the stories, I was totally cautious and diligent in not overstating anything. In this sense I didn't allow the emotions to do anything but help tell the objective story before us—in all its outrageousness."[23]

Anne Hull said in my interview with her that she and Priest gradually worked their way into the fabric of the life in Walter Reed by talking to wives first. "They were the most frustrated because in a sense they had to pick up all the pieces," said Hull. "Their husbands were injured and they had to deal with the injuries, with their kids, with everything. The wives had been fed up. They talked first. Some went on the record sand some did not want their names used. Little by little, we got to the soldiers this way.

It meant hanging around Walter Reed every day for months. I would never approach a soldier in a group of guys. I would wait until one went off by himself to smoke or to go to the cafeteria. I would not go up to a soldier and say, 'I am Anne Hull of the *Washington Post*.' I would find a way to speak to a soldier, you know, 'I overheard you complaining about not being able to see a psychologist,' and he would say, 'Yes.' I would say, 'I am a reporter.' I never gave my name.

We spent a lot of time watching, I could tell who was discontented or was having the most problems. I hung out where they smoked. I hung out at the bar. I could tell which ones were more eager to talk. I hung out where they lived at the Mologne House. I was embedded with the troops. We crossed the threshold because I had been hanging around so long I just became part of the scenery."[24]

What did you learn from spending so much time with the troops? I asked Hull. "You can't interview someone and ask what they are going through," Hull responded. "You have to be watching it. And when they get up in at five in the morning doped from all their tranquilizers and pain medications. I had to go with them to morning formation at 6 A.M. I could see it. The formation was dicey. That was a close call a few times. Dana and I both went separately. I guess I just looked like any other wife or girlfriend."

Story number 8 came out a few months later, on September 15. Its headline read: "Almost Home, but Facing More Delays at Walter Reed." This piece put the spotlight on Staff Sgt. John Daniel Shannon, who had been staying at Walter Reed as an outpatient for nearly three years. He was given a month's leave to move his family to Suffolk, Virginia.

Shannon had sustained a "traumatic brain injury from an AK-47 round that shattered one eye and half his skull." The aftereffect was chronic PTSD, which overwhelmed him for a time. He spent his first couple of weeks at home taking care of his two children, cleaning house and cooking, but not for long. Within a short time, his disability papers had expired, and he returned to Walter Reed to be reexamined. His medical summaries had to be rewritten because, as the *Post* story reported, "the sergeant in charge of his disability paperwork had not stayed on top of his case."[25]

The outlook was bleak: Nobody in the hospital could tell him when he would be able to go back to his family. Shannon was an outgoing man and "became an informal spokesman for his fellow patients." In fact, before he was forced to return, he had testified at a congressional hearing about his feelings that the Army was obligated to take care of its wounded. The story stated:

> Members of Congress and generals shook Shannon's hand and thanked him for his courage, while President Bush and Defense Secretary Robert M. Gates promised swift changes. Three panels were set up to study not only Walter Reed's failures, but the entire overburdened military medical-care system for returning soldiers and Marines five years into the war.

Despite all of this rhetoric, Shannon's records were mishandled, and he was back in the hospital

> "It's like being kicked in the teeth by a horse," Shannon said this week in a phone interview, alone in his room at Walter Reed. "I've been sitting here for three years. I don't even know

what 'going on with my life' means. I want to scream at the top of my lungs, I'm at the end of my rope."

The *Post* reporters noted that his case manager was "hard to reach." The story continued:

> Shannon and his wife were plunged into despair. Torry Shannon, who had spent two years caring for her husband and children at Walter Reed, had just started a house-cleaning business in Suffolk.
>
> The delay and sense of neglect seemed an echo of their early days at Walter Reed, when Shannon, with a bandaged head from surgery and on heavy pain medications, was released from the hospital with nothing more than a map and told to find his room across post by himself. He had sat for weeks without appointments and without anyone to check on him. The family had almost gone broke. At one point they lived five to a tiny room.
>
> Shannon, struggling with post-traumatic stress, was so angry that he broke things around the house, including his new Bluetooth earphone, which he smashed just thinking about all the new obstacles. His PTSD had been triggered, as it had been before, by the thought of soldiers treated disrespectfully. "It's about whether we're important enough," he said.

The ninth story, "A Wife's Battle," was published on October 14. The *Washington Post* reporters decided to go beyond Walter Reed to see what was happening, if anything, to a soldier as a result of the revelations at Walter Reed. Had any reforms caught up with former GIs? How were they being helped, if at all? These are only a few of the questions for which they sought answers.

Hull and Priest visited the home of Michelle and Troy Turner in Romney, West Virginia. Troy had served for a year in the Army in Baghdad and returned with PTSD and a possible brain injury. As the reporters entered their home, Michelle was on the telephone with the utility company, pleading with someone to keep their power on. "Can't you tell them I'm a veteran?" asked her 38-year-old husband. "Troy," she replied, "they don't care."[26]

After the disclosures by the *Post* of the VA wrongdoings, the article noted, "President Bush appointed a commission to study the care of the nation's war-wounded." The commission had made some "bold recommendations, including the creation of a national cadre of caseworkers and a complete overhaul of the military's disability system that compensates wounded soldiers."

"But so far," the story went on,

> little has been done to sort out the mess of bureaucracy or put more money in the hands of newly disabled soldiers who are fending off evictions and foreclosures.
>
> In the Turner house, that leaves an exhausted wife with chipped nail polish to hold up the family's collapsing world. "Stand Together," a banner at a local cafe reminds Michelle. But since Troy came back from Iraq in 2003, the burden of war is now hers.

The story went on to explain that Michelle "has spent hundreds of hours at the library researching complicated VA policies and disability regulations. 'You need two college degrees to understand any of it,'" she told the reporters. She had no college degree. Yet at the same time, she had the full responsibility for getting their two children ready for school, while attending to a husband whom the reporters described as "placidly medicated or randomly explosive." "He can't deal with the stress of living," she told them. "He can't make decisions. He's a worrywart. Fearful. It's like they took Troy and put him in a different person." Hull and Priest summed up the powerful vignette: "Troy's one-year war has become his wife's endless one."

Once again, through the experience of one couple, the two journalists told a compelling story that was designed to send an important message to the readers: the government had not yet done its job, even after months and months of newspaper stories, panels, commissions, congressional hearings, and promises of help for the VA from just about everyone appointed or elected to a government post who was empowered to do something. There was, in fact, no evidence anything had changed, in this one household, at least. And by using themselves as conduits of taking in everything they could absorb and then writing about it, Priest and Hull continued to perform a public service that must have been appreciated by veterans across the country. The reader could come to only one conclusion from this story: America had let this veteran down.

In an interview with me, Hull talked about how she followed Troy Turner home to West Virginia. "I found him later in the year and I wanted to write about how soldiers were getting stiffed on their disability and families were falling on near poverty status after they served their country. And I went to his home and spent a lot of time with the Turners." "Everybody in that town had a connection to Walter Reed," she said.[27]

The tenth and final story was headlined "A Patient Prosecuted" and was published on December 2, 2007. This was the climactic, and perhaps the most poignant, article in the series. It focused entirely on an officer whose promising military career, and even her life, nearly came to an end because of psychiatric problems that the Army could not deal with adequately.

The officer, 1st Lt. Elizabeth Whiteside, was accused of attempting suicide and of endangering the life of another soldier while serving in Iraq. Much has been written about similar incidents in the intervening years, but this particular story was extraordinary at the time because it was perhaps the first to concentrate on one officer who had turned on herself and her comrades. The account demonstrated the reporters' enterprising journalism and ability to obtain highly classified documents. The story opened with Lieutenant Whiteside in Walter Reed Hospital in a plain conference room first hearing the charges against her read aloud:

> Her hands trembled as Maj. Stefan Wolfe, the prosecutor, argued that Whiteside, now a psychiatric outpatient at Walter Reed, should be court-martialed. After seven years of exemplary service, the 25-year-old Army reservist faces the possibility of life in prison if she is tried and convicted.
>
> Military psychiatrists at Walter Reed who examined Whiteside after she recovered from her self-inflicted gunshot wound diagnosed her with a severe mental disorder, possibly triggered by the stresses of a war zone. But Whiteside's superiors considered her mental illness "an excuse" for criminal conduct, according to documents obtained by the *Washington Post*.[28]

The story then pointed out that beyond the Pentagon, there was no system for dealing with mental problems for military personnel—that the Army did it in an "ad hoc" manner, often depending on the views of tough military commanders who expected soldiers to do their jobs, no matter what the circumstances.

The two reporters found out that "under military law, soldiers who attempt suicide can be prosecuted under the theory that it affects the order and discipline of a unit and brings discredit to the armed forces." However, they reported that "criminal charges are extremely rare unless there was evidence that the attempt was an effort to avoid service or that it endangered others." At the time the story was published no decision had been made regarding Whiteside's case. The Army had to decide whether there was sufficient evidence to initiate a court-martial.

The reporters learned that Whiteside's father had also served in the Army and that she had enlisted in the Army Reserve in 2001 and later joined Reserve Officer Training Corps (ROTC) at the same time she was taking courses in economics at the University of Virginia. Ironically, her first assignment was at Walter Reed, where she was put in charge of 150 soldiers and officers. She was given a high evaluation with expectations that she would have a distinguished career.

> "This superior officer is in the top 10 percent of Officers I have worked with in my 16 years of military service," wrote her rater, Capt. Joel Grant. She "must be promoted immediately, ahead of all peers."
>
> Maj. Sandra Hersh, her senior rater, added: "She's a Soldier's Officer. . . . She is able to get the best from Soldiers and make it look easy."

With such an outstanding record, the *Post* piece went on, she felt she should volunteer to fight in Iraq. "Whiteside was assigned as a platoon leader" in a medical company based "at the Camp Cropper detainee prison near Baghdad International Airport." The *Post* story went into some detail: "The hot light from the Abu Ghraib abuse scandal still charged the atmosphere at Cropper, which housed 4,000 detainees and included high-security prisoners." She was nick-named "Trauma Mama," supervising medics on the night shift at the prison.

"I loved our mission," the story quoted Whiteside, "because it represented the best of America: taking care of the enemy, regardless of what they are doing to us." But there were problems: the long hours, only one meal a day, and seven days a week on shifts. Still, she was given high marks by her commanders. Then tensions developed between some of her women officer colleagues and a male officer; there were charges that the females were not being promoted, according to Army investigative documents the *Washington Post* obtained.

"As the tensions with the officer increased," the story went on,

> she began suffering panic attacks. She stopped sleeping, she
> said, and started self-medicating with NyQuil and Benadryl,
> but decided against seeking help from the mental health clinic
> because she feared that the Army would send her home, as it
> had recently done with a colonel.

Eventually, Whiteside resigned with a "general under honorable
conditions" discharge that would mean she would fail to receive
any benefits, according to her pro bono civilian attorney, Matthew J.
MacLean, the story continued. But it was not over yet.

The *Post*'s story added that Whiteside "still had the innate ability
to motivate soldiers. . . . Whiteside also offered encouragement over
the phone to her friend Sammantha Owen-Ewing, the soldier she
befriended on Ward 54 who had been abruptly dismissed from
the Army." What happened to Whiteside? I later inquired of Hull.
"She was exonerated of the charges," Hull said. The Army dropped
the case. "She left Walter Reed to go back to her home in Nevada.
It was a really tough case."[29]

When I interviewed the two reporters later,[30] I asked Anne Hull:
"What has happened to change procedures at Walter Reed since
the *Washington Post* series?" She responded: "A lot more money
has been put into caring for the wounded from the psychological
aspect. There is no such thing as Medical Housing Company.
It was done away with. Now it is called the Warrior Transition
Brigade. That's one result of our story. That is a progressive way
for the Army to care for the wounded and keep track of the
wounded."

I then asked her if she was satisfied that the military was stepping
up to the job. Hull replied without hesitating: "Not all. There is still
a lot of work left to be done. And the war is keeping it going. The
Army has been given a ton of money, but has not used it as wisely
as it could have. They are spending money on bureaucracy." Hull
added: "They are spending more money on psychologists, but they
are not willing to pay the market rate for psychologists, so they are
getting contract workers who don't know anything about the Army
and don't know anything about combat stress."

Looking back on the series with the passage of time, I asked Hull
how she viewed the whole assignment. How did it affect her views
of the war and the soldiers? "First of all," she explained, "Dana and

I worked on the story for months with hardly anyone at the paper knowing it. We worked on the story, and we were both senior reporters at the paper, so we had the freedom to spend time and not report to an editor every day. So we really worked under the radar of not just Walter Reed but also in the *Washington Post*. We wrote the story with the great help of our editor, David Maraniss [at the time an associate editor at the *Washington Post* and the author of four critically acclaimed and best-selling books]. He's a wonderful guy and he had just come off his own book on Vietnam, so he understood the veterans' psyche very well.

We really worked under the radar at our paper until the first stories broke, and then we had the support of the paper to continue on the story all year long. We could never have imagined the powerful response the story had. We get thousands of e-mails after the first stories ran, and to this day—it's nearly a year later—and I get 10 e-mails a day from soldiers and Marines looking for help. The *Washington Post* has come to 'own' the story of wounded soldier care."

I asked Dana Priest, "What should good investigative reporters learn from their experience?" like hers at Walter Reed. She said: "One of the things that I learned in doing this story is the importance of listening. The art of listening is so fundamental to what we do. And if you have a heightened ability to do that you can pick up so much. That person standing there, reading his body language, not a complainer, macho guy, not supposed to be wounded, not feeling comfortable enough to tell us the whole truth about the building because he didn't even know us. But there is just so much in his voice, and in the voices of a lot of people that we would talk with even though we didn't know their whole stories.

"Another thing is patience, in terms of building sources in particular. And it's people like we were dealing with who are not going to tell you everything. They don't know who you are exactly, and what you're doing exactly, and you don't want to actually tell them what you're doing. You might want to express an interest in finding out more about their life, but to be patient building those people as sources. When you're asking people to go deep into their personal lives or, in this case, stand up in a small or large way against their institution—which many of them depended on, loved, thought themselves a part of, and now they're being disillusioned by it—you just can't expect that to come out right away. So be patient, start with easy questions, easy subjects, and work to the harder things.

We took months to cultivate a lot of our sources and to get what we were really after. In this story and so many others, it's about context, context, context. The anecdotes you have, the personalities that you develop, the sources that you build—to me, they obviously all have a context. And we could only do that at Walter Reed after understanding, not only all of the anecdotes and systems, but then, too, the larger context of the Army and the war in Iraq."

In my interview with Hull, I inquired about how they went about writing their stories. Said Hull: "We wrote our own sections. We wrote our stories. Dana would write on one day, and I'd write the next. And then we went through that inevitable process of having to redraft, which we did a couple of times with the great help of David Maraniss, our editor, and this helped the pieces to have a unified voice. We didn't think so much about creating a beautiful piece of writing as we did accomplishing a goal, and that was to expose what the Army was doing. So we were not being super conscious of the writing, per se, other than the organization of it to maximize our anecdotes and to hit certain themes and to kind of tie it up that way."

How did they remain "under the radar" without anyone tipping off the Army? "We made sure that we stressed with each person we talked to, please don't tell anyone you're talking to us, especially your supervisor, but other people, too. And if you see us in public, don't acknowledge us. We pretty much lived and breathed that story for four or five months," Hull told me. "And even after its publication, we lived and breathed it because of the outpouring. For every e-mail that came in, there was often a tip, and we had to follow it up, so it never stopped, really. It still goes on. We are up there all the time."

"We often went there separately," Hull added, "because we could accomplish twice as much work and, if one got caught, it's better than two getting caught. So there was a strategy to how we went into the place. And we just reported like crazy for about three and a half months. And then spent a month writing and redrafting but continuing to report while we were writing and getting the piece redrafted and edited."

Curious about the details of how they reported, I asked: "As you were reporting, were you continuously writing notes?" Hull said they were. "We're both pretty good about keeping up with our notes, and we're both very organized. So when we would have a full notebook, or we had a day of reporting, we transcribed that night, and then we'd share with each other what we had. So everything was open between us, and we'd talk 15 times a day. If I went two hours without talking to Dana, it was really strange. And it still is really strange."

Did they have cameras? Priest answered: "We only used a camera once, without anyone noticing. We are both pretty low-tech. We took notes in certain ways when we were there so we would not draw attention to ourselves. We did tape-record some interviews with people that we had off post. And we had to learn the bureaucracy, since this is all about a bureaucracy failure, and then we had to learn about the Army structure. There were a lot of details we could scribble down, but they were still so murky. That was why sometimes it was good to have a tape recorder. And then we had some inside sources who could explain things, like how the brigades are organized and who the platoon sergeants are.

Other than one time when we did use a camera, we didn't take cameras or notebooks or other things that would identify us. If we did get caught and someone wasn't thinking you were a reporter, they're just wondering, well, why are you there? Or maybe someone would ask to look in your bag, which did happen. And you wouldn't have things that would stand out as identifying you with the paper. Then, hopefully, they wouldn't ask, 'Well, who are you with?' I mean, like, 'What organization are you with?' If you were with a soldier, you've got to brief the soldier so they don't lie about who you are, but maybe they don't totally disclose who you are, either. And so finding that phraseology is the key."

How did they handle having conversations with soldiers who did not want to be identified? Said Priest: "We did not identify those people. We made sure that they couldn't be identified when we used the quote. Everything else is completely attributed. It has to be." Priest added: "There are privacy rights involved, and so we were never going to put somebody's name, or even a descriptor with a blind quote, unless that person allowed us to do that. We have to respect that people there don't want everybody to know they're even there. So we had to use those rules."

Did the experience give her satisfaction? I asked Hull. "It was tremendously gratifying in that very rarely does a series get published and real reforms happen," Hull answered. "The Army cleaned up its act, and there is still a lot to do. The story appeared, all Hell broke loose, and the Army fired three high-ranking officials, including the secretary of the Army, and the Army approached the way wounded soldiers were handled from then on in a much better way."

Did she ever imagine that they would be able to accomplish so much as a result of being a reporter? "You're only as good as the story you working on," said Hull. "It's such an honor to be able to make a difference in people's lives. We've been given so many awards for these stories, but the real reward has come when individual soldiers and parents write us letters because their kid is in Iraq and is coming home. That kind of gratification you can never find." And the remarkable part of it all was that they had to travel no farther than nearby Walter Reed Hospital to gather their complete stories.

Hull said that Secretary of Defense Robert Gates "had a lot to do with a lot of reforms. [Secretary of Defense Donald] Rumsfeld never accepted any blame. Gates said a remarkable thing in May of 2007 at the Naval Academy. He gave the convocation and said, without the *Washington Post*, the public would never have known about all the problems about the Army Veterans Administration."

I asked Hull what she thought the future of investigative reporting would be for newspapers. "You really worry that there will be no room for this kind of investigative story in the future," she replied. "We were given the luxury of four months, two reporters, of working on a story that brought about incredible reform. It was a public service to our country. And I am worried now that, with all the newsroom staff cutbacks, this kind of reporting will not be invested in any more. That is really what I am worried about. Dana and I can still do it, but there are not a lot of reporters doing a follow-up on these investigative stories. I think for a small group of reporters this will be possible, but by and large it is going to become a diminished thing."

About Anne Hull

Anne Hull, who joined the *Washington Post* in 2000 after working for 15 years as a reporter for the *St. Petersburg Times*, has written broadly about a number of subjects ranging from the Iraq war to immigration. She has a reputation for becoming deeply involved in the lives of her stories' subjects. She is a Pulitzer Prize finalist many times over, and most recently won a Pulitzer Prize in 2008, for a series written with Dana Priest that investigated Walter Reed. Hull is a graduate of Florida State University and was honored as a Niemen Fellow at Harvard University in 1995. She also served on the Board of Trustees at the Poynter Institute for Media Studies. Her work has been used in academia, journalism textbooks, and journalism anthologies.

Notes

1. Author's interview with Anne Hull, September 8, 2008.

2. Dana Priest and Anne Hull, "Soldiers Face Neglect, Frustration at Army's Top Medical Facility," *Washington Post*, February 18, 2007.

3. Author's interview with Dana Priest, September 3, 2008.

4. Anne Hull and Tamara Jones, "The War after the War," *Washington Post*, July 20, 2003, and "Moving Forward, One Step at a Time: After Iraq, Wounded Soldiers Try Out New Lives," *Washington Post*, July 21, 2003. The two articles described the painful physical and psychological challenges soldiers who had returned from Iraq with missing limbs had to endure facing amputations and being fitted for prosthetics.

5. "Creating an Investigative Narrative, Based on a Q&A with Priest and Hull at the Nieman Foundation's 2008 Conference on Narrative Journalism, July 4–6, 2008," *Nieman Reports*, summer 2008.

6. Author's interview with Priest.

7. Anne Hull and Dana Priest, "The Hotel Aftermath," *Washington Post*, February 19, 2007.

8. Author's interview with Priest.

9. "Creating an Investigative Narrative."

10. Hull and Priest, "Hotel Aftermath." Additional quotes follow from this article.

11. Dana Priest and Anne Hull, "Hospital Investigates Former Aid Chief," *Washington Post*, February 20, 2007.

12. Dana Priest and Anne Hull, "Swift Action Promised at Walter Reed," *Washington Post*, February 21, 2007. Additional quotes follow from this article.

13. Anne Hull and Dana Priest, "It's Just Not Walter Reed," *Washington Post*, March 5, 2007. Additional quotes follow from this article.

14. Michael Luo, "Bush Appoints Dole and Shalala to Head Inquiry on Military Health Care," *New York Times*, March 7, 2007. The following March, the Veterans Affairs Department started deployment of an online comprehensive health care and benefits portal recommended by the President's Commission on Care for America's Returning Wounded Warriors.

15. Peter Baker, "At Walter Reed, Bush Offers an Apology," *Washington Post*, March 31, 2007.

16. George W. Bush, interview with Judy Woodruff, *The NewsHour with Jim Lehrer*, PBS, March 31, 2007.

17. Dana Priest and Anne Hull, "The War Inside," *Washington Post*, June 17, 2007. Additional quotes follow from this article.

18. Dana Priest and Anne Hull, "Soldier Finds Comfort at Dark Journey's End," *Washington Post*, June 17, 2007. Additional quotes follow from this article.

19. Anne Hull and Dana Priest, "Little Relief on Ward 53," *Washington Post*, June 18, 2007. Additional quotes follow from this article.

20. Author's interview with Hull.

21. Hull and Priest, "Little Relief on Ward 53." Additional quotes follow from this article.

22. Author's interview with Priest.

23. "Anatomy of a Pulitzer: Q&A with Hull and Priest," interview by Al Tompkins, *PoynterOnline*, 2008, http://www.poynter.org/column.asp?id=101&aid=141080.

24. Author's interview with Anne Hull, September 15, 2008.

25. Dana Priest and Anne Hull, "Almost Home, but Facing More Delays at Walter Reed," *Washington Post*, September 15, 2007. Additional quotes follow from this article.

26. Anne Hull and Dana Priest, "A Wife's Battle," *Washington Post*, October 14, 2007. Additional quotes follow from this article.

27. Author's interview with Hull.

28. Dana Priest and Anne Hull, "A Patient Prosecuted," *Washington Post*, December 2, 2007. Additional quotes follow from this article.

29. Author's interview with Hull.

30. Quotes in the remainder of the chapter are from the author's interviews with Dana Priest on September 3 and 8, 2008, and with Anne Hull on September 8 and 15, 2008.

CHAPTER 10

GUANTANAMO DETAINEES' STORIES

Reported by Tom Lasseter,
Miami Herald, *2008*

After interviewing detainees in their home countries following their release from Guantanamo, it became clear early on that there were a lot of detainees in that prison who did not have the sorts of intelligence the U.S. was seeking.
—Tom Lasseter, in an interview, 2009

In the years since 9/11 and the arrest and detention of hundreds of alleged terrorists at the controversial Guantanamo Bay Detention Camp in Cuba,[1] nobody from the media had ever pursued the idea of interviewing the detainees following their release from that prison and return to their countries. Nobody, that is, except for McClatchy Newspapers, and its *Miami Herald* in particular. Many influential Americans see the creation of a detention center at Guantanamo as one of the historic blunders in American legal and political history. President Barack Obama announced on his second day in office in 2009 that he was ordering that it be closed. But shutting the prison down and eliminating or cutting back on many of the so-called enhanced interrogation techniques, which many critics call torture, did not prove quite that easy.

The *Miami Herald*'s vivid, detailed profiles of the detainees and the moving stories they told after their release is now a significant part of journalism history. It was launched on Sunday, June 15, 2008, when McClatchy Newspapers' Washington Bureau released "Day 1" of a five-part series on "Guantanamo: Beyond the Law" for publication. It got major page 1 play around the country and was picked up and run by the broadcast media as well. Its summary minces few words:

> An eight-month McClatchy investigation of the detention system created after the September 11 terrorist attacks has found that the U.S. imprisoned innocent men, subjected them to abuse, stripped them of their legal rights and allowed Islamic militants to turn the prison camp at Guantanamo Bay, Cuba into a school for jihad.[2]

There were Senate hearings under way at the time about the treatment of Guantanamo detainees, and the White House was defending its policy by saying that the International Red Cross was able to go into Guantanamo Bay and other prisons and check out what was going on. The public had been aware of the issue of torture since the Bush administration approved it for selective use as far back as 2002. Two days after the *Miami Herald*'s first story hit the stands, on June 17, Assistant Press Secretary Tony Fratto was asked at a White House press briefing about the many abuses allegedly suffered by the detainees at Guantanamo. His pat answer reflected the fact that the Bush administration remained in denial: "I'm telling you that abuse of detainees has never been, is not, and will never be the policy of this government. The policy of this government has been to take these detainees and to interrogate them and get the information that we can get to help protect this country, which we have been very successful at doing, and we've been very successful at getting the information that has saved lives and prevented attacks on this country and on our allies."[3]

The groundbreaking concept of a series of interviews with 66 ex-Guantanamo detainees—published in the newspapers and online—was the brainchild of Roy Gutman and Mark Seibel, both McClatchy Washington bureau editors. Gutman told me in an interview that on his first day of work as foreign editor of the *Miami Herald* in the Washington, D.C., office in the National Press Building, December 18, 2006, he was asked to lunch by Mark Seibel, international editor for foreign news. They ate at Shelley's Backroom across the street from their offices. Seibel described the restaurant in a separate interview with me as "basically a tavern and cigar bar, somewhat out of place in Washington."[4]

In 2006, Gutman had just come from his job as diplomatic correspondent for *Newsweek*. He recalled: "We were just talking about what my job amounted to and I suggested to Mark that we ought to do a Guantanamo project on the former detainees. I think he had that idea, as well. It was a natural because at the time of the lunch, [Secretary of Defense Robert] Gates had just been in office for a few weeks and he had said he wanted to close Guantanamo. At *Newsweek*, we had just published a series of articles on Guantanamo and habeas corpus. Following the detainees home was a logical follow-up. I told Mark: 'I think we ought to find out where these people [detainees] are and interview them [about their experiences].' He agreed.

I had gone to Guantanamo when I was with *Newsweek* to talk to the commanders and to see everything I could see, which was next to nothing. That convinced me there are a huge number of people who should not have been in Guantanamo. I had a pretty good knowledge of the history of Guantanamo and what we would find. We started looking for those cases where detainees had lawyers, so we could track as many down as possible. I thought this was an immense injustice—to be holding people against their will."

After some discussion with the other editors, reporter Tom Lasseter was selected to be the lead reporter for the assignment. A tall, friendly, level-headed, Mississippi-born graduate of the University of Georgia, Lasseter had had a stint with the *Lexington* (Kentucky) *Herald* from 1999 to 2004. In March 2003, he also began going to Iraq on a regular basis for the Knight Ridder Washington bureau. During the spring of 2004, Lasseter was hired by the *Miami Herald*, but before moving to Miami, he was sent back to Iraq for two months, at the end of which the Knight Ridder Washington bureau hired him as a full-time Iraq correspondent. He started his Guantanamo project in the spring of 2007, at the age of 31. The two editors were confident Lasseter was up to the job.

They also got in touch with Matt Schofield, who was their European bureau chief at the time. The editors divided up the assignments, with Schofield covering Europe and Lasseter doing the interviewing in South Asia and the Persian Gulf area. Schofield, for his part, wrote 13 profiles or stories about individuals he interviewed, all of which were online. "I'm proud of the work that Tom did," Schofield shared with me. "When we started, we were hopeful of finding maybe 25 to 30 former detainees who would talk with us. When I reached 13, Tom was crushed, as we had made it a good-natured contest, who could find the most, and when we talked he was convinced he'd never catch up. But he left for Central Asia and worked himself to the bone. He did amazing work."

Gutman agreed: "Tom is an absolute genius as a reporter. He establishes a rapport very quickly with average people. He finds a way to make people comfortable. His reporting as an 'imbed' in Baghdad, which I had read before I got to McClatchy, was just stunning. He had already earned himself a special distinction as a great reporter. Mark [Seibel] suggested Lasseter would be a good person." Seibel added: "Lasseter is a digger. We wanted the person who would know how to do that best. It was a lot of legwork."

What was Lasseter's reaction? "Well, Gutman was my boss. I said that I'd do it, but I asked him for a better sense of how extensive a project he wanted to do. I asked him what's involved. And he said, 'What's involved is, it's going to be very involved.'"

"Roy called me in my hotel in Jordan," Lasseter continued. "And I had just gotten out of Iraq. My first reaction was that it was going to be complicated. That it would be hard. Having worked in Iraq off and on for three years, I knew there would be security issues of me being worried about detainees and they being worried about me. I told Roy on the phone that I saw it coming. It was weird. I had had a hunch I might be tapped for such an assignment. I knew from working in tribal areas in Iraq it would be hard. Afghanistan, a place I had never been to, would be a lot different but I suspected there would be some similarities in the difficulties of navigating tribal areas. I knew there would be a lot of suspicion on their side.

"Roy and I spoke on the phone a couple more times and he said, 'We're interested in investing a significant amount of time.' I said, 'I have a significant amount of time.' I was in Yemen with my wife, Megan Stack, a reporter for the *Los Angeles Times* who was working on some stories. That was it."

How did the editors go about planning the interviews of the ex-detainees? One might expect that they might have spent hours, if not days, laying out a specific plan about who should go where, how long the assignment would be, and exactly what they were looking for. In fact, they left all of that up to Lasseter, whose previous investigative reporting experience was invaluable; they knew that he would figure out how to go about such a challenging assignment—and he did. Lasseter dispatched himself with a list of detainees and the places they had fled to after being released.

"How did you get the entire list of detainees who were released?" I asked Gutman. "That was easy," he said. "When I did my earlier work at *Newsday*, those lists did not exist. In the interim, the ACLU [American Civil Liberties Union] and the AP [Associated Press] had forced the release of the list through the FOIA [Freedom of Information Act], and the *Miami Herald*'s Carol Rosenberg had the files on Guantanamo," he explained.

Rosenberg told me that she kept an extensive filing system on each detainee, which she had developed during the years that she covered Guantanamo starting with the arrival of the first detainees on January 11, 2002.[5] "It was during the years when the captives were nameless, nationless jumpsuits," she explained. "I started building the files with their military internment numbers. I figured out the identities of many long before the Department of Defense [DOD] finally released the document known as 'The List' in 2005 in response to various litigation and, more importantly, a leak by the staff judge advocate at Joint Task Force Gitmo [slang for Guantanamo]. By then, there were also habeas corpus petitions available. By the time Knight Ridder decided to do the series, I had leads on the whereabouts of some, and lists of folks who had been released and on what date by compiling DOD documents, transfer announcements, regional news stories, Saudi Press Agency reports in Arabic, court filings, and, in some instances, the ACLU and AP documents." She said she passed them on to Gutman, and he gave them to Lasseter and Schofield.

Lasseter said he initially got a list of detainees from Warren P. Strobel, in the D.C. bureau, who contributed to the series by gathering some information from his Washington sources. Lasseter called Strobel's list a great starting point, but there was some confusion about which detainees had been released. At the beginning, Lasseter said, he set up interviews through Western lawyers who had represented Guantanamo detainees who were released, and then in Afghanistan began finding the former detainees through a variety of means, including an Afghan government office that registered the men after they were released from Guantanamo. He cross-referenced the men he had interviewed with the first list of all Guantanamo detainees that the DOD had released.

I asked Gutman how he guided Lasseter in determining the truth of the statements coming from the detainees. "The best answer is in the profiles," he replied. "I asked Tom: 'Walk us through them. Imagine you are the reader. Tell the reader what the men said, and give your best judgment about the facts.' The proof is in reading the profiles. Somebody says this. Somebody else says that. Where is the truth? That's the only thing you can do in a case like this. Get as much information as possible from as many different sources as possible and let the reader make up his or her mind. The U.S. government probably doesn't know the truth—or could care less."

Mark Seibel responded to the same question this way: "We had a lot of discussion here about that. And the way that ultimately wound up being decided was that those stories are their accounts, so we were going to let their words be the way we told the story. But whenever possible, we looked for documents that gave the U.S. side of the story, or somebody else who might have some recollection of it. In the end, the profiles would have to be pretty much their version of events."

How did he feel about the Department of Defense failure to respond to Lasseter's questions? I asked Gutman.

He said: "Tom sent questions to DOD a good six months in advance, then three months. Did anybody from administration try to interfere? Nope. Nor did they ever comment on the results. My hunch is that [Secretary of Defense Robert] Gates and company in the higher reaches of the civilian side of DOD knew that we had it right. That was the basis for his decision to close Guantanamo as a prison.

My hunch is they might have been willing to answer our questions but they were under the thumb of the White House. We know where Gates was coming from. We know that Bush said one thing and Gates does another. We know that the White House manages messages closely. I have to guess it was a White House decision to in no way cooperate with us in doing the series. It was to their embarrassment.

It's important to note that nobody denied it. That gave us credibility. The truth is that two-thirds of the people at Guantanamo—maybe more—should have never been there. To admit this massive lie and this massive crime would have been political suicide."

The series was so comprehensive that not only did 25 of the 30 McClatchy newspapers run them in page 1, but many of its corporate subscribers across America did the same. Lasseter and Schofield filed a total of 180,000 words, much of which was edited down for purposes of sending the series out online, with the assistance of online editor, Beryl Adcock on the copy desk.

McClatchy also listed a guide on its Web site that enabled readers to tap into a description of the project; the full content of the five major stories that were published on June 15–19; an archive of documents obtained by McClatchy in the course of the investigation, as well as videotapes of the questioning of 10 key detainees; and a detainee profile database containing 66 profiles obtained by McClatchy in the basic file section of the investigation. In the interviews section, a reader can browse or search each of the individual detainees, whose photos appear on cards compiled by reporter Lasseter. In addition, there is another browser for images of detainees held at Guantanamo, detainees held in Afghanistan, and the faces of all the detainees that Lasseter interviewed.

Lasseter started out with this list of about 100 men in 11 countries—and that's as far as he could plan ahead. Over time, in travels that included everything from nearly being killed by a bomb to being entertained with warm hospitality by a few of the detainees' families, he would wind up successfully persuading, cajoling, pursuing, and convincing 66 of these men to bare their souls to him. Some of the interviews, which he conducted with pad and pencil rather than a tape recorder so as not to arouse any suspicions, took hours, even days—many former detainees would get up in the middle of an interview and leave, only to come back the next day. It was completely unpredictable, Lasseter said.

"There was a lot of distrust and apprehension," Lasseter told me. "I found that it was always best to be very clear and very honest and not to try and be clever. I would talk to them as I would talk with anyone else, particularly guys who had been through a series of interrogations. I think they would have picked up pretty quickly if I was being overly friendly or trying to ingratiate myself. We would sit down and I would pour them tea. If I was in their home, I would be a good guest. Like in Pakistan, several of the interviews I did at my hotel. I would invite them into my room, you know, I would treat them just like anyone coming into my hotel room in that culture."

As Gutman recalled: "Tom threw himself into it. He took a 12-hour train ride into Kazakhstan to get to one person there. He was willing to try everything. He throws himself into something with total alacrity. There are no limits for this guy. If there was somebody out there, he'd say, Well, maybe I will try that guy. One guy in Russia would not see him, but submitted to a five-hour phone interview from Afghanistan. After a good many interviews, we discovered a pattern: Saudi Arabia, Yemen, Afghanistan, and Pakistan were the primary countries from which they had come."

When asked about his first impressions, Lasseter responded: "It was pretty clear early on that there were a lot of people in Guantanamo who did not have, who were in no position to offer the sorts of intelligence the U.S. was looking for. Some of them were Taliban conscripts, some of them were Taliban grunts, some of them were criminals, some had killed the wrong guy's cousin and had gotten set up, some of them were in the wrong place at the wrong time. There was a myriad of reasons for people being in Guantanamo."

He continued: "There were frustrations within the intelligence and Defense Department in some quarters that the wrong guys were being sent to Guantanamo. It was also a problem because you had them there for two to three years, and in discouraging conditions, next to pretty serious radical jihadists who were only too happy to preach them sort of the word of radical jihad, and that's not constructive. If you're going out to kill or catch terrorists, you certainly don't want to run the risk of creating them. Particularly in places like Bagram and Kandahar, where the former detainees said the physical treatment was worse than the treatment in Guantanamo, and sending them to Guantanamo for years, where they were exposed to radical Islam, in many cases, was not constructive. Not only for the men, but not constructive for U.S. interests."

Following is a summary of each of the five major articles.

The initial headline read: "Day 1: America's Prison for Terrorists Often Held the Wrong Men." The story focused on one militant in Gardez, Afghanistan: Mohammed Akhtiar, who "was among the more than 770 terrorists imprisoned at the U.S. naval base at Guantanamo Bay, Cuba, after the Sept. 11, 2001, terrorist attacks. They are the men the Bush administration described as 'the worst of the worst,'" Lasseter wrote. Akhtiar told the *Miami Herald* reporter he had been mistakenly arrested in Afghanistan. Lasseter quickly confirmed this fact. "He was not an enemy of the government, he was a friend of the government," Lasseter was told by a senior Afghan intelligence officer. "Akhtiar was imprisoned at Guantanamo on the basis of false information that local antigovernment insurgents fed to U.S. troops, he said."[6]

Not only was Akhtiar not part of the Taliban, but he had escaped to Pakistan after the Islamist group took power in 1996, the Afghan intelligence officer told Lasseter. Akhtiar's house had been torched by the Taliban after he refused to ally his tribe with their government, Lasseter wrote. "The U.S. government had the wrong guy." Lasseter reported that Akhtiar had told him that during his military review board hearing at Guantanamo, Akhtiar addressed the U.S. officers in front of him and said: "I wish that the United States would realize who the bad guys are and who the good guys are."

The reporter also confirmed the long-held theory that instead of gathering intelligence, U.S. detention policies resulted in the opposite—support for extremist Islamist groups. "For some detainees who went home far more militant than when they arrived, Guantanamo became a school for jihad, or Islamic holy war," wrote Lasseter, while conceding that Guantanamo also held Khalid Sheikh Mohammed, "the alleged mastermind of the Sept. 11 attacks, who along with four other high-profile detainees faces military commission charges." He pointed out, however, that because the prisoners were allowed to be held indefinitely under the Bush administration's special rules, it was virtually impossible to learn how many of the men held in Guantanamo actually were terrorists.

As it turned out, Lasseter's timing on the first story was good. He included in this piece the fact that, just a week before he filed it,

> the [Bush] administration's attempts to keep the detainees beyond the law came crashing down. . . . The Supreme Court ruled . . . that detainees have the right to contest their cases in federal courts, and that a 2006 act of Congress forbidding them from doing so was unconstitutional. "Some of these petitioners have been in custody for six years with no definitive judicial determination as to the legality of their detention," the court said in its 5–4 decision, overturning Bush administration policy and two acts of Congress that codified it.

Gutman told me that Lasseter then called a former administration official—whom he promised anonymity because of the legal and political sensitivities of the issue—for comment. This source, Lasseter wrote, said that

> the legal decisions "probably made instances of abuse more likely. . . . My sense is that decisions taken at the top probably sent a signal that the old rules don't apply . . . certainly some people read what was coming out of Washington: The gloves are off, this isn't a Geneva world anymore."

Lasseter then did "due diligence" by calling the Pentagon for comment on his first story. The Pentagon declined to discuss his findings, but issued a statement to the effect that the all prisoners of the U.S. military are always treated "humanely" and that its policy is "to investigate credible complaints of abuse and to hold people accountable." The statement added that an al Qaeda manual it had obtained instructs prisoners not to tell the truth after they are released. "We typically do not respond to each and every allegation of abuse made by past and present detainees," the Pentagon statement added.

In order to convey the full impact of his story, Lasseter told his readers that the newspaper "in many cases did more research than either the U.S. military at Guantanamo, which often relied on secondhand accounts, or the detainees' lawyers, who relied mainly on the detainees' accounts." This could also be construed as a form of self-promotion, but that was not unusual with an extraordinary series like the one Lasseter was writing.

Lasseter reported that, of the 66 detainees he interviewed, his findings showed that "34 of them, about 52 percent, had connections with militant groups. At least 23 of those 34, however, were Taliban foot soldiers, conscripts, low-level volunteers or adventure-seekers who knew nothing about global terrorism." He said only seven of the detainees knew any terrorists of importance. Lasseter confirmed these findings by talking to high-ranking Defense Department officials, anonymously, sources he had developed even before leaving on the assignment. They confirmed, he reported, that "most of the prisoners at Guantanamo weren't terrorist masterminds but men who were of no intelligence value in the war on terrorism."

Lasseter was successful in getting former Army secretary Thomas White to talk on the record: White told him that "many detainees were 'swept up in the pot' by large operations conducted by Afghan troops allied with the Americans." Another former Pentagon official told Lasseter that he was shocked at times by the backgrounds of men held at Guantanamo. "Captured with weapons near the Pakistan border?" the official said. "The screening, the understanding of who we had was horrible," he added. "That's why we had so many useless people at Gitmo." Lasseter also put the story in perspective by reminding his readers:

> The Bush administration didn't launch a formal review of the detentions until a 2004 Supreme Court decision forced it to begin holding military tribunals at Guantanamo. The Supreme Court ruling last week said that the tribunals were deeply flawed, but it didn't close them down.

Lasseter's second story was headlined "Day 2: U.S. Abuse of Detainees Was Routine at Afghanistan Bases." In this article, published on June 16, Lasseter laid out in detail just how common the abuse of detainees was in Afghanistan, even before they were taken to Guantanamo. The dateline this time was Kabul, Afghanistan.

The story reported that the detainees were herded by U.S. soldiers "into holding pens of razor-sharp concertina wire."

> The guards kicked, kneed and punched many of the men until they collapsed in pain. U.S. troops shackled and dragged other detainees to small isolation rooms, then hung them by their wrists from chains dangling from the wire mesh ceiling.[7]

Lasseter reported that former guards whom he interviewed told him that Bagram prison in Afghanistan was also a "center of systematic brutality" for nearly two years. Lasseter's investigation found that Bagram, an old Soviet airstrip about 30 miles outside Kabul, was the most violent of the major U.S. detention centers. "The brutality at Bagram peaked in December 2002," Lasseter reported, "when U.S. soldiers beat two Afghan detainees . . . to death as they hung by their wrists."

Lasseter wrote that even though other national newspapers—including the *New York Times*—had previously disclosed some of what had happened at Guantanamo, "the extent of the mistreatment, and that it eclipsed the alleged abuse at Guantanamo, hasn't previously been revealed." The young reporter also noted that even in two cases where detainees died after they had been beaten by American guards, no serious punishments had been handed out.

The article told the grim story of how one prisoner had "been hit in his leg so many times that the tissue was 'falling apart' and had 'basically been pulpified,'" according to Lt. Col. Elizabeth Rouse, the Air Force medical examiner who performed the autopsy on him.

Lasseter wrote that many of the atrocities that he discovered had not been officially reported "because President Bush loosened or eliminated the rules governing the treatment of so-called enemy combatants." He also stated that the Bush administration was refusing to release full records of detainee treatment, and nobody from the administration would agree to an on-the-record interview to respond to the findings published in his stories.

"Although they were at Bagram at different times and speak different languages, the 28 former detainees who told [Lasseter] that they'd been abused there told strikingly similar stories": of troops chaining them to the ceiling by their hands or feet while they were punched repeatedly; of being kicked in the head like a soccer ball; of being beaten; of guards threatening to rape them. Lasseter quoted Sgt. Selena Salcedo, a U.S. military intelligence officer, saying that she saw another interrogator "pull down the pants of a detainee and leave his genitals exposed."

And so it went, story after story—all geared to vividly describe the suffering and complete stripping of human dignity of the detainees. Lasseter named the detainees and quoted all of them. It was tough reading, especially in light of the fact that, Lasseter revealed, most of the American soldiers themselves were "untrained and undisciplined." Lasseter cited chapter and verse of the military police rulebook—but few, if any, of those inflicting torture had ever seen or read it.

"Good order and discipline had evaporated," he concluded. He summed up this article by quoting an American soldier: "Really, nobody was in charge . . . the leadership did nothing to help us. If we had any questions, it was pretty much 'figure it out on your own.' When you asked about protocol they said it's a work in progress."

Once again, Lasseter noted, Army officials refused to be interviewed. In response to written questions, Col. Gary Keck, a Defense Department spokesman, released this statement: "The Department of Defense policy is clear—we treat all detainees humanely. The United States operates safe, humane and professional detention operations for unlawful enemy combatants at war with this country."

"Day 3" of the Guantanamo detainee series, on June 17, 2008, started off with a bang:

> GARDEZ, Afghanistan—Mohammed Naim Farouq was a thug in the lawless Zormat district of eastern Afghanistan. He ran a kidnapping and extortion racket, and he controlled his turf with a band of gunmen who rode around in trucks with AK-47 rifles.
>
> U.S. troops detained him in 2002, although he had no clear ties to the Taliban or al Qaida. By the time Farouq was released from Guantanamo the next year, however—after more than 12 months of what he described as abuse and humiliation at the hands of American soldiers—he'd made connections to high-level militants.
>
> In fact, he'd become a Taliban leader. When the U.S. Defense Intelligence Agency released a stack of 20 "most wanted" playing

cards in 2006 identifying militants in Afghanistan and Pakistan—with Osama bin Laden at the top—Farouq was 16 cards into the deck.[8]

One U.S. military officer conceded that he had to make "the assumption that there's a fully functional al Qaida cell here at Guantanamo." Further, he confirmed that Afghan and Pakistani officials, too, were aware that Guantanamo was creating militant leaders. Lasseter also latched on to a classified 2005 Pakistani intelligence review of 35 prisoners which stated unequivocally that the majority of prisoners had been subjected to "severe mental and physical torture" and that they had built up "extreme feelings of resentment and hatred against USA."

Lasseter added that, in the course of his scores of interviews of U.S. officials, DOD officers acknowledged the mushrooming problem of turning the detainees against America, but nobody would go on the record. Lasseter's conclusion: "U.S. officials mistakenly sent a lot of men who weren't hardened terrorists to Guantanamo, but by the time they were released, some of them had become just that." And the recruiting continued after the detainees were released, his story said.

The Americans tried to separate the prisoners into groups. "The idea," he wrote, "was that detainees who presented graver threats and were uncooperative would be separated from those with looser ties to international terrorism." But once again, the U.S. plan was undermined, he reported. Many of the hardened detainees pretended to go along with the plan, but remained quiet. "As a result," Lasseter continued, "some senior radicals ended up in Camp Four [the facility for the 'best-behaved detainees'], free to preach their message of international jihad to petty criminals, Taliban conscripts and detainees who had little or no previous affiliation with Islamic militancy."

A sidebar appeared next to this article on June 17, with a dateline from Kuwait City, where Guantanamo detainees told stories that were now very familiar to Lasseter of American soldiers and interrogators disrespecting the Quran in detention facilities at Bagram, Kandahar, and Guantanamo. Lasseter heard from former detainees in Jordan, Russia, Kuwait, Pakistan, and Afghanistan that from late 2001 to early 2002, "soldiers at Kandahar dropped Qurans into buckets used as latrines."[9]

Lasseter wrote about a Russian detainee who was held at Kandahar for about six months in 2002 before he was transferred to Guantanamo. The Russian related this story to him: "I approached a guard one time and said it was no good to do this because it would provoke unrest amongst the prisoners; that while we were unarmed, this book was the most holy thing in the world for us, and that it would be better for them if they stopped doing these things."

To put this in perspective, however, Lasseter cautions his readers that these stories were repeated so many times by so many people that it was virtually impossible to fasten onto the truth of the matter. Lasseter did say that nine incidents of alleged mishandling of the Quran at Guantanamo were reported by U.S. officials, five of which were confirmed.

The issue of abuse of the Quran at Kandahar and elsewhere was one of the questions that Lasseter submitted to the Defense Department for comment. Senior defense officials repeatedly turned down requests for interviews, but Pentagon spokesman Col. Gary Keck said—amazingly—"We heard many times the allegations about Qurans thrown into buckets that were used as latrines. There have been some [instances] where it's been substantiated, I think." He obviously caught the officer off guard, because afterward, wrote Lasseter, "Keck quickly sent a follow-up e-mail saying that he assumed that the conversation wasn't for reporting purposes."

But that was not the end of this tricky incident, which turned out to be a lesson in reporting for the Army official, who found himself backpedaling. As Lasseter wrote the story:

> Told that the reporter considered all conversations with public-affairs officials to be on the record—but that there were no immediate plans to use the interview material—Keck sent a second note, saying, "My only concern here is that I have researched nothing specifically on the information we discussed, so if you need an on-the-record quote, I would have to try to determine the facts. I was speaking in general on the subject of detention operations, it is not my expertise. I would hate for you to use inaccurate information."
>
> Keck didn't supply any additional information in subsequent conversations.

What's most fascinating about this account, however, is the fullness of reportage—especially the candor and honesty with which Lasseter related exactly what happened.

"Day 4: Deck Stacked against Detainees in Legal Proceedings" was published on June 18, 2008. This time Lasseter filed his story from

Khost, Afghanistan, and it dealt mainly with what detainees told him about how one-sidedly the so-called military tribunals were handled. Lasseter reviewed the tribunal transcripts and then interviewed those detainees he could find who had gone through them. He wrote that, on the basis of his readings and his interviews, he concluded that "the tribunals consistently failed to distinguish hard-core international terrorists from low-level fighters and innocents."[10]

At about this time, it should be noted, the U.S. Supreme Court "sharply criticized the tribunals, [but] stopped short of ruling them illegal."

The "most serious flaw" in the process, Lasseter reported, was that none of the detainees "was able to submit testimony from witnesses outside" Guantanamo. In an action not normally carried out by a reporter—newsmen are not supposed to get involved with the stories they cover—Lasseter took it upon himself to find one witness: Mohammed Mustafa, who was the Afghan Interior Ministry's security chief for Khost from late 2001 to mid-2003. He confirmed much of a story of one detainee, Swatkhan Bahar, whom Lasseter said was begging for help. Bahar had been accused of helping the Taliban attack American soldiers, according to an unclassified transcript of the proceedings. Bahar—who had been held at Guantanamo for more than four years—pleaded with him to speak with someone from Afghanistan "and you will find out who I am. I am an employee of the Afghan Interior Ministry in Khost, and a friend of the Americans." A Marine colonel had said that there were no witnesses available outside of the prison to testify in his behalf. Lasseter believed otherwise and found Mustafa.

Lasseter questioned the officers in charge of the hearing processes and found that there were no specific criteria to go by in terms of prisoners who were released or who were referred to military commissions. "There are no specific criteria," Brig. Gen. Thomas Hartmann, a legal adviser to the convening authority for the office of military commissions, told Lasseter. "There's no specific science, but it is based on experience and the seriousness of the war crimes."

Lasseter's reporting left no doubt that the system was deeply flawed. His ability to get uniformed officers to speak to him on the record reflects Lasseter's powers of persuasion, and also points to the honesty of some American soldiers.

The fact that Lasseter went far out of his way to find witnesses outside of Guantanamo to support some of the detainees can be seen as a marked departure from objective journalism. But without question, Lasseter himself got wrapped up in the scene he was covering and felt compelled to seek justice even if it meant compromising the journalistic process. Many of his colleagues have told Lasseter they would have done the same thing.

A sidebar published with this article stated that the United States had not apologized to or compensated any of the ex-detainees.[11]

The fifth and final article of the series was published on June 19. It concentrated on how a Taliban ambassador wielded power within Guantanamo. Filed with a dateline from Kabul, it led off with this anecdote:

> When U.S. guards frog-marched Abdul Salam Zaeef through the cellblocks of Guantanamo, detainees would roar his name, "Mullah Zaeef! Mullah Zaeef!" Zaeef, in shackles, looked at the guards and smiled. "The soldiers told me, 'You are the king of the prison.'"[12]

Lasseter explained that Zaeef was the former Taliban ambassador to Pakistan known "for his defiant press conferences after 9/11, in which he said that the militant Islamist group would never surrender Osama bin Laden."

Zaeef told Lasseter that "Pakistani intelligence officers dragged him out of his house in Islamabad in late December 2001 or January 2002 and took him to Peshawar. 'Your Excellency, you are no longer Your Excellency,' he recalled one of them saying." He was then handed over to U.S. troops, a sack thrown over his head, and flown to a warship, "where he was held for about a week in a small cell that reminded him of a dog kennel," Lasseter wrote. He told Lasseter in an interview in Kabul that "I was afraid about what would happen to me. . . . I don't know if it was a dream or not. I never imagined this would happen to me."

But, as Lasseter related, during the next three years as a prisoner in Guantanamo, "Zaeef became a leader again. He helped orchestrate hunger strikes and exploit the missteps of a U.S. detention system that often captured the wrong men, mistreated them, and then incarcerated them indefinitely without legal recourse." Toward the end of this interview, Lasseter asked Zaeef if his time in Guantanamo had changed him, and he told Lasseter that "it only further convinced him that America was the enemy of Islam."

The entire article about Zaeef illustrates how a journalist with initiative can pick out one individual and, through that individual, tell a major story. In the case of Abdul Salam Zaeef, it brought to readers the full emotional and physical impact of this detainee's experience and how it only served to make him a great deal more bitter toward the United States than he was before he was taken prisoner.

Looking back on how he imagined the series and how it turned out, Roy Gutman observed: "It takes a special kind of investigative reporter to do this kind of thing. What are the special qualifications an individual should have to do this? Tenacity is a key element. Patience. Curiosity. A knowledge of war. And a familiarity with the history of the country in which he is involved. He has to have the guts to go into areas which are unsafe.

"I thought at times he was taking big risks, and I just told him to minimize the risks. I asked him to check in with me every day. He is sure-footed. He doesn't make many mistakes. What I found most fascinating with Tom is that this was his kind of story. He was talking to average people and trying to construct a little facet of a very big picture. He was always working on the big picture, so he was comparing notes between individuals and building rapport with individuals, and moving from one interview to the next guy. Always building. Tom really was evolving a story. The major themes that came out of it were really out of his reporting.

The thing I most admire about the product today is that it emerged from the ground up from pieces that were collected painstakingly in the field at some risk. But the mosaic is something that Tom assembled piece by piece until you could see the picture. You've got to have a mind that is good at assembling information. I knew enough of the basics—I knew the essence of the story, I thought. But I didn't know the details, and I didn't know the design. Take the 'school of jihad' day. We had all heard this. You can imagine this being the case, but to prove that it actually produced jihadists rather than reduced the number of them. . . . I could not imagine that piece coming out of this series. And the 'King of Guantanamo'—I could have never imagined that."

For himself, Lasseter, calm and cool as ever, responded to my question about whether he ever felt his life was in danger this way: "Yes. Absolutely. That's something to keep in mind in a place like Afghanistan or depending on where you are. You have to keep in mind that some of these guys had ties with militants who had been released, and that you are operating in areas where there is a considerable security threat, particularly kidnapping threat. It's very real in places like Afghanistan."

Were there any moments when he thought he was in imminent danger, when he thought somebody might kidnap him? How close did he come to real danger? Lasseter recalled this story: "One day I was driving, and we ended up getting stuck behind a U.S. convoy. I've got a beard and a hood, and I'd never driven from Galabad to Kabul before. We were behind this convoy, and a couple of times I got too close by mistake and the gunner in front of me swiveled his gun around and pointed at me, and I kept wishing there was some signal I could give to tell him who I was. But at the same time, I didn't want the cars around me to know who I was. I slowed down. I kept hoping the convoy would turn off. I was behind that thing forever. I was worried about getting too close to this convoy and getting shot."

I asked him if he worried about improvised explosive devices (IEDs). "The only time I worried about that was when I was close to a convoy that might get targeted. I had a driver and a translator most of the time," he responded.

Did he ever come across or come near a scene of battle or combat? I followed up. "When we were in Kandahar, we would hear shooting at night. And in Gardez. But we didn't get caught in firefight or anything like that.

Another time, we were in Gardez. We were staying in this tribal guest house and the guard came down, very wide-eyed and said: 'You have to leave right now. We cannot guarantee your safety,' which is sort of against a culture like Afghanistan. It was a big deal. But it was too late at night. I told them it would have been instructive to tell us earlier. We wake up at 5 o'clock in the morning and leave, but we're not going anywhere tonight. The problem is the interviews took so long like in Gardez, where we were the host. Kandahar, you were going someplace and sitting for some time. But the security environment was such that you were not supposed to be in one place for too long. I was inside most of the time—hotels, their houses, tribal guest houses, coffee shops, restaurants."

Lasseter said he took notes most of the time, but occasionally used a tape recorder after he felt he had the confidence of the detainee he was interviewing. "Notes? I did both. If I got their trust, I would use tape recorders. When I had digital recordings, I put them on the Internet to McClatchy. Of the 66 detainees, I interviewed 50 and maybe 6 to 7 hours per interview per person.

"We did a Web package through the D.C. bureau where you can call up a guy's profile and record a snippet. You could move to the audio on their profile, and we had a videographer come to Afghanistan with me in late April of 2008 to shoot some pictures and some video."

"Looking back on the whole thing, how do you view your whole experience?" I asked Lasseter. He responded: "I had worked with a team of reporters about drugs in eastern Kentucky when I was working at the paper in Lexington, Kentucky. I broke out a chunk and did a narrative project where I spent a lot of time with con-victed but not yet sentenced drug traffickers. The format pieced together a narrative of this one drug dealer's sort of odyssey. I thought about that project a lot during the Gitmo series because a lot of the time I told them I had spoken with others detainees. . . . It involved a lot of times going through not-well-worn paths. Driving up to a drug dealer's house reminded me of going to meet some-body in Afghanistan."

Did he find anyone who was only too happy get things off their chests?

"No. It was not a cathartic experience. There was a lot of suspicion to begin with. One of them said he was waterboarded in Jalalabad in Afghanistan. Waterboarding was more a technique used by the CIA, and most of these guys had gone through the DOD chain of custody."

I asked: "Did they say they were tortured?" "Many of them did, yes," he said.

How did he go about it in such an anecdotal way?

"I went through many drafts. Initially we were going to have two versions of each story—a much longer version and a shorter version for the Internet. We decided that was too much to move all of that, so we ended up melding those two versions. It ended up being an awful lot of drafts and multiple versions. Eight months of reporting and a few months of writing and editing, and then when it came about to run, I went over the stories in the D.C. bureau five days a week just going through all of this stuff with Roy [Gutman] and our fantastic copy desk chief Beryl Adcock. Mark Seibel had worked at drafts and written up a memo offering conceptual guidance. I was more involved with editors, discussing what to run and in deciding where the sidebars should go."

After the release of many detainees at the prison in Guantanamo Bay, the reporters at McClatchy set out to track down as many freed prisoners as possible to see what had become of them. Who were the men imprisoned in this facility? How had they been treated? This series explored these questions, and found that a majority of the prisoners were at Guantanamo based on faulty evidence or testimony. They were not even involved in the terrorist attacks.

The award-winning project,[13] which included five major articles and numerous sidebars, comprised 78 stories totaling 108,000 words. Perhaps the most incisive comment that could be made about this extraordinary series came from the one man who was most responsible for creating and guiding it from start to finish: foreign editor Roy Gutman. He told me: "It contributed to public knowledge and understanding of America's shameful policies in a way you can't quite measure. It was worth every bit of energy the entire team put into it."

About Tom Lasseter

Born in 1976 in Biloxi, Mississippi, Tom Lasseter graduated from the University of Georgia in 1999 and then went to work at the *Lexington* (Kentucky) *Herald-Leader* from 1999 to 2004. He began covering Iraq for the Knight Ridder Washington bureau in March 2003, and continued rotating there on a regular basis. He was hired by the *Miami Herald* in the spring of 2004, went back to Iraq for two rotations, and then, before heading to Miami to start his job, was hired on full-time by the Knight Ridder Washington bureau. After completing his series on the Guantanamo detainees, he was assigned to Moscow in April 2008. In 2005, he and his fellow news team members won a National Headliners Award for "How the Bush Administration Went to War in Iraq."

Notes

1. Guantanamo Bay is the location of a major U.S. naval station, leased to the United States in 1903.

2. "About This Series," *Guantanamo: Beyond the Law,* http://www.mcclatchydc.com/guantanamo/.

3. Tony Fratto, White House press briefing, June 17, 2008.

4. Unless otherwise noted, quotes in this chapter are from the author's interviews with Mark Seibel on April 6, 2009; Roy Gutman on April 11, 2009; Tom Lasseter on April 17, 2009; Matt Schofield on April 20, 2009; and Carol Rosenberg on April 25, 2009.

5. Rosenberg said she reconstructed the detainee files in Guantanamo, first through internment serial numbers (ISNs), and later with names. Rosenberg also proposed a systematic effort in a bid to learn a number of things, the basis of which became the outlines of their effort. A survey was developed that the freed detainees would understand. Rosenberg reported that she wound up with a 66-detainee sample, "some of whom had never spoken with other reporters or human rights groups."

6. Tom Lasseter, "Day 1: America's Prison for Terrorists Often Held the Wrong Men," *Miami Herald*, June 15, 2008. Additional quotes follow from this article.

7. Tom Lasseter, "Day 2: U.S. Abuse of Detainees Was Routine at Afghanistan Bases," *Miami Herald*, June 16, 2008. Additional quotes follow from this article.

8. Tom Lasseter, "Day 3: Militants Found Recruits among Guantanamo's Wrongly Detained," *Miami Herald*, June 17, 2008. Additional quotes follow from this article.

9. Tom Lasseter, "Ex-detainees Say U.S. Troops Abused Quran," *Miami Herald*, June 17, 2008. Additional quotes follow from this article.

10. Tom Lasseter, "Day 4: Deck Stacked against Detainees in Legal Proceedings," *Miami Herald*, June 18, 2008. Additional quotes follow from this article.

11. Tom Lasseter, "Day 4: U.S. Hasn't Apologized to or Compensated Ex-detainees," *Miami Herald*, June 18, 2008.

12. Tom Lasseter, "Day 5: Taliban Ambassador Wielded Power within Guantanamo," *Miami Herald*, June 19, 2008. Additional quotes follow from this article.

13. The Investigative Reporters and Editors (IRE), a prestigious organization of watchdog journalists, gave an award to McClatchy, stating: "The five-part series included an extensive Internet component, with a searchable database, individual stories on each detainee, videos of the detainees and an official archive of official U.S. documents. It allowed the American public to find out what really happened at Gitmo and other American detention camps."

Epilogue

The scandals analyzed in this book are intended to offer a sampling of some of the finest investigative journalism in America at the close of the 20th century and the beginning of the 21st. While this extraordinary group of journalists stands out among the icons of investigative reporters in recent decades, scores of other investigative reporters were digging up scandals and writing about the abuse of power at all levels of government, as well as in business and finance and in other walks of life across America.

These reporters have been recognized, wherever they worked, by their colleagues in the profession for their achievements not only in newspaper reporting but also in radio, television, magazines, and increasingly in the "new journalism" of the blogosphere.

For those who thrived during that era, the transformation from lengthy, well-researched series of stories exposing wrongdoing to another form of investigative reporting online that is in the process of being shaped can be traumatic. There is a great deal of handwringing going on in the early phase of a new century about exactly what the future of newspapers—and by the same token, the future of investigative reporting—will be like. No doubt, we are living through a historic transition of the news business on a worldwide scale that will change radically in generations to come.

We have already touched on the inevitable move to online journalism and cited some of the fears and perceived downsides in the profession. But there is an upside—a quest for an innovative way of continuing investigative journalism online.

In their landmark "The Reconstruction of American Journalism," Leonard Downie Jr. and Michael Schudson offer a detailed roadmap for what could happen to journalism in the future.

> The questions that this transformation raises are simple enough: What is going to take the place of what is being lost, and can the new array of news media report on our nation and our communities as well as—or better than—journalism has until now? More importantly—and the issue central to this report—what should be done to shape this new landscape, to help assure that the essential elements of independent, original, and credible news reporting are preserved? We believe that choices made now and in the near future will not only have far-reaching effects but, if the choices are sound, significantly beneficial ones.[1]

The report states that some of the answers are already in existence: the Internet makes it much easier and faster to "gather and distribute news more widely in new ways." This is already under way in those major newspapers still publishing and in commercial television, Downie and Schudson point out, as well as in start-up online news organizations, nonprofit investigative reporting projects such as ProPublica, public broadcasting stations such as PBS, university-run news services, community news sites with citizen participation, and bloggers. "Together, they are creating not only a greater variety of independent reporting missions but different definitions of news."[2]

Perhaps Linda Winslow, executive producer of *The NewsHour with Jim Lehrer*, a professional broadcast veteran who, along with Jim Lehrer and Robin MacNeil, dates back to 1973 when she produced the pair's coverage of Watergate for what was then called the National Public Affairs Center for Television (NPACT), expressed it best when she said: "It's an exciting time to be a journalist, similar to the moment when the first Gutenberg bible rolled off the presses, a similar upheaval."[3]

Notes

1. Leonard Downie Jr. and Michael Schudson, "The Reconstruction of American Journalism," *Columbia Journalism Review*, October 19, 2009, 5.

2. Ibid., 6.

3. Linda Winslow, *116 & Broadway* (Fall 2009): 7.

Selected Bibliography

Books

Adams, Sherwood. *Firsthand Report: The Story of the Eisenhower Administration*. New York: Harper, 1961.

Anderson, Dale. *Watergate: Scandal in the White House*. Minneapolis: Compass-Point Books, 2007.

Anderson, Jack, and James Boyd. *Confessions of a Muckraker: The Inside Story of Life in Washington during the Truman, Eisenhower, Kennedy and Johnson Years*. New York: Random House, 1979.

Bamford, James. *The Shadow Factory: The Ultra-Secret NSA from 9/11 to the Eavesdropping on America*. New York: Doubleday, 2008.

Bausum, Ann. *Muckrakers: How Ida Tarbell, Upton Sinclair, and Lincoln Steffens Helped Expose Scandal, Inspire Reform, and Invent Investigative Journalism*. Washington, DC: National Geographic, 2007.

Benston, George J., Michael Bromwich, Robert E. Litan, and Alfred Wagenhofer. *Following the Money: The Enron Failure and the State of Disclosure*. Washington, DC: Brookings Institution Press, 2003.

Bernstein, Carl, and Bob Woodward. *All the President's Men*. New York: Simon & Schuster, 1974.

Bogart, Leo. *Press and Public: Who Reads What, When, Where, and Why in American Newspapers*. Hillsdale, NJ: Erlbaum, 1989.

Bradlee, Ben. *Guts and Glory: The Rise and Fall of Oliver North*. New York: Donald I. Fine, 1988.

Brewer, Lynn, and Matthew Scott Hansen. *Confessions of an Enron Executive: A Whistleblower's Story*. Bloomington, IN: Author-House, 2004.

Bryce, Robert. *Pipe Dreams: Greed, Ego, and the Death of Enron*. New York: PublicAffairs, 2003.

Bunyan, John. *Pilgrim's Progress*. Edited with introduction by Roger Sharrock. Harmondsworth, Middlesex, UK: Penguin Books, 1987.

Burke, John P., Fred I. Greenstein, Larry Bermen, and Richard H. Immerman. *How Presidents Test Reality: Decisions on Vietnam, 1954 and 1965*. New York: Sage Foundation, 1989.

Castro, Fidel, and José R. Fernandez. *Playa Girón: Bay of Pigs, Washington's First Military Defeat in the Americas*. New York: Pathfinder, 2001.

Castro, Fidel, and Ignacio Ramonet. *Fidel Castro, My Life: A Spoken Autobiography*. New York: Scribner, 2006.

Chalmers, David Mark. *The Social and Political Ideas of the Muckrakers*. New York: Citadel Press, 1964.

Chomsky, Noam. *Necessary Illusions: Thought Control in Democratic Societies*. Boston: South End Press, 1989.

Collins, Denis. *Behaving Badly: Ethical Lessons from Enron*. Indianapolis: Dog Ear, 2006.

Corn, David. *The Lilies of George W. Bush: Mastering the Politics of Deception*. New York: Three Rivers Press, 2003.

Cruver, Brian. *Anatomy of Greed: Telling the Unshredded Truth from an Enron Insider*. New York: Carroll & Graf, 2002.

DeFleur, Margaret H. *Computer-Assisted Investigative Reporting: Development and Methodology*. Mahwah, NJ: Erlbaum, 1997.

Douglass, James W. *JFK and the Unspeakable: Why He Died and Why It Matters*. Maryknoll, NY: Orbis Books, 2008.

Drudge, Matt, and Julia Phillips. *Drudge Manifesto*. New York: New American Library, 2000.

Eichenwald, Kurt. *Conspiracy of Fools: A True Story*. New York: Broadway Books, 2005.

Ellsberg, Daniel. *Papers on the War*. New York: Simon & Schuster, 1972.

———. *Risk, Ambiguity and Decision*. Studies in Philosophy. New York: Garland, 2001.

———. *Secrets: A Memoir of Vietnam and the Pentagon Papers*. New York: Viking, 2002.

Epstein, Edward Jay. *Between Fact and Fiction: The Problem of Journalism*. New York: Vintage Books, 1975.

Ettema, James S., and Theodore Lewis Glasser. *Custodians of Conscience: Investigative Journalism and Public Virtue*. New York: Columbia University Press, 1998.

Felt, W. Mark. *The FBI Pyramid: From the Inside.* New York: Putnam, 1979.

Felt, W. Mark, and John D. O'Connor. *A G-Man's Life: The FBI, Being "Deep Throat," and the Struggle for Honor in Washington.* New York: PublicAffairs, 2006.

Filler, Louis. *The Muckrakers.* Stanford, CA: Stanford University Press, 1993.

Fox, Loren. *Enron: The Rise and Fall.* Hoboken, NJ: Wiley, 2003.

Franken, Al. *Lies and the Lying Liars Who Tell Them.* New York: Dutton, 2003.

Fusaro, Peter C., and Ross M. Miller. *What Went Wrong at Enron: Everyone's Guide to the Largest Bankruptcy in U.S. History.* Hoboken, NJ: Wiley, 2002.

Gant, Scott. *We're All Journalists Now: The Transformation of the Press and Reshaping of the Law in the Internet Age.* New York: Free Press, 2007.

Garment, Leonard. *In Search of Deep Throat: Greatest Political Mystery of Our Time.* New York: Macmillan, 2000.

Garment, Suzanne. *Scandal: The Crisis of Mistrust in American Politics.* New York: Times Books, 1991.

Grandin, Greg. *Empire's Workshop: Latin America, the United States, and the Rise of the New Imperialism.* New York: Metropolitan Books, 2006.

Grossman, Mark. *Political Corruption in America: An Encyclopedia of Scandals, Power, and Greed.* New York: Delacorte Press, 2003.

Hammer, Richard. *The Court-Martial of Lt. Calley.* New York: Coward, McCann & Geoghegan, 1971.

Hersh, Seymour M. *Chain of Command: The Road from 9/11 to Abu Ghraib.* New York: HarperCollins, 2004.

———. *Cover-up: The Army's Secret Investigation of the Massacre at My Lai 4.* New York: Random House, 1972.

———. *My Lai 4: A Report on the Massacre and Its Aftermath.* New York: Random House, 1970.

Hess, Stephen. *News and Newsmaking: Essays.* Washington, DC: Brookings Institution, 1996.

Higgins, Trumbull. *The Perfect Failure: Kennedy, Eisenhower, and the CIA at the Bay of Pigs.* New York: Norton, 1987.

Hofstadter, Richard. *The Age of Reform: From Bryan to FDR.* New York: Knopf, 1955.

Hume, Brit. *Inside Story Tales of Washington Scandals by the Young Reporter Who Helped Jack Anderson Dig Them Out.* Garden City, NY: Doubleday, 1974.

Isikoff, Michael. *Hubris: The Inside Story of Spin.* New York: Crown, 2006.

———. *Uncovering Clinton: A Reporter's Story.* New York: Crown, 1999.

Jensen, Carl. *Stories That Changed America: Muckrakers of the 20th Century.* New York: Seven Stories Press, 2000.

Jones, Alex S. *Losing the News: The Future of the News That Feeds Democracy.* Oxford, UK: Oxford University Press, 2008.

Kaplan, Justin. *Lincoln Steffens: A Biography.* New York: Simon & Schuster, 1974.

Klein, Woody. *Let in the Sun.* New York: Macmillan, 1964.

Kornbluh, Peter, ed. *Bay of Pigs Declassified: The Secret CIA Report on the Invasion of Cuba.* New York: New Press, 1988.

Krajicek, David J. *Scooped! Media Miss Real Story on Crime While Chasing Sex, Sleaze and Celebrities.* New York: Columbia University Press, 1998.

Lawson, Don. *Famous Presidential Scandals.* Hillside, NJ: Enslow, 1990.

Lichtblau, Eric. *Bush's Law: The Remaking of American Justice.* New York: Pantheon, 2008.

Long, Kim. *Almanac of Political Corruption, Scandals and Dirty Politics.* New York: Delacorte Press, 2007.

McCartney, Laton. *Teapot Dome Scandal: How Big Oil Bought the Harding White House and Tried to Steal the Country.* New York: Random House, 2008.

McCombs, Maxwell E. *Setting the Agenda: The Mass Media and Public Opinion.* Malden, MA: Blackwell, 2004.

McIntyre, Bryce Telfer. *Advanced Newsgathering.* New York: Praeger, 1991.

McLean, Bethany, and Peter Elkind. *The Smartest Guys in the Room: The Amazing Rise and Scandalous Fall of Enron.* New York: Portfolio, 2003.

Miraldi, Robert, ed. *The Muckrakers: Evangelical Crusaders.* Westport, CT: Praeger, 2000.

Mitchell, Jack. *Executive Privilege: Two Centuries of White House Scandals.* New York: Hippocrene Books, 1992.

Olson, Keith W. *Watergate: The Presidential Scandal That Shook America.* Lawrence: University Press of Kansas, 2003.

Parry, Robert. *Lost History: Contras, Cocaine, the Press and "Project Truth."* Arlington, VA: Media Consortium, 1999.

———. *Secrecy and Privilege: The Rise of the Bush Dynasty from Watergate to Iraq.* Arlington, VA: Media Consortium, 2004.

Parry, Robert, Sam Parry, Nat Parry. *Neck Deep: The Disastrous Presidency of George W. Bush.* Arlington, VA: Media Consortium, 2007.

Patai, Raphael. *The Arab Mind.* Rev. ed. New York: Hatherleigh Press, 2002.

Payne, Phillip G. *Dead Last: The Public Memory of Warren G. Harding's Scandalous Legacy.* Athens: Ohio University Press, 2009.

Pfeiffer, Jack, and David M. Barrett. *The Bay of Pigs Operation*, vol. 3, *Evolution of CIA's Anti-Castro Policies, 1950–January 1961.* Villanova, PA: Villanova University Press, 2005.

Pilger, John, ed. *Tell Me No Lies: Investigative Journalism That Changed the World.* New York: Thunder's Mouth Press, 2005.

Priest, Dana. *The Mission: Waging War and Keeping Peace with America's Military.* New York: Norton, 2003.

Prochnau, William. *Once upon a Distant War.* New York: Times Books, 1996.

Protess, David L., Fay Lomax Cook, Jack C. Doppler, James S. Ettema, et al. *The Journalism of Outrage: Investigative Reporting and Agenda Building in America.* New York: Guilford Press, 1992.

Protess, David, and Maxwell E. McCombs, eds. *Agenda Setting: Readings on Media, Public Opinion and Policymaking.* Hillsdale, NJ: Erlbaum, 1991.

Rapoport, Nancy B., and Bala G. Dharan. *Enron: Corporate Fiascos and Their Implications.* New York: Foundation Press, 2004.

Regier, C. C. *The Era of the Muckrakers.* Chapel Hill: University of North Carolina Press, 1992.

Risen, James. *State of War: The Secret History of the CIA and the Bush Administration.* New York: Free Press, 2006.

Ritchie, Donald A. *Reporting from Washington: The History of the Washington Press Corps.* Oxford, UK: Oxford University Press, 2005.

Rosenberg, Jerry Martin. *Inside the* Wall Street Journal: *The History and Power of Dow Jones & Co. and America's Most Influential Newspaper.* New York: Macmillan, 1982.

Rozell, Mark J., and Clyde Wilcox. *The Clinton Scandal and the Future of American Government.* Washington, DC: Georgetown University Press, 2000.

Safire, William. *Scandalmongers: A Novel.* New York: Simon & Schuster, 2000.

Salter, Malcolm S. *Innovation Corrupted: The Origins and Legacy of Enron's Collapse.* Cambridge, MA: Harvard University Press, 2008.

Schrag, Peter. *Test of Loyalty: Daniel Ellsberg and the Rituals of Secret Government.* New York: Simon & Schuster, 1974.

Schultz, Jeffrey D. *Presidential Scandals.* Washington, DC: CQ Press, 2000.

Shapiro, Bruce. *Shaking the Foundations: 200 Years of Investigative Journalism in America.* New York: Thunder's Mouth Press/Nation Books, 2003.

Shapiro, Herbert. *The Muckrakers and American Society.* Boston: D.C. Health, 1968.

Sheehan, Neil. *After the War Was Over: Hanoi and Saigon.* New York: Random House, 1992.

———. *A Bright Shining Lie: John Paul Vann and America in Vietnam.* New York: Random House, 1988.

Silberdick, Barbara Feinberg. *Watergate: Scandal in the White House.* New York: Watts, 1990.

Smith, Rebecca. *24 Days: How Two* WSJ *Reporters Uncovered the Lies That Destroyed Faith in Corporate America.* New York: HarperBusiness, 2003.

Steffens, Lincoln. *The Autobiography of Lincoln Steffens.* New York: Literary Guild, 1931.

———. *The Shame of the Cities.* American Century series. New York: Hill & Wang, 1957.

Stewart, James B. *Blood Sport: The President and His Adversaries.* New York: Simon & Schuster, 1996.

Streitmatter, Rodge. *Mightier Than the Sword: How the News Media Have Shaped American History.* Boulder, CO: Westview Press, 1997.

Stuart, Iris, and Bruce Stuart. *Ethics in the Post-Enron Age.* Mason, OH: SouthWestern/Thomson, 2004.

Swartz, Mimi, and Sherron Watkins. *Power Failure: The Inside Story of the Collapse of Enron.* New York: Doubleday, 2003.

Szulc, Tad. *Fidel: A Critical Portrait.* New York: Morrow, 1986.

Szulc, Tad, and Karl Ernest Meyer. *The Cuban Invasion: The Chronicle of a Disaster.* Westport, CT: Praeger, 1962.

Tarpley, Webster Griffin, and Anton Chaitkin. *George Bush: The Unauthorized Biography.* Washington, DC: Executive Intelligence Review, 1992.

Tiffen, Rodney. *Scandals: Media, Politics and Corruption in Contemporary Australia.* Sydney: University of South Wales Press, 1999.

U.S. Department of Defense. *The Pentagon Papers: Senator Mike Gravel Edition.* 4 vols. Boston: Beacon Press, 1971–1972.

Webb, Gary. *Dark Alliance: The CIA, the Contras and the Crack Cocaine Explosion*. New York: Seven Stories Press, 1998.

Weinberg, Arthur, and Lila Weinberg. *The Muckrakers: The Era in Journalism That Moved America to Reform*. New York: Simon & Schuster, 1961.

Wells, Tom. *Wild Man: The Life and Times of Daniel Ellsberg*. New York: Palgrave, 2001.

Willis, William James. *The Shadow World: Life between the News Media and Reality*. New York: Praeger, 1991.

Woodward, Bob. *The Secret Man: The Story of Watergate's Deep Throat*. New York: Simon & Schuster, 2005.

ARTICLES

Adams, Sherman. "The Administration: O.K., S.A." *Time*, January 9, 1956: 18–22.

Boylan, James. "Muckraking! The Journalism That Changed America." *Columbia Journalism Review* 41, no. 2 (2002): 72.

Carlson, Margaret. "The Letter Formerly Known as Scarlet." *Time*, September 28, 1998, 44ff.

Chicago Tribune. "A History of White House Scandals." October 28, 2005.

DeLong, Brad. "Torture and Rumors of Torture." http://www.j-bradford-delong.net.

Dettmer, Jamie. "Partisan Smear Called Investigative Reporting." *Insight on the News*, July 13, 1997.

Ellsberg, Daniel. "Dan Ellsberg: The *Rolling Stone* Interview." *Rolling Stone*, November 8, 1973.

Epstein, Edward Jay. "Recovered Memories." Review of *The Dark Side of Camelot* by Seymour M. Hersh. *Los Angeles Times*, December 28, 1997.

Feldstein, Mark. "A Muckraking Model: Investigative Reporting Cycles in American History." *Harvard International Journal of Press/Politics* 11, no. 2 (2006): 105–20.

Gonzalez, Roberto J. "We Must Fight the Militarization of Anthropology." *Chronicle of Higher Education* 53, no. 22 (2007): 22.

Hersh, Seymour M. "Chain of Command: How the Department of Defense Mishandled the Disaster at Abu Ghraib." *New Yorker*, May 17, 2004, 38.

———. "The General's Report: How Antonio Taguba Who Investigated the Abu Ghraib Scandal Became One of Its Casualties." *New Yorker*, June 25, 2007, 58–69.

———. "Torture at Abu Ghraib." *New Yorker*, May 10, 2004: 42–47.

Hitchens, Christopher. "Minority Report: 1980 Origins of Iran Contra Affair." *Nation* 245 (August 1, 1987): 80.

Kennedy, John F. "The President and the Press." *Vital Speeches of the Day* 27, no. 15 (May 15, 1961): 450–52.

Mayer, Jane. "The Black Sites: A Rare Look Inside the CIA's Secret Interrogation Program." *New Yorker*, August 13, 2007, 46–57.

McLean, Bethany. "Is Enron Overpriced? It's in a Bunch of Complex Businesses . . . Its Financial Statements Are Nearly Impenetrable. So Why Is Enron Trading at Such a Huge Multiple?" *Fortune*, March 5, 2001, 122–26.

———. "Why Enron Went Bust: Start with Arrogance. Add Greed, Deceit and Financial Chicanery, What Do You Get? A Company That Wasn't What It Was Cracked Up to Be." *Fortune*, December 24, 2001, 58–68.

McNamara, Laura A. "Notes on an Ethnographic Scandal: Seymour Hersh, Abu Ghraib and the Arab Mind." *Anthropology News* 48, no. 7 (October 1, 2007): 4.

Mitchell, Greg. "Four Years Later: Why Did It Take So Long for the Press to Break Abu Ghraib Story?" *Editor & Publisher*, May 8, 2008.

Pitney, John J., Jr. "Scandal Time: History Suggests White House Scandals Won't Help Republicans as Much as They Expect." *Reason* 26, no. 3 (July 1, 1994): 44–45.

Powell, Bonnie Azab. "Investigative Journalist Seymour Hersh Spills the Secrets of the Iraq Quagmire and the War on Terror." October 2004. http://www.berkeley.edu/news/media/releases/2004.

Rich, Frank. "All the Presidents Stink." *New York Times Magazine* (New York edition), August 18, 1999, 42ff.

Shepard, Alicia C. "The Isikoff Factor." *American Journalism Review* 20 (December 1, 1998): 34–35.

Sherman, Scott. "The Avenger: Sy Hersh, Then and Now." *Columbia Journalism Review* 42, no. 2 (July/August 2002): 34.

———. "Enron: Uncovering the Uncovered Story." *Columbia Journalism Review* 40, no. 6 (March/April 2002): 22–28.

Sobel, Robert. "(Monkey) Business as Usual? White House Scandals Normally Make Good Reading, Not Bad Markets." *Barron's*, February 9, 1998.

Sudo, Phil. "Crisis in the White House." *Scholastic Update* 30, no. 10 (February 23, 1998): 18ff.

Suellentrop, Chris. "Sy Hersh Says It's Okay to Lie (Just Not in Print): The Runaway Mouth of America's Premier Investigative Journalist." *New York Magazine*, April 18, 2005, 38–42.

Summers, John H. "What Happened to Sex Scandals? Politics and Peccadilloes, Jefferson to Kennedy." *Journal of American History* 87, no. 3 (2000): 825–54.

Szulc, Tad. "Cuba on Our Mind." *Esquire*, February 1, 1974, 90–91.

———. "Friendship Is Possible, but . . ." *Parade*, April 1, 1984.

———. "The Politics of Assassination." *New York Magazine*, June 23, 1975, 58–60.

Taheri, Ami. "Many Sources but No Meat: Amir Taheri on Anti-Bush Expose That Contains Assertions and Allegations Aplenty . . . but No Evidence." *Sunday Telegraph* (London), September 22, 2004.

Thomas, Evan. "The Tripp Trapp?" *Newsweek*, July 13, 1998, 23.

Wolff, Michael. "Spread Thin." *New York Magazine*, March 4, 2002, 35–36.

INDEX

A

Abramson, Jill, 131

Abu Ghraib prison scandal, xxxii, 105–119, 188; abuses in, 106, 110; Americans view of torture in, 115; Bush awareness of torture in, 111–112; Hersh on torture at, 108–109; Rumsfeld and, 109–110; Taguba's investigation on, 110–111, 117

Adams, Sherman, xxxi–xxxii, 1–18; on Eisenhower, 15; Ewald on, 16; memoir of, 12; on relation with Goldfine, 13; resignation of, 15–16

Adams–Goldfine scandal, 1–18; Anderson on, 5–6, 8; Federal Trade Commission (FTC) and, 6–8; proof for, 8

Adcock, Beryl, 202, 215

Akhtiar, Mohammed, 204

Alcorn, Meade, 15, 16

Alliance Base, 154, 158

All the President's Men, 43, 48, 58–59, 67, 126, 142

al Qaeda, 124, 125, 126, 129, 133, 140, 153, 156, 159, 206, 209

American Civil Liberties Union (ACLU), 108–109, 146, 200, 201

American Journalism Review, 79–80, 88

American Newspaper Publishers, 30

Anderson, Arthur, 97

Anderson, Jack, xxxi–xxxii, 1–18; Hume on, 2–3; on investigative reporting, 17

anti-Castro movement, 28

Anti-Castro Revolutionary Council, 24

The Arab Mind, 113

Arabs, sexual humility and, 113

Army's Family Medical Assistance Center, 175

Ashcroft, John, 126

Associated Press (AP), 200–201

B

Bagram Air Base, 150, 207

Baker, James, 92

Batista, Fulgencio, 28

Bay of Pigs fiasco scandal, xxxii, 21–38, 129

Bernstein, Carl, xxxii, 40, 41, 44, 56, 63, 64, 66, 68n21, 69–70n53, 126, 146; books of, 67; on Felt, 48; on Watergate scandal, 44–45, 61

"The Biggest Secret," xxxii, 123–143

Bin Laden, Osama, 137

"The Black Sites," 160

Blackwood, Lt. Sylvia, 179–180

Bradlee, Ben, 43–44, 57, 84; tribute
  to Cronkite, 55–56; on Watergate
  scandal, 45–46, 60–61, 65
Brinkley, Alan, 77
Buffet, Warren, 100
Bunyan, John, xxvii, xxviii
Bush, George W., 67, 91, 96, 109,
  120*n*17, 123, 151, 153, 177,
  185–186, 207; admonition to
  media, 165; excerpts of, 138–140;
  link between Lay and, 98–99; on
  treatment of Iraqi prisoners, 113;
  on Walter Reed, 176
*Bush's Law: The Remaking of
  American Justice*, 124
Bush Torture Memo, 152

C
Califano, Joe, 45
Calloway, PFC Joshua, 180, 181
Campbell, Deborah, 114
Canavan, Charles, 7
Castro, Fidel, xxxii, 21, 22, 23–24,
  26–27, 28–29, 31, 32–33, 35
CBS Evening News, 140
Central Intelligence Agency (CIA),
  22, 41, 42, 136, 142, 147, 150, 152,
  154–156, 164
*Chain of Command: The Road from
  9/11 to Abu Ghraib*, 117, 119
Chanos, James, 93
Cheney, Dick, 98
Chotiner, Murray, 45
Chotiner theory, 45
Cille, Michel Du, 170
"citizen journalism," xxvi
Clinton, Bill, xxxii, 74, 75, 87, 89*n*1;
  interview with press, 78–79,
  80–81; Isikoff on, 82–83, 84; Jones
  charges against, 82; on Lewinsky
  allegations, 79; sexual affair with
  Lewinsky, 75
Clinton, Hillary, 81, 86
Colson, Charles W., 42

Columbia Journalism Review, 76
Committee to Reelect the President
  (CREEP), 42
Corbett, Rebecca, 130
Counterterrorist Intelligence
  Centers (CTICs), 157, 158
Criminal Investigation Command,
  175
Cronkite, Walter, 55–56
Cruz, Jeans, 178, 179
Cuban missile crisis, 29, 33–34
Cuban Revolution, 23
Currie, Betty, 90*n*10

D
Darby, Joseph, 113
Dean, John, 60
Deep Throat, 47, 48, 60, 63, 64
Democratic Leadership Conference,
  85
Democratic National Committee,
  42, 62
Dobbs, Michael, 63
Dole, Bob, 177
domestic eavesdropping, 123–143
Donaldson, Sam, 75
Downie, Leonard Jr., xxiv, 84, 149,
  220
Drudge, Matt, 73, 76, 77
Dryfoos, Orville, 21–22

E
Eisenhower, Dwight D., xxxi, 3, 4,
  8–9, 11, 13, 14, 23, 30
Elkind, Peter, 100, 102
Enron corporation scandal, xxxii,
  91–102, 103*n*8, 103*n*10; decline of
  share price, 97; financial
  statements, 93–94, 95; growth of
  corporation, 94–95; McLean on,
  92, 93, 100–101; negative cash
  flow, 95; Rich on, 102
*Enron: The Smartest Guys in the
  Room*, 100, 102

Enrongate, 64

Ewald, William Bragg Jr., 16, 17, 19*n*33

F

Fastow, Andrew, 96

Federal Trade Commission (FTC), 6–7

Feingold, Russ, 135

Feldstein, Mark, 17–18

Felt, W. Mark, 48, 49–50, 51–52, 53, 54, 60, 64, 67

Fidel Castro, My Life: A Spoken Autobiography, 30

Fiske, Robert B., 87

Flowers, Gennifer, 84

Foreign Intelligence Surveillance Act (FISA), 126, 133

Forsten, Lt. Col. Robert, 181

Fortune, 91, 100

Fratto, Tony, 198

Freedom of Information Act (FOIA), 201

"The Future of Newspapers: The Impact on the Economy and Democracy," xxiv

G

Gant, Scott, xxvi

Garment, Suzanne, xxx

Gates, Robert, 193

Geneva Conventions, 145, 146, 153

Gibney, Alex, 100

Graham, Katharine, 59

Gray, L. Patrick, 50, 51, 65

Greenspan, Alan, 67

Griswold v. Connecticut (1965), 142

Goldberg, Lucianne, 75

Goldfine, Bernard, 3, 6–7, 8, 10, 13

Gonzalez, Alberto R., 141, 152

Gorbachev, Mikhail, 93

Guantanamo Bay Detention Camp, xxxiii, 146, 163, 197–216; articles on, 204–216; interviews with detainees, 198–199

Gutman, Roy, 198–199, 200, 201, 203, 205, 213, 216

H

Hadley, Stephen, 132, 156, 157

Hagerty, Jim, 7, 13, 14

Haldeman, H. R., 60

Harlow, Bryce, 12

Harrison, John M., xxix

Harvey, Francis, 175–176

Hayden, Gen. Michael, 129, 137

Hearst, William Randolph, xxvii

Hersh, Seymour, 59, 105, 114, 118–119; on Americans view of Abu Ghraib prison, 115; on Bush awareness of Abu Ghraib torture, 111–112; on investigative reporting, 106; on Karpinski's lax management of prison, 112; Remnick on, 107–108; Sullentrop on, 107, 108; on torture at Abu Ghraib prison, 108–109

Hines, Charles, 115

Holbrook, Hal, 126

Hoover, J. Edgar, 18, 50, 60

Howard, Roy Wilson, xvii*n*7

Howrey, Edward, 7

Hull, Anne, xxxii–xxxiii, 169–170, 176, 178, 181, 183, 185, 186–187, 192–193; on future of investigative reporting, 193; report of Building 18 in Walter Reed, 172, 174; Walter Reed medical administration, 170–172, 189–190; on writing articles, 191

Hume, Brit, 2–3

Hunt, Howard E., 42

Hussein, Saddam, 105, 178

I

Impoco, Jim, 96–97

International Red Cross, 198

Interstate Commerce Commission (ICC), 3
investigative reporters, 17, 62, 83, 106, 127, 190–191, 193
Investigative Reporters and Editors (IRE), 217*n*13
investigative reporting, xxvi–xxvii, 63
Isikoff, Michael, xxxii, 22, 77, 86, 88–89; on Clinton, 81–85; on investigative reporters, 83; report of Monicagate scandal, 73–75

J
Johnson, Andrew, 89*n*1
Jones, Paula, 83–84, 85
Jordan, Vernon, 90*n*10
journalism, xxiii, xxiv; American, xxv, xxx; Gant on, xxvi; investigative, xxvii, 219

K
Katrinagate, 64
Keck, Col. Gary, 208
Keller, Bill, xxiii, 131
Kennedy, Caroline, 77
Kennedy, John F., xxxii, 18, 21, 22, 29, 129; on Cuban situation, 27; defamation campaigns against Cuba, 23; Reston on peace conference of, 25
Kennedy, Robert F., 34
Kerry, John, 125
Kirkland, Rik, 99
Kissinger, Henry, 92
Koenig, Mark, 96
Kristol, William, 75, 77
Krock, Arthur, 14
Kurtz, Howard, 63–64, 70–71*n*64, 77, 98, 99
Kuwait Times, 136

L
Lasseter, Tom, xxxiii, 197, 199, 200, 201, 203–204, 209, 211, 213–214, 215, 216

Lawrence, William H., 11
Lay, Kenneth, 91, 96, 97, 98, 99, 103*n*8
Lehrer, Jim, 220
Lewinsky, Monica, xxxii, 75, 86, 87, 90*n*10
Lewis, Al, 45
Lewis, Alfred E., 39–40
Lichtblau, Eric, xxxii, 124, 125, 127–128, 129–130, 131, 132, 134–135, 141, 143
Liddy, G. Gordon, 53
Los Angeles Times, 98

M
MacNeil, Robin, 220
Mandela, Nelson, 92
Masri, Khaled, 159
Mayer, Jane, 160
McArdle, Megan, xxv
McClatchy Newspaper, 197, 202–203, 215–216, 217*n*13
McCord, James, 42, 62
McLean, Bethany, xxxii, 91, 95, 102; on Enron experience, 101–102; Kurtz praising, 99–100; on link between Lay and Bush, 99; on profit of Enron Corporation, 92, 93–94; on Skilling's role in scandal, 98
Meyer, Karl E., 28
Miami Herald, 76, 197, 198, 199, 201, 204
Miller, Maj. Gen. Geoffrey, 112
Millett, Doug, 93
Miraldi, Robert, xxv
The Mission: Waging War and Keeping Peace with American Military, 166
Mitchell, John, 42, 46, 47, 65
Mohammed, Khalid Sheikh, 205
Mollenhoff, Clark, 5
Monicagate scandal, 64, 73–90; outbreak of, 73–75; Porter on, 76

Montgomery County Sentinel, 41
Moorer, Thomas H., 49
The Muckrakers, xxv
muckraking, xxv; definition, xxix;
    interpretation of term, xxviii;
    origin of term, xxvii
muckraking movement, xxvii
Murray Eagle, 18
Mustafa, Mohammed, 211
Myers, Gen. Richard, 112
My Lai massacre, 106

N
National Magazine Award, 88
National Public Affairs Center for
    Television (NPACT), 220
National Security Administration
    (NSA), 123, 124, 128, 130, 133,
    134, 140
National Security Council (NSC), 4
The NewsHour with Jim Lehrer, 177,
    220
newspaper industry, xxiii;
    newspaper scandals, xxv;
    technology in, xxiv
Newsweek, 77, 80, 81–82, 86, 88, 89,
    199
New York Times, 12, 14, 15, 21, 29,
    31, 36, 82, 88, 100, 106, 129, 140,
    207
Nieman Foundation, 172–173
Nixon, Richard M., xxxii, 15, 41, 46,
    53, 56–57, 60, 66, 89*n*1, 129, 135,
    146
Nocera, Joe, 96, 100

O
Obama, Barack, 145, 197
O'Reilly, Bill, 112

P
Palmer, Mark, 96
Patai, Raphael, 113
Pearson, Drew, 1

Phelps, Robert H., 65
Pilgrim's Progress, xxvii, xxviii
Plamegate, 64
political scandals, xxx–xxxi
Porter, Evan, 76
Powell, Colin, 92–93
Priest, Dana, xxxii, xxxiii, 145–166,
    169, 176, 182, 183, 185, 192; on
    CIA, 147, 148–150; on
    investigative reporters, 190–191;
    on policy of releasing
    information after 9/11, 165–166;
    relation between reporter and
    government, 163–164; on
    rendition, 146, 149–160; report
    of Building 18 in Walter Reed,
    172–174; state secrets, reporting,
    162–163; on Walter Reed medical
    administration, 170–172

Q
Quran, 210

R
Rakes, Adams, 12
Rathergate, 64
Ray, Robert W., 87
Rayburn, Sam, 4
Reagan, Ronald, 18, 147
"The Reconstruction of American
    Journalism," xxiv, 220
Redford, Robert, 59
Reeves, Richard, 34–35
Regier, C. C., xxviii–xxix
Remnick, David, 107–108
Rendition, 166
renditions, 145–166
Reno, Attorney General Janet, 87
Reserve Officer Training Corps
    (ROTC), 188
Reston, James, 24–25
Rich, Frank, 82, 102
Ridder, Knight, 201
Riis, Jacob A., xxviii

Risen, James, xxxii, 123, 128, 129, 130, 131, 132, 135, 141, 142, 143; on CIA and Bush administration, 136–138; on investigative reporting, 127; phrase "the biggest secret," 124
Rodriguez, Richard, xxiii–xxiv
Roosevelt, Franklin D., 51
Roosevelt, Theodore, xxvii
Rose, Charlie, 83
Rosenberg, Carol, 201, 217n5
Rosenfeld, Harry M., 45
Rosenstiel, Tom, xxiv
Rouse, Lt. Col. Elizabeth, 207
Rumsfeld, Donald, 109–110, 112, 113, 115, 116
runaway investigation, 5
Rusk, Dean, 30

S
Sachs, Goldman, 91
Sanchez, Lt. Gen. Ricardo S., 115
Schlesinger, Arthur M., 29
Schofield, Matt, 199
Schudson, Michael, 220
Schultz, Jeffrey D., xxx
Schumer, Chuck, 176–177
Schwartz, Bernard, 4–5, 15
The Secret Man: The Story of Watergate's Deep Throat, 48–49
Securities and Exchange Commission (SEC), 3, 93
Seibel, Mark, 198, 202, 215
September 11, 2001, attack, 126, 130, 136, 148, 156
Shacklette, Baron L., 5, 10–11
Shalala, Donna, 177
The Shame of the Cities, xxviii
Shannon, John Daniel, 184–185
Shield Law, xxvii
Skilling, Jeffrey, 92, 95, 96, 97–98
Simons, Howard, 41–42, 45, 68n21
Smith, R. Jeffery, 151
Smith, Robert M., 65

"smoking gun," 60
Snow, Tony, 176
Sola Pool, Ithiel de, xxiv
Spygate, 64
Stanzel, Scott, 120n17
Starr, Kenneth W., 74, 85–86, 87
Stars and Stripes, 18
State of War, 123, 130
Steffens, Lincoln, xxvii–xxviii, 61
Stein, Harry H., xxix
Stephanopoulos, George, 77, 84, 85
Stevenson, Adlai, 8
Strobel, Warren P., 201
Sullentrop, Chris, 107, 108
Sulzberger, Ochs, 123, 131
Sussman, Barry, 41–42, 57
Szulc, Tad, xxxii, 35–36; on Castro, 27, 29, 31, 32–33; on Cuban rebel leaders and Kennedy, 25–26; invasion of Cuba exiles, 21–22, 24, 28; Miami stories, 24; on missile crisis, 29, 33; Reeves on, 34–35

T
Taguba, Lt. Gen. Antonio M., 110, 111, 117, 120n17
Taliban, 124, 153, 203–204, 206
Tenet, George J., 147, 148, 158
Thomas, Evan, 77
Thomas, Helen, 80
Times, 26, 30, 36, 129
Travelgate, 64
Tripp, Linda, 86
Truman, Harry S., 11–12, 128
Turner, Troy, 185, 186

U
Uncovering Clinton: A Reporter's Story, 81, 83, 88
Ungar, Sandy, 54
U.S. Patriot Act, 126, 130, 131, 133, 135
U.S. Supreme Court, 211

V
Vicuña coat scandal, 3
Vietnam War, 83

W
Wagner, Michael J., 175
Wall Street Journal, 98, 100
Walter Reed Veterans
    Administration scandal, xxxii–
    xxxiii, 169–182; articles published
    on, 174–175, 176–179, 185–187;
    poor conditions of building, 170;
    report on Building 18 of, 172–174
war on terror, 164
Washington Post, 39, 40, 77, 80, 81,
    89, 98, 99, 146, 155, 162, 163, 166,
    169, 172, 174, 180, 188, 190, 193
Washington Star, 40
waterboarding, 155
Watergate scandal, xxxii, 39–67,
    126; Bernstein report of, 42–43;
    Bradlee on, 45–46; Felt's role in
    investigation of, 48–50, 51–53;
    impact on national psyche, 65,
    66; impact on other political
    scandals, 64; Lewis report of,
39–40; as model for investigative
    reporting, 61; sources of, 43;
    Woodward on, 47–48
Weightman, Army Maj. Gen.
    George W., 172
Welch, Carrie, 100
White, Thomas, 206
Whiteside, Elizabeth, 187, 188, 189
"Whitewater" drama, 87
Will, George F., 77
Willey, Kathleen, 90*n*10
Williams, Edward Bennett,
    57
Winslow, Linda, 220
Wolfowitz, Paul, 109
Woodward, Bob, xxxii, 40–41, 44,
    45, 54, 56, 63, 64, 66, 81, 82, 126;
    books of, 67; on grand juror,
    57–58; on investigative reporters,
    62; relationship with Felt, 48–50,
    51–52; on Watergate scandal,
    47–48, 61–62

Z
Zaeef, Abdul Salam, 212–213
Ziegler, Ron, 42

About the Author

Woody Klein is a former award-winning political and investigative reporter for the *Washington Post and Times-Herald* and the *New York World-Telegram & Sun*, an adjunct professor of journalism, and an award-winning historian. He served as press secretary to New York mayor John V. Lindsay and then as editor of *Think*, IBM's international magazine. He is the author of *Westport, Connecticut: The Story of a New England Town's Rise to Prominence*, winner of the Connecticut League of History Organizations' Book Award; *Toward Humanity and Justice: The Writings of Dr. Kenneth B. Clark, Scholar of the Brown v. Board of Education Decision in 1954*, winner of the Best Book of the Year award from the Connecticut Press Club; *Liberties Lost: The Endangered Legacy of the ACLU*; *All the Presidents' Spokesmen: Spinning the News—White House Spokesmen from Franklin D. Roosevelt to George W. Bush*, winner of the Best Book of the Year award from the Connecticut Press Club; *Lindsay's Promise*; and *Let in the Sun*. He has taught journalism at New York University, the New School, the University of Bridgeport, Fairfield University, and Iona College. Klein has a B.A. from Dartmouth College and an M.S. from the Graduate School of Journalism, Columbia University. Now a freelance author and writer, he lives with his wife Audrey in Westport, Connecticut.

Foreword author **Jeff Greenfield** is an award-winning senior political correspondent for CBS News. He is principally known for his coverage of domestic politics and media.